WARFARE
in the
OLD TESTAMENT

WARFARE
in the
OLD TESTAMENT

The Organization, Weapons, *and* Tactics
of Ancient Near Eastern Armies

BOYD SEEVERS

With line drawings by Josh Seevers

Kregel
Academic

Warfare in the Old Testament: The Organization, Weapons, and Tactics of Ancient Near Eastern Armies

© 2013 by Boyd Seevers

Published by Kregel Publications, a division of Kregel, Inc., P.O. Box 2607, Grand Rapids, MI 49501.

The Hebrew font New JerusalemU is available from www.linguistsoftware.com/lgku.htm, +1-425-775-1130.

ISBN 978-0-8254-3655-0

Printed in the United States of America
13 14 15 16 17 / 5 4 3 2 1

To Karen, my beloved wife of more than thirty years, including many in the lands that witnessed the events described herein

Contents

CHAPTER 9 / PERSIA:
Final Rulers from the East   273

For Further Reading   299

Figures and Maps Index   305

Subject Index   311

Scripture Index   321

Figures and Maps

Abbreviations

ABC	*Assyrian and Babylonian Chronicles.* A. K. Grayson. TCS 5. Locust Valley, New York, 1975
ABD	*Anchor Bible Dictionary.* Edited by D. N. Freedman. 6 vols. New York, 1992
AEL	*Ancient Egyptian Literature.* M. Lichtheim. Berkeley, 1971–80
AMMO	"Ancient Mesopotamian Military Organization," by Stephanie Dalley. 1:413–22 in *Civilizations of the Ancient Near East.* Edited by J. Sasson. New York, 1995.
ANET	*Ancient Near Eastern Texts Relating to the Old Testament.* Edited by J. B. Pritchard. 3d ed. Princeton, 1969
ARCT	"Assyrian Rule of Conquered Territory in Ancient Western Asia," by A. Kirk Grayson. 2:959-68 in *Civilizations of the Ancient Near East.* Edited by J. Sasson. New York, 1995
ARE	*Ancient Records of Egypt.* Edited by J. H. Breasted. 5 vols. Chicago, 1905–1907. Reprint, London: 1988
ARI	*Assyrian Royal Inscriptions.* A. K. Grayson. 2 vols. RANE. Wiesbaden, 1972–1976
AWBL	*The Art of Warfare in Biblical Lands in the Light of Archaeological Study.* 2 vols. Y. Yadin. New York, 1963
BAR	*Biblical Archaeology Review*
BASOR	*Bulletin of the American Schools of Oriental Research*
CAH	Cambridge Ancient History
CANE	*Civilizations of the Ancient Near East.* Edited by J. Sasson. 4 vols. New York, 1995
CBQ	*Catholic Biblical Quarterly*
CLS	*The Conquest of Lachish by Sennacherib.* D. Ussishkin. Tel Aviv, 1982
COS	*The Context of Scripture.* Edited by W. W. Hallo. 3 vols. Leiden, 1997–2002

Cyr.	*Xenophon's Cyropaedia: With an English Translation by Walter Miller.* The Loeb Classical Library. T. E. Page, et al, eds. Cambridge, MA: Harvard, 1960
HALOT	Koehler, L., W. Baumgartner, and J. J. Stamm, *The Hebrew and Aramaic Lexicon of the Old Testament.* Translated and edited under the supervision of M. E. J. Richardson. 4 vols. Leiden, 1994–1999
Her.	*Herodotus: With an English Translation by A. D. Godley.* The Loeb Classical Library. T. E. Page, et al, eds. Cambridge, MA: Harvard, 1960
JAOS	*Journal of the American Oriental Society*
JEA	*Journal of Egyptian Archaeology*
JETS	*Journal of the Evangelical Theological Society*
JNES	*Journal of Near Eastern Studies*
MRTO	*Military Rank, Title, and Organization in the Egyptian New Kingdom.* A. Schulman. Berlin, 1964
NEAEHL	*The New Encyclopedia of Archaeological Excavations in the Holy Land.* Edited by E. Stern. 5 vols. Jerusalem, 1993, 2008
NEASB	*Near East Archaeological Society Bulletin*
PEQ	*Palestine Exploration Quarterly*
RIMA	The Royal Inscriptions of Mesopotamia, Assyrian Periods
Strabo	*The Geography of Strabo: With an English Translation by Horace Leonard Jones.* The Loeb Classical Library. T. E. Page, et al, eds. Cambridge, MA: Harvard, 1961
ZÄS	*Zeitschrift für ägyptische Sprache und Altertumskunde*

Acknowledgements

The author expresses his sincere appreciation to the following:

- The entire publishing team at Kregel, especially Jim Weaver, former director of academic books, and Paul Hillman, senior project manager, for their guidance and work on this project.

- Colleagues at the University of Northwestern - St. Paul—Michael Wise and Jason DeRouchie for their help and encouragement early in the project, and Charles Aling for reviewing this work, particularly the chapters on Egypt.

- My highly capable teaching assistants Elyse Kallgren, Sarah Schock, and Abigail Zerrien for their encouragement and help editing the text.

- Sergeant Joshua A. Draveling, United States Marine Corps, for many stimulating exchanges about military concepts and practices and for his helpful review of the text.

- *Accordance* Bible software, for use of maps from their atlas module. Most maps in this book were developed using a map from *Accordance* as the base.

- The administration at the University of Northwestern - St. Paul, for the sabbatical that allowed time to research and write much of this book.

- Paul and Diane Wright at Jerusalem University College in Israel, for the opportunity to serve as Visiting Professor and work on this project during my sabbatical in spring 2010. It was a wonderful privilege to write about events of the Bible in the always-fascinating world of the Bible.

- Barry J. Beitzel and Richard E. Averbeck, readers of my doctoral dissertation at Trinity Evangelical Divinity School, on which much of this book is based.

- Osprey Publishers, for the rights to use color illustrations by Angus McBride.

- And last but not least, artist and son Josh Seevers, for his skill and enthusiasm in illustrating this project, as well as for many enjoyable discussions about warfare.

INTRODUCTION:
"I CAN'T IMAGINE LIFE WITHOUT THE ARMY."

IMPORTANCE OF THE MILITARY IN THE LAND OF THE BIBLE

A number of years ago, my wife and I moved with our infant son to Israel for what would turn out to be several years of working and ministering in the land of the Bible. One of my first experiences in Israel involved an interview by the general manager of the company where I would be employed. This gentleman was a native Israeli, the son of a Holocaust survivor, a former intelligence officer in the Israeli army, and now the head of a growing company. I remember little of the interview except its conclusion, which, as I would later learn, typically included an inquiry into an applicant's experience in the Israeli military. Knowing that I grew up in America, however, the general manager asked if I had even *been* in the military. I had not. Hearing this, he paused, shook his head, and said, "I can't imagine life without the army."

"I can't imagine life without the army." Having grown up after the abolishment of the draft in an America still reeling from its divisive experience in the Vietnam War, I could hardly imagine life *with* the army. My subsequent years in Israel showed me, however, just how normal my interviewer's statement would seem for the typical modern Israeli. Most young men and women enter the military after high school and serve for the next two or three years. Then for as long as several more decades, most Israeli men serve in the reserves for ten to sixty days a year. Military service seemed a normative part of life in that modern Middle Eastern country—your relatives and friends do their part, and you are expected to do yours. It seemed to me that most modern Israelis couldn't imagine life without the army.

Looking back into history through the Bible and other ancient Near Eastern texts has caused me to wonder if the ancient Israelites, Egyptians, Assyrians, and others would also have said, "I can't imagine life without the army." Accounts of military campaigns and battles abound in their texts. Ancient kings set out, frequently at the command of their god(s), to fight for their freedom or to assert their rightful dominance over a rebellious nation. Scribes often recorded the results of these wars in accounts usually intended to exalt the king and/or the nation's god(s). Military information even permeates non-military texts. Warfare clearly pervaded much of the ancient Near Eastern world.

The scriptural accounts of ancient Israel fit this pattern well. Joshua, David, and other leaders led armies into battle, often with Yahweh's blessing. Israel typically fought to do God's will, and honored him with the result. The Bible, like other contemporary literature from this period, often includes interesting but brief accounts of those wars and battles.

The biblical authors normally write about warfare for some theological purpose, such as illustrating faith—or lack thereof—in God by some Israelite leader or the nation as a whole. Such was the case with Israel's remarkable victory at Jericho, reportedly won because of Israel's obedience to Yahweh's precise instructions (Josh. 5:13–6:27). The same holds true for King Hezekiah, who prayed that God would deliver Judah from the Assyrians so that "all the kingdoms of the earth may know that you, alone, LORD, are God" (2 Kings 19:19). Along with illustrating proper faith in God, the biblical authors also include accounts of battles and campaigns to show the fulfillment of prophecy, as David's conquests in 2 Samuel 8:1–14 fulfilled God's promise of a great kingdom (Josh. 1:4).

But when battles—even significant battles—did not fit into the author's theological purpose, they received little or no mention. For example, the major powers of the time fought a great battle at Carchemish on the Euphrates River in northern Syria in 605 BC. This battle changed the balance of power in the entire ancient Near East at that time, but it is only hinted at in 2 Kings 23:29. This brief mention appears to serve more as an explanation of why King Josiah's religious reform ended (with the king's death), rather than recording how the battle of Carchemish was changing the face of contemporary political realities.

This brevity and seeming disinterest in military and other non-theological matters often leaves the modern reader of the Bible without a clear picture of how certain biblical events such as battles and military campaigns took place. For example, shortly after David's ascension to the Israelite throne in the late 11th century BC, the Bible records that he led his armies to conquer the surrounding nations. Although these victories helped transform the politically insignificant nation of Israel into arguably the greatest power of its day, they are summarized in just fourteen verses in 2 Samuel 8.[1] Such brevity may mask the importance of the events to the modern reader and leave many questions unanswered. The text can leave the reader wondering: How did nations like Israel practice warfare? Did David fight the same way Joshua had years before? How big were the armies? How did they move? What weapons and tactics did they use? And, most importantly, what role did religion and faith play in the practice of warfare?

PURPOSE AND STRATEGY OF THIS BOOK

In order to help us better understand the world and message of the Old Testament, this book will seek to describe the military practices of David, Joshua, and other Israelites, as well as those of the Egyptians, Philistines, Assyrians, and others known from the Old Testament. God, in his infinite wisdom, chose to communicate and work with people as they lived in the context of the contemporary culture. Often then, God's Word is inextricably bound up in the regular cultural practices known to the original participants, authors, and readers. These cultural contexts, as we have seen, often included warfare.

The great distance in location, time, culture, and language separating us from the original events and writings often causes problems. Because our understanding and mindset often differ greatly from those of the ancients, we can find it difficult to understand what God was saying and doing in their distant world. Learning about the ancient culture, including the practice of warfare, can help us better understand the biblical message.

This book seeks to help bridge the gap between the modern reader and the world of the Old Testament by using textual and physical evidence to describe ancient military practices. Primary historical documents, written at or near the times of the events, will serve as the main support. Archaeological evidence such as artifacts and pictures will support and supplement the written material wherever possible. These should hopefully paint a realistic picture of how Israel and the surrounding nations did battle, adding helpful depth and impact to the relevant biblical accounts.

This book will describe the military practices of the following kingdoms from the time of the Old Testament: Israel (Chaps. 1–2), Egypt (Chaps. 3–4), Philistia (Chap. 5), Assyria (Chaps. 6–7), Babylon (Chap. 8), and Persia (Chap. 9). The treatment of each nation will start with some historical fiction describing a soldier's participation in one of the nation's major historical battles. It will continue by describing the historical backdrop for the nation during that time, and then its military organization, weaponry, and tactics. Line drawings and color illustrations based on actual ancient drawings and reliefs will illustrate the written descriptions of the military in these ancient nations—nations whose soldiers, like my modern Israeli boss, probably couldn't imagine life without the army.

NOTES

1 Compare the following comments by authors David Howard and Rolf Rendtorff: "Following this theological highlight (the promise of the Davidic covenant), we have *a rather mundane catalog of David's further military victories . . .*" (Emphasis added. David M. Howard, "David," *ABD* 2:44). Similarly, Rendtorff notes that "It is striking that the Old Testament account notes this side of David's activity only in passing" (*The Old Testament: An Introduction.* Philadelphia: Fortress Press, 1991, 33).

ISRAEL:
THE ARMY OF THE KINGDOM OF GOD—PART 1

1

THE ISRAELITES CONQUER JERICHO: "YOU DON'T HAVE TO UNDERSTAND; JUST OBEY"

Judah ben-Eliezer (Judah son of Eliezer; see Fig. 1.1[1]) awoke in a tent, as he had every morning for his entire twenty-one years, and remembered to move his torso very, very slowly. Only two days had passed since Judah and the other Israelite soldiers had undergone circumcision in their camp near the enemy city of Jericho (Josh. 5:2–9), and most were still sore.[2] After the sound of the trumpeter blowing a ram's horn to stir the troops, sharp groans from some in Judah's and other nearby tents gave notice that many were not so careful. The resulting pain jolted them awake and elicited some choice Hebrew[3] words.

Judah lay still a few more moments, as he liked to do in the morning, and thought again how he couldn't understand the timing of the circumcision. Judah usually tried to understand why things happened as they did, but Eliezer, his more spontaneous father, often grew impatient with his son. "You don't have to understand; just obey!" By contrast, Judah's more reflective mother appreciated this quality

Fig. 1.1—Head of Israelite male from later military relief

23

in their youngest son, thinking that it resulted from Judah's above-average intellect. He truly enjoyed the mental challenge of discerning connections between events.

Now, Judah saw a problem with circumcising his nation's army. He didn't question the act itself. He understood well the need to get circumcised—his people descended from their forefather Abraham, and God had commanded that all of Abraham's male descendants undergo this delicate operation in a very private area. The pain wasn't the problem, either. Surviving the challenges of living in a desert for years had made him and his people tough. Thus, his problem wasn't with the act or the resulting pain. What Judah wrestled with was the timing. Why do it now? Why didn't they do it a few days earlier when they would have been so much safer?

A few days earlier, the Israelite army was still camping on the pleasant, green plain across the Jordan River from Jericho (Map 1.1), preparing to invade. After decades of traveling through the huge desert of Sinai on their way to Canaan, the land promised to Abraham's descendants, the Israelites had finally come to where they could see their goal. They had camped across the Jordan for several weeks while their great leader, Moses, led the people to review their journeys, renew their national covenant with their God, and prepare for life in the much-anticipated Promised Land (book of Deut.). All of this Judah understood, too.

Then Moses died, and the younger warrior Joshua had assumed the mantle of leadership. Joshua commanded the army to prepare to invade (Josh. 1:10–11), and they waited several more days while spies sneaked into Jericho to gather information (Josh. 2). The spies returned with an encouraging report, and the army prepared to cross the Jordan River. Judah and the entire nation then witnessed how God stopped up the river so the army could easily cross what had been a flooding river just hours before[4] (Josh. 3). What a miracle! As children, Judah's parents had witnessed and often told how God had opened a great body of water by Egypt to let the Israelites through, then closed it again to destroy the pursuing Egyptian chariots (Ex. 14–15). Now Judah and his generation watched God do a similar miracle.

Although it was the greatest thing Judah had ever seen, he hadn't understood God's instructions for that event, either. Joshua said God commanded the army to cross the river even though it was still at spring flood stage. The Israelites were at a natural ford where the river was usually relatively shallow, but during flooding, it was far too deep and wide to cross even at the ford.[5]

Judah voiced his confusion during the family meal after the command had spread through the camp. Eliezer responded, "You don't have to understand; just obey. God can make this river like the great water back in Egypt." *You don't have to understand; just obey.* Judah admired his father's simple trust. Judah realized that sometimes his thinking made trusting harder. But he could still trust, and he did. When the time came and the army was ready, he marched with his unit toward the river. They watched as the priests carrying the Ark of the Covenant approached and stood in the edge of the river, and the water slowly dropped until they all could cross. Judah and the Israelites hadn't understood how they could cross the river at flood stage, but they obeyed, and God opened the river so the invasion could begin.

Judah and the rest of the soldiers crossed the Jordan, erected a memorial to commemorate the miracle (Josh. 4), and advanced toward Jericho. Up until now the entire nation had traveled together, the soldiers along with their families and animals and other possessions. Now the non-combatants plus guards stayed in the camp across the Jordan while the bulk of the army moved into enemy territory. They advanced the few miles toward Jericho, but Joshua led them to a site just to the north (Map 1.1) that they would call Gilgal, where they would camp a short but safe distance away from the city.

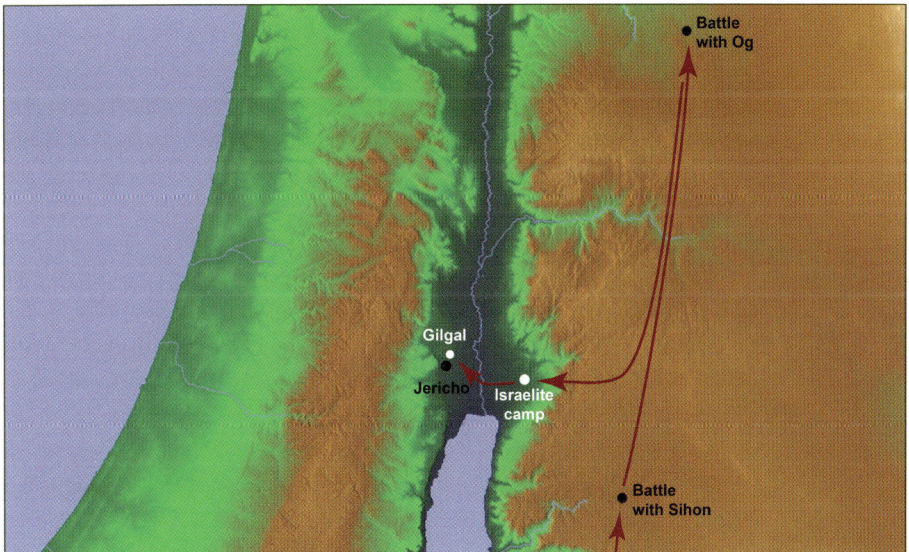

Map 1.1—Israel's journey to Canaan and Jericho

The men were nervous even though they had faced battle before. They had fought nomads in the desert (Ex. 17:8–13) and later against kings Sihon and Og as the Israelites had passed through the highland across the Jordan (Num. 21; see Map 1.1). But now the situation had grown more serious. The earlier fighting had taken place while the Israelites were on their way toward the land they intended to conquer and occupy. Now they had entered that land, and the locals knew that the invaders intended to kill and replace them. Such was the way of life in that part of the world. The gods of many peoples commanded them to take lands and goods from others, and they took as much as they were able (Deut. 2:12, 20–23). They then gave a portion of those goods back to their gods as an expression of thanks. Israel would do the same. In some ways their actions were not unusual, but in other ways what they did was quite different. The Israelites worshipped a single God, unlike the other peoples, and their God could part great waters and rivers and defeat the military of Egypt, the greatest in that part of the world. The other gods couldn't do that, and everyone knew it; Israel's enemies heard the stories and feared (Josh. 2:8–11; 5:1).

Now events took a surprising turn. Almost as soon as they made camp near Jericho, down came the order that Judah ben-Eliezer really couldn't understand. All the soldiers needed to be circumcised. The nation hadn't been following that ancient commandment during their years in the desert, and now they needed to correct it (Josh. 5:2–9). Again, Judah understood the command; he just couldn't understand the timing. Why now? Why didn't they do this a few days ago when they were camped across the swollen river that offered excellent protection from their enemies? Judah knew that as soon as they completed the circumcision, the Israelites would be quite sore and unable to defend themselves for several days (note the story of the circumcised Shechemites in Gen. 34). If their enemies at Jericho knew what the invaders were doing, they would surely attack and the Canaanites would have many obedient but very dead Israelites to present as an offering to their gods. The Israelite conquest would end before it ever started.

Judah, along with many others, didn't understand the timing. But the miraculous crossing of the Jordan had reinforced the truth that they didn't have to understand; they just had to obey. So they did. They all went through the operation and prayed that God would keep their enemies at bay while they healed. And he did. No one attacked, and the Israelites began to anticipate the next step, which they assumed would be attacking Jericho.

However, God had a few more things for the Israelites to address first. He commanded them to celebrate Passover, the holiday commemorating their national deliverance from slavery. They obeyed, and the celebration used up the last of the food they had brought with them. Thus, the following day they sent out units to gather local grain and other food (Josh. 5:10–11). Judah thought this hard luck for the Canaanites who had raised these crops, but such were the rules of the game. Those same Canaanites would do the same to the Israelites or others if they had the chance, and now the Israelite God was giving his people that opportunity. Then the Israelites saw that God also stopped the miraculous provision of food they called manna (Josh. 5:12), which they had eaten every day for the last forty years. Judah found it hard to imagine life without manna, but he quickly figured out why God stopped the manna now. Cutting off their food should further motivate the invaders—if they wanted to eat, they must conquer and take.

With these matters addressed, Joshua and the Israelites turned their attention to Jericho. Joshua went out to conduct one last review of the site and came back with an exciting report. God had physically appeared to him near Jericho, promised the attack would succeed, and gave him specific instructions on how to attack (Josh. 5:13–6:5). This news encouraged the army, but Judah had an uneasy feeling that the instructions might fit into the "I don't understand, so I'll just obey" category.

Indeed they did. God commanded the Israelites to use some very strange tactics (Josh. 6:1–7). They were to march around the city once a day for six days. The seventh day, they were to march around seven times, then shout as the priests blew their trumpets of rams' horns, and the walls would collapse. Judah knew that he wasn't the most experienced military strategist around, but he figured anyone could see problems with that plan. Marching the whole army around the city in broad daylight would give the enemy excellent opportunity to take measure of the invaders and their capabilities. Their full number and weaponry would be on display for the defenders to analyze and scheme against. And if the defenders weren't sure of all they had seen on the first day, the invaders would come back again to make the same display the following day, and the day after that, and the day after that. Wouldn't it be better to disguise at least part of their numbers and weaponry?[6] And what would it accomplish to start out with an extra long, tiring march of several hours into and through the heat of the day on the day of the attack,[7] and then rely on an attack that pitted noise against solid fortifications? Truly, this strategy fit into the "I don't understand, so I'll just obey" category. Only God could make such strategy work. Judah assumed that was the point and committed himself to doing his part.

The next morning, Judah ben-Eliezer awoke before the morning trumpet call. He lay still and thought for a few minutes. He moved his torso carefully to confirm that the effects of the circumcision had passed. Good. Then his mind turned to what lay ahead. The Israelites would begin to engage the Canaanites today, though perhaps they would just attack each other with words from a safe distance, if he was anticipating correctly. Even that seemed like a watershed. For his entire life Judah had looked forward to the chance to conquer Canaan, as had his father and those of his generation. His father's father and countless generations before that had longed for this opportunity but knew that they wouldn't see it. God had promised his people centuries ago that they would return to Canaan and take the land, but always it had been too far away to become reality for them. Today Judah would see that distant promise begin to merge with very real current events, and he knew that blood and death were needed to bring the promises to life. His generation would see the divine promises come true, and many would pay the price in blood. These were great concepts that even Judah's nimble brain struggled to fully comprehend and synthesize.

Soon the blowing of the ram's horn announced the time to rise, and the day began. The men ate a breakfast of unleavened bread, dates, and wine, courtesy of the unwilling locals, and packed roasted grain and dried dates[8] to carry along with skins of water or wine. They somberly donned their protective gear and weapons, modest though they were. Judah looked around at his close and distant kinsmen preparing for battle. Many wore plain garments with no extra protection beyond simple wooden shields covered with leather that all had fashioned for themselves. Others, like Judah, substituted simple leather garments for their regular clothing. Leather could not stop a direct blow from a spear, sword, or even an arrow, but it did lessen and even deflect entirely some indirect blows. His mother had made leather garments for Judah and his brothers, and Judah thought the extra protection worth the discomfort from the added weight and heat. Plus, it made mother feel like she was helping protect her boys.

The Israelites' offensive weapons also appeared quite modest compared to the spears, swords, axes, and composite bows that Egyptian troops or soldiers of other great armies would carry. Many Israelites had only basic weapons they could fashion themselves—slings or simple bows for long range fighting, and sharpened sticks for spears to use at close range.

Though they had to start with simple weapons, Israelite troops upgraded their weaponry at the expense of enemy citizens or troops whenever they had opportunity. They raided metal tools from enemy farmers to use as is or adapt as weapons. Farmers' cutting tools became soldiers' daggers or spearheads. Farmers used metal ox goads on the ends of sticks to prod their animals when plowing; soldiers took and sharpened them for piercing weapons (Judg. 3:31). Every enemy nomad or Transjordanian soldier that had fallen in battle against Israel had served as a potential source for better weaponry or protective gear, and some yielded fine weapons. Because of this, a few Israelites carried nice metal weapons crafted by skilled artisans. Someday after they settled in their homeland, the Israelites would be able to produce their own effective metal weapons, but for now they had to watch for chances to take them from others who may well have obtained them in similar fashion from other enemies. Indeed, it was often impossible to know who had originally produced the weapons and how many hands they had passed through over time.

Judah was fortunate. He wore the leather protective gear fashioned by his mother and carried a good leather-covered shield made from strong wood that had grown on the Transjordanian highlands. In addition, he had tricked and killed a large but not-so-clever Moabite soldier in a small skirmish some weeks earlier and inherited the Moabite's beautiful spear. The spearhead was long, fairly new, and still in good condition, made of bronze,[9] of course. Judah appreciated that it had a central rib running the length of the blade for strength, as well as a reinforced metal "mouth" at the base that swallowed the end of the long, wooden handle (Fig. 1.2[10]). Most spearheads were not so strong and ended in a simple metal tail that had to fit inside of the wooden handle, weakening it. (In modern terminology, Judah had a socketed spearhead rather than one with a tang.) Others envied Judah's fine weapon.

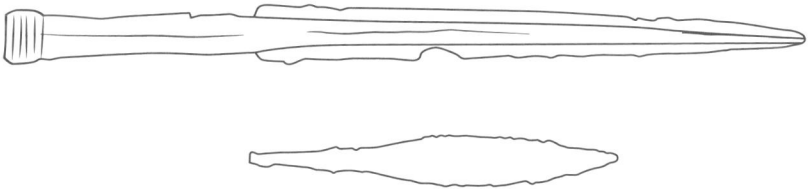

Fig. 1.2—Socketed and tanged spearheads

The Israelite soldiers finished their preparations, and when they next heard the ram's horn, they mustered in their units. Nearly all of these units were comprised of men from the same familial clan, serving under the relative who led the clan in peacetime as well as war. Judah thus marched and fought alongside his three older brothers and their many cousins, as well as their fathers. The eldest of the fathers led the unit. After the units assembled, the ram's horn sounded again, and the numerous units formed into their order of march. The assembled Israelite army couldn't compare to the armies of nations like Egypt, but for an emerging people without a homeland to serve as a base, they were fairly well organized, somewhat experienced, and highly motivated.

Israel's soldiers were all motivated to win themselves homes and a homeland, of course, but they had other motivations as well. Many were fighting to bring glory to their God and to themselves. Most also wanted to add to their possessions and always had their eyes open for enemy goods they could claim for themselves and their families (Deut. 20:14). Others had at least one eye open for attractive enemy women they could take as wives (Deut. 21:10–14). Judah thought the idea of taking an enemy woman ridiculous, in part because a certain attractive cousin named Naomi had looked at Judah with large brown eyes before the army crossed the Jordan River, and pled with him to be careful and return soon. Judah thought again of Naomi and his other reasons for fighting as he awaited the command to begin advancing toward Jericho.

The ram's horn sounded yet again and the formation set out. Nearly all were silent, alone with their thoughts. Most dreamt of wealth and glory, fought to suppress fear, and wondered what lay ahead, both today and beyond. Soon Jericho came into view. The city looked smaller than Judah had anticipated, but had a clear, double line of strong mud-brick walls protecting it[11] (Fig. 1.3). Someone gave out a low whistle, and everyone understood why. Israel's young army had already won a number of victories, but none against such a well-fortified target. This should prove challenging.

For any other nation-less army, conquering such a target would probably have proved overwhelming. For the Israelites, it seemed overwhelming, but their God had a good track record of helping them through overwhelming situations as long as they were obedient. They were obedient now, including following God's orders about placing him at the head of the march. Many armies carried symbols of their gods at the front to symbolize their gods' leadership and protection (note Fig. 3.8 and accompanying discussion, as well as 2 Chron. 13:8). The Israelites also carried a symbol of their God, except that their priests bore a gold-covered holy box, the Ark of the Covenant, rather than a statue or mounted standard of their God. In front of the Ark marched an honor guard and seven priests blowing seven rams' horns to announce God's

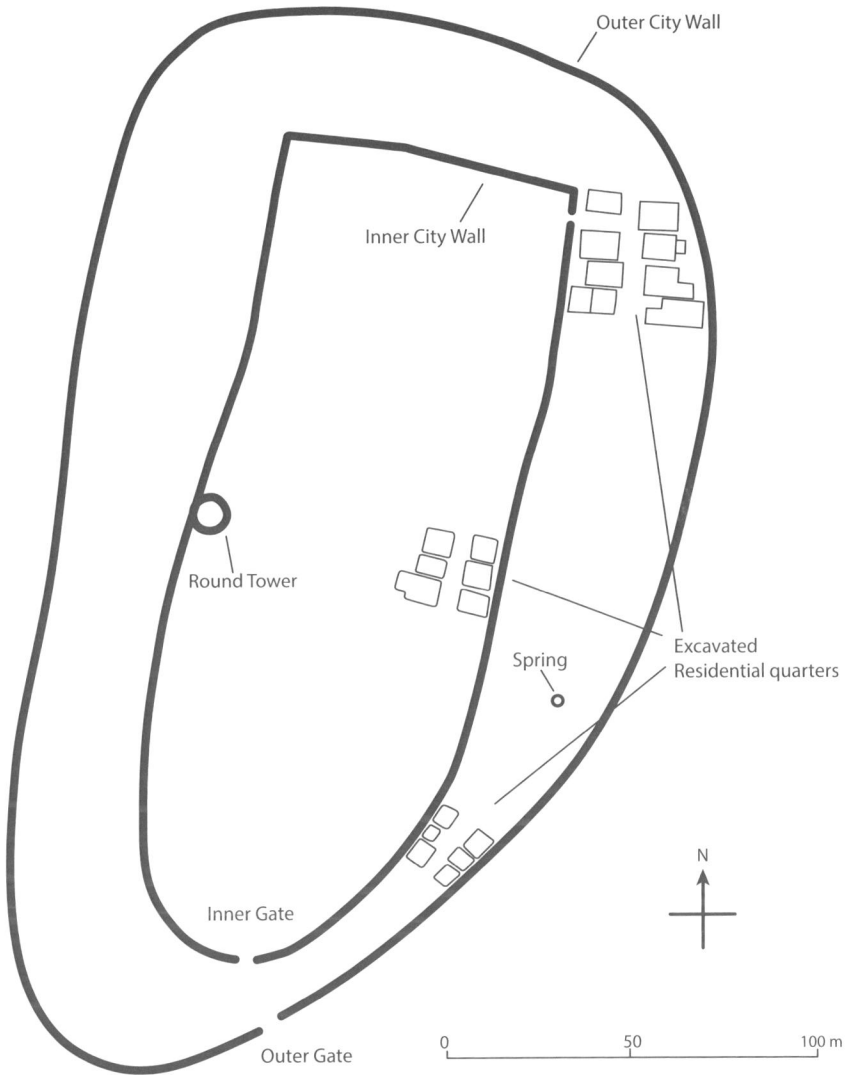

Fig. 1.3—Ancient Jericho as it may have appeared at the time of the conquest

presence. Israel's God wanted his army and their enemies to know that he would lead Israel to victory.

As per divine orders, Joshua led the army not directly toward the city but slightly to the side so they could go around it without engaging. They would circle the city once, close enough to observe as much as they could, but far enough away to stay out of range of enemy archers manning the ramparts on top of the walls. The Israelites couldn't make out archers or any other defenders clearly yet, but everyone knew they were there.

The long line of Israelites continued to advance, and soon they could hear the first of the enemy's taunts between the blasts of the Israelites' rams' horns. No one knew whether the enemies' jeers came more from confidence in their defenses or from fear because of the reputation of the attackers, both of which were substantial. Taunts were a typical part of the game, except that the order had come down that the Israelites were not to return them here at Jericho. Judah figured that their unusual silence would confuse the defenders at least a bit, adding to the odd presentation the Israelites were making. The attackers continued their circuit, with their full number eventually forming a complete, albeit thin, ring around the city.[12] The defenders continued taunting, along with launching a few arrows, undoubtedly from their strongest archers. The taunts increased when the defenders saw the head of the attackers' column heading off to return to their camp at the end of the circuit. Soon Judah's unit had finished the circuit and began moving toward Gilgal. Judah and his relatives relaxed a bit, relieved that the action, such as it was, had ended for the day.

The day's events repeated themselves six times, though each day the tension decreased for the attackers and the confusion and taunts increased for the defenders. The soldiers at Jericho wondered when the actual attack would finally begin, and the attackers wondered what would happen when they employed the very strange tactics ordered for day seven.

The fateful seventh day finally arrived. For the Israelites, it began like the others, but they knew it would not end at all like the others. The defenders at Jericho knew it was different as soon as the Israelites turned to begin their second circuit of the city. The defenders' vigilance heightened, then gradually diminished as the attackers made circuit after circuit and the morning passed to and beyond midday. Finally the Israelites stopped and faced their target. The defenders remaining on the walls snapped back to full alert, and called for reinforcements. Most of their comrades had been dismissed during the Israelites' long march, and had descended to rest in the shade of buildings next to the wall.[13] Now they scrambled to don their equipment and weapons, and retake their places. But that took time, and the Israelites and their God didn't give it to them.

The priests sounded the rams' horns a final time, Joshua shouted a command, and the troops shouted their battle cries. At that moment, the Israelites all felt the earth begin shaking, and saw that Jericho shook the most.[14] The thick mud-brick walls teetered and cracked, then collapsed in multiple places. The Israelites heard the city's defenders and inhabitants cry out in terror. They watched many in Jericho get buried in the collapse of parts of the walls and numerous buildings before an increasing cloud of dust shielded their view. The stunned Israelites hesitated until Joshua commanded them to charge. The attackers let out another battle cry and charged at full speed. Amazement, excitement, fear, and courage all coursed through their minds and hearts as they raced the short distance to the city.

Minutes ago, capturing the city had seemed nearly impossible; now it had become a foregone conclusion. The Israelites clamored up the piles of mud bricks from the collapsed walls, and Judah noted the irony that the bricks that were intended to keep out attackers now helped them to enter. This battle, like most, broke down quickly into countless small skirmishes between individuals or small groups. The Israelites fought bravely and effectively, doing more slaughtering than fighting. Many defenders had lost their lives or their weapons, or at least their will to resist, with the earthquake. Like the attackers, the defenders understood the earthquake as the work of Israel's God, and what mortal can defeat a god? Most of the defenders fell quickly at the perimeter of the city, and the attackers penetrated deeper into the city to find and slaughter the civilians as well. Most of the Israelites didn't relish this part, but such were their orders from their commander and their God, and they understood what they needed to do. Many peoples in this era dedicated entire conquered cities with their populations to their god or gods,[15] and total destruction was one way they converted something into a divine offering. God was beginning to give Canaan to the Israelites, and the Israelites would give back Jericho and its inhabitants as the "firstfruits."

Thankfully, the carnage didn't last long, and the battle transitioned to the after-battle activities. Normally the troops would be taking food, goods, and people for their own, but in this case the people were nearly all dead, and most of the goods were off limits. Only the local woman who had aided the Israelite spies was spared, along with her family (Josh. 6:22–23). As commanded, the troops collected all the metal objects they could find to donate to the national treasury (Josh. 6:19). The food, clothing, and other valuables had to be left behind to be consumed when the attackers set the city ablaze.

The soldiers found it difficult to forego the plunder, and Judah thought through what obedience to these commands would cost the Israelites. Soon Judah and his countrymen would have new homes in Canaan and would need to supply them. Destroying good materials and food seemed impractical, especially now. God had asked that they donate the precious gold and silver objects to him—no problem. But asking soldiers in desperate need of good metal weaponry to turn over nice weapons to be melted down or used for other purposes was extremely difficult. Nevertheless, Judah and the Israelites understood their divine orders, and obeyed (but see Josh. 7). They also knew that such plunder would probably be off limits just this once. Future victories would surely produce good plunder to which they would be welcome, and their divinely aided, stunning success at Jericho bode well for the rest of the conquest. Apparently all they needed to do was obey.

You don't have to understand; just obey. As Judah watched the city burn, he thought again how wisely his father had spoken. It seemed that events in life usually went according to ways one could naturally understand. At other times—like when crossing swollen rivers, disabling troops after entering enemy territory, and attacking solid walls with noise and obedience—obeying their faithful God seemed the key to Israel's success. *Maybe this conquest really will work,* thought Judah, *and maybe I will return whole and soon to Naomi.* The future looked bright and promising for this thoughtful and obedient Israelite. He was part of an army and people that were forming a nation that was supposed to obey God as their king. Israel was to be the kingdom of God, and obedience was vital to build such a kingdom. So far, so good.

HISTORICAL BACKGROUND

The preceding story is set at the beginning of the Israelite conquest of Canaan, but the history of that people and their involvement in warfare had begun much earlier. Assuming the authenticity of the Bible's historical texts, the Israelite people and warfare began at the time of Abraham, who may have lived about 2000 BC. Genesis 14 records the most meaningful military account from the stories of Abraham and the other patriarchs. In that event, the powerful leader Abraham mustered hundreds of troops from his clan and joined with a few allies to attack a coalition of armies that had successfully plundered the region and taken Abraham's kinsmen as captives. The account tells us nothing of his weaponry and little of his tactics except that Abraham and his forces "divided against them" (Gen. 14:15*) for an attack at night, apparently using guerilla tactics typical for an outmatched force, successfully attacking a superior foe.

After the patriarchs, the Bible presents the Israelites spending several centuries in Egypt, at the end of which they had to free themselves from a nation whose military was at or near its quite impressive peak (see chap. 3). Israel succeeded, though clearly not because of its own strength or military capability. Indeed, the Israelites didn't seem to even have engaged the Egyptians militarily. Rather they seem to have simply watched as their God worked dramatically and successfully on their behalf against Egypt's chariots that were pursuing them (Ex. 14–15). Obviously, Yahweh was "fighting for them against Egypt" (Ex. 14:25).

As the Israelites then journeyed through the Wilderness of Sinai on their way to Canaan, their need and opportunity to gain military capability increased. They would have skirmished with nomadic groups in the desert (Ex. 17:8–13), and needed to organize, equip, and train for such encounters as well as future battles against the established populations in the areas they intended to settle (Num. 14:39–45). The earlier victory over the Egyptians at the time of the Exodus probably provided an opportunity to plunder good weapons and equipment from the Egyptian chariotry (Ex. 14:7), the best of the Egyptian military (see chap. 3). During the following years the Israelites would have had ample time to fashion and practice using bows, slings, and other simple weapons as they journeyed through the desert, undoubtedly hunting game and defending themselves from bandits. The Israelites also made trumpets to signal commands for marching and battle (Num. 10:1–10). Their formations while camping (Num. 2) and on the march (Num. 10:11–36) reflect military organization, with the leadership in the center for command and control, and a clear organization of surrounding groups of tribes protecting the core.

The Bible next records a number of battles involving the Israelites at the edges of Canaan as they approached their Promised Land. The king of Arad at the southern tip of Canaan made a preemptive and initially successful attack against the invaders. The account (Num. 21:1–3) tells little of the tactics except that Israel vowed to completely destroy this enemy as a gift to their God if he would grant them success. He did, and they fulfilled their vow by completely destroying the attackers' villages, rather like Israel would do at Jericho later. Victories over two kings and their forces at two locations in the Transjordan (Num. 21:21–31, 33–35; see Map 1.1) broke the ability of these forces to resist, and opened up the region for settlement by several of the Israelite tribes. As usual, the accounts include little military data.

Next the Bible records the conquest of Canaan, a significant achievement for an emerging nation without an established homeland. Even though questions about the factuality and timing of the conquest continue to foster much scholastic debate, the Bible appears to present the conquest as taking place in the latter half of the 2nd millennium BC, perhaps in the early 14th or later 13th centuries.[16] Following the unusual tactics commanded at the Jordan River and Jericho as portrayed in the earlier story, the Israelites continue their conquest of at least parts of Canaan. The biblical accounts of these battles are the longest and most detailed at the beginning of the invasion (Josh. 1–10:28) when the Israelites would have been most inexperienced. Likely the author(s) emphasized these early events to highlight the Israelites' obedience of their divinely directed strategies, and especially to make clear how God was helping them accomplish an otherwise seemingly impossible task.

A careful reading of the conquest, along with a good map, reveals the overall Israelite/divine strategy. The attackers first penetrated in east-central Canaan, then gained a hold in the central highlands through victory at Ai and unintentionally by treaty with Gibeon (Josh. 7–9). They finished cutting across the heart of the central hill country with their victory over the enemy coalition attacking Gibeon and driving them westward out of the hills into the western foothills. After thus dividing the country, they conquered the parts, making a swing through the southern foothills and high ground, and then defeating a coalition gathered in the north (Josh. 10–11).

Although the conquest allowed the Israelites to settle in parts of Canaan centered around the central highland, the subsequent period of the Judges demonstrated the often tenuous nature of their hold on the land. The book of Joshua presents the Israelites as acting in unison during the conquest, but now during the book of Judges, the twelve tribes often operated independently and "everyone did as they saw fit" (Judg. 21:25). The resulting general chaos and apostasy within Israel reflected both on the Israelites' spiritual condition and on the general conditions around Israel. During the latter part of the 2nd millennium BC, the ancient Near East witnessed great upheavals among peoples and nations, a significant decline in population, and the destruction of previously great cities and civilizations. Apparently Egypt's control over Canaan went through a corresponding decline, perhaps allowing, in part, for the initial Israelite conquest as well as contributing to the general anarchy reflected in the book of Judges.

Militarily, the Israelites fought numerous defensive wars during the time of the Judges, in which the objective was simply to survive. Many peoples, including the Philistines on the west, Amalekites in the south, and Ammonites, Moabites, and Edomites in the west (Map 1.2), pressured Israel by plundering food and other goods. In response to these challenges, charismatic leaders that the Bible calls judges would arise and call for a muster of ablebodied Israelites to follow and help repulse the latest invader. Although some of these exploits are recorded in colorful and interesting stories, the deeply flawed judges reflect the deeply flawed nation as it struggled to avoid extinction.

This ongoing pressure to survive these military challenges contributed to the Israelites' desire for a centralized authority in a king who "go out before us and fight our battles" (1 Sam. 8:20). The prophet Samuel warned clearly that a centralized government would come at a high price—the king would take the Israelites' sons for

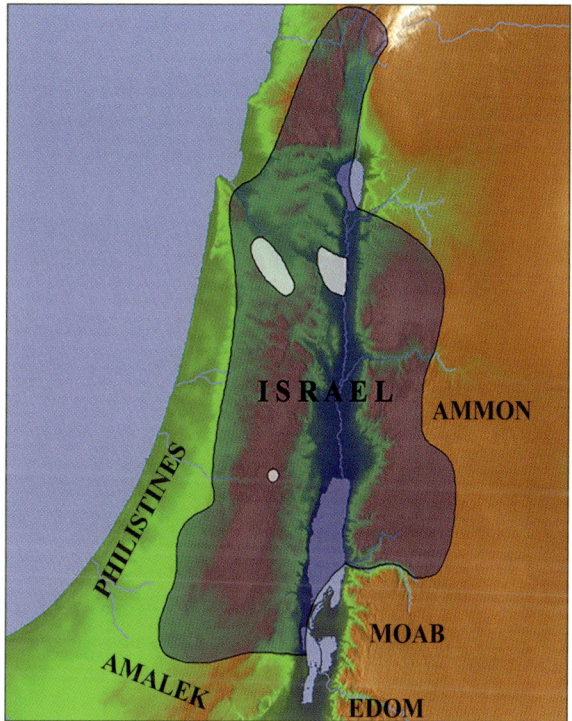

Map 1.2—Israel and its oppressors during Judges. Blue shows area of Canaan under Israelite control after conquest (portrayed optimistically). Light areas represent enclaves of non-Israelites.

military service and for making implements of war, as well as taking the best of their property and imposing heavy taxes to pay soldiers and other officials (1 Sam. 8:10–18). Despite these warnings, the nation proceeded with the change to a monarchy during the latter part of the 11th century. During the reign of Saul, the largely unsuccessful first king, the nation continued to limp along in defensive wars, fighting for survival. When Saul's reign came to its inglorious end (see story at the beginning of chap. 5), the nation nearly did as well.

Fortunately for Israel, Saul was succeeded by David, who not only managed to keep Israel alive, he led it in conquests until he and son Solomon would command an empire that stretched from Egypt to the Euphrates River (Map 1.3). The record of David and Israel's rise from the brink of annihilation to domination of the ancient Near East in less than the span of a generation represents one of the most dramatic stories to come from the ancient Near East. David combined military, political, economic, and theological skills that carried him and his nation to glory. He also benefited from ruling at a time when neither Egypt nor the Mesopotamian kingdoms such as Assyria or Babylon could exert their usual dominance. David and Solomon's Israel dominated the ancient Near East during a rather small window of opportunity when a nation like theirs could take charge. Not long after the death of Solomon, that window would close.

Israel's military obviously played a major role in the nation's rise and dominance during the time of David and Solomon, and one can see elements of the transformation of Israel's military during this time (see further discussion in chap. 2). The army evolved from a militia made up of part-timers who served during an emergency with a small standing army at its core, to a force with a strong standing army, supplemented by a militia. David also seems to have added the beginnings of a chariot force, or at least have begun preparations for such a force, and his son Solomon developed a powerful chariotry, typical of the great militaries of the time. During the reigns of these two kings, the number of Israelites involved in the military would have increased dramatically, along with the national resources needed to staff and support such a force. Likely resentment over these costs helped foster the division during the second half of the 10th century that resulted in the separate kingdoms of Israel and Judah.

After that division, the fortunes of the two nations rose and fell in accordance with the greater political realities in the ancient Near East, as well as with the political and economic skill and theological fidelity of the two nations and their kings. Israel and Judah sometimes wasted their resources in civil wars that accomplished little more than

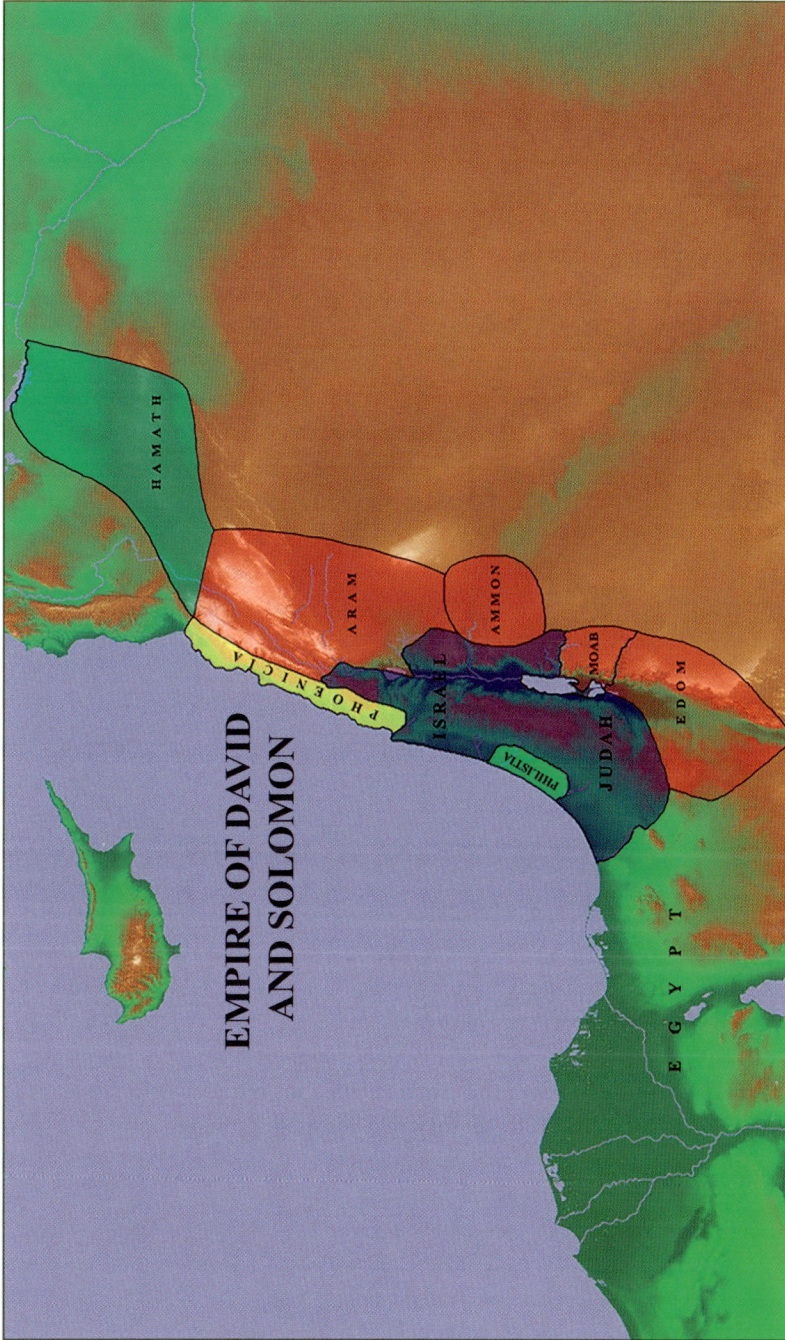

Map 1.3—Empire of David and Solomon at its peak. Dual kingdom of Israel and Judah shown in blue, conquered nations that brought tribute in red, nations subjected to a lesser degree in green, and allied nation in yellow.

distracting them from more important matters. Nearby nations such as Aram to the north and Egypt to the south periodically sent in armies to plunder or to conquer and annex. The more distant nation of Assyria threatened the kingdoms in the Levant or eastern Mediterranean in the 9th century, but had to withdraw. Unfortunately, they would return.

As described in chapter 6, Assyria did return to the eastern Mediterranean and conquered nearly all of the Levantine kingdoms in the second half of the 8th century, including Israel and most of Judah. Although Israel had developed into a relatively wealthy nation with a sizeable and effective military, it could not hold off a superpower such as Assyria, even when aligned with other nations in the region. This expansion of Assyria into the eastern Mediterranean began a period of regional dominance by Mesopotamian powers that would run until the end of the Old Testament and beyond, during the empires of Assyria, Babylon, and Persia. Curiously, the lesser, weaker Judah withstood the Mesopotamian forces nearly a century and a half longer than Israel, which the Bible attributes to the mercy of God and his fidelity to his earlier promises to David.

Ultimately Judah would fall, despite God's promises and character. The moral and religious failures of Judah's kings and people would cause God to withdraw his protection. The God who had stopped up the flooding Jordan River years before so Israel could invade at the nation's birth would not stop the flood of Mesopotamian power at the nation's death. God had helped young Israel because young Israel had obeyed the covenant and commands of its God, and it had become the kingdom of God. A much older Israel had long since abandoned that obedience, and would pay the heavy price of conquest and exile. Fortunately, the Israelites worshipped a merciful and faithful God who would first punish and purify, but then forgive and restore, and Israel's history would continue.

NOTES

1 Image is an Israelite male from a relief done by artists of the Assyrian king Sennacherib portraying the conquest of the Judean city of Lachish at the end of the 8th century. It postdates the time of the Israelite conquest of Canaan and the fictitious Judah by several centuries, but it includes one of the few apparently genuine portrayals of ancient Israelites.
2 Compare the experience of a modern US marine who underwent circumcision

during a tour of duty. After he was circumcised, the doctors ordered a week of bed rest, then six weeks of light duty for Corp. Phil Bolanos. When one of his stitches ruptured, he was given three additional weeks of light duty. Thus, this marine, with the advantages of modern health care, was out of commission for ten weeks. The Bible states simply that the newly circumcised Israelite army remained in camp "until they were healed" (Josh. 5:8). However long that took, they would have been highly vulnerable to enemy attack.

3   The Israelites apparently spoke one of the dialects of what the Bible calls "the language of Canaan" (Isa. 19:18). After they settled in their homeland, the Israelites became one of several different groups in the region that spoke variations of the same root language of that area, and these dialects would later be called names like Hebrew, Moabite, and Edomite.

4   The text states that the water stopped "a great distance away, at a town called Adam" (Josh. 3:16). There the Jordan runs below a bluff on its east bank, which periodically collapses and cuts off the flow of the Jordan for a time before the water cuts through and resumes its southward course. This is known to have occurred in AD 1927 (for twenty-one hrs.), 1906, 1834, 1546, 1267 (for sixteen hrs.), and 1160.

Adam is located approximately sixteen miles north of Jericho, so the Israelites would not have been able to see the collapse. It would also have taken many hours for the water level to drop so dramatically so far away, allow the army to cross, and then return to normal.

5   A tributary flowing into the Jordan River at this spot deposited enough silt to create the shallower ford. At the ford the water was typically three to four feet deep, but at flood stage the river could be ten to twelve feet deep and 140 feet across (John A. Beck, "The Narrative-Geographical Shaping of Joshua 3–4," *JETS* 48/4 (Dec. 2005) 694–96). The modern Allenby Bridge (called the King Hussein Bridge by the Jordanians) connecting the countries of Israel and Jordan near Jericho continues the tradition of crossing the Jordan River at this point.

6   The oldest known military treatise in the world was written by the Chinese general Sun Tzu ca. 500 BC. One of his well-known maxims states, "All warfare is based on deception," emphasizing that one can better defeat an enemy that doesn't know what to expect. God apparently wanted the Israelites to ignore this normally sound principle for the attack at Jericho.

U.S. Marine Sergeant Joshua Draveling commented as follows on the Israelite tactic of marching around Jericho in plain view of the enemy: "If that's what God commanded them to do, then that's what they needed to do. But just on a human level, it's pretty ridiculous. It's like playing poker—you can't win if you show your hand. Showing your numbers and weapons to the enemy would help them plan how to defeat you, and instill confidence in them that they can win."

7   This author's personal march around the outer perimeter of the relatively small site of Jericho took approximately fifteen minutes. If one assumes the Israelites would have stayed at least a bowshot (up to 200 yards) away from the walls while encircling the city, the march might have taken some three times as long. A roughly forty-five minute circuit times seven circuits on the seventh day would suggest many hours of marching in increasingly warm conditions, stretching to midday in a place that gets quite warm even in the spring (summer temperatures reach 120 degrees F). This suggests that God was asking the Israelites to tire themselves appreciably before beginning the attack—indeed strange tactics.

8   Joshua 5:11 notes that the Israelites had begun eating unleavened bread and roasted grain from Canaan by this point, and dates have always been a common food in the region of Jericho. The city is even called the "City of Palms" (Deut. 34:3; Judg. 1:16; 3:13; 2 Chron. 28:15), undoubtedly for the date palm trees that flourish in the region.

9   Bronze remained the primary metal for making such objects at this time, though iron would begin to replace it during the 12th century (see Amihai Mazar, *Archaeology of the Land of the Bible 10,000–586 B.C.E.* (New York: Doubleday, 1990), 264–66, 359–61).

10   The two spearheads depicted were found at Tell Al Umayri (biblical Abel Keramim—see Judg. 11:33) and Megiddo. Both were bronze and dated to Iron Age I, perhaps shortly after the Israelite conquest. Rodriquez, *Arsenal,* pl. 18 (H60), 21 (H2).

11   The archaeological remains at Jericho continue to foster debate, with some arguing that no Canaanite city stood at Jericho at the time the Bible apparently portrays that Joshua would have attacked. The inner, higher city wall shown in Fig. 1.3 originally dates to the Early Bronze Age (3200–2200 BC), and the outer wall apparently was built in the latter part of the Middle Bronze Age (2000–1550 BC). Both predate the Israelite conquest, but both could still have been in use until that time.

12   According to U.S. Marine Sergeant Joshua Draveling, a force of even 5,000 troops could form a complete circle 200 yards out around a target like Jericho, though the line would be too strung out to appear intimidating.

13   Thanks to Sergeant Draveling for his insights on how the defenders may have responded to the long wait, and how that response could have greatly eroded their numbers at the moment of attack.

14   Jericho is located along a major geological fault, and the region has witnessed many earthquakes throughout history, including earthquakes of magnitude 5.3 in February 2004 and of 4.5 in November 2007. This story suggests that a divinely directed earthquake caused the city's walls to collapse at this point in the conquest.

15   For example, the Moabite king Mesha (2 Kings 3:4–27) boasted about such an event: "And Kemosh [the Moabite god] said to me, 'Go! Seize Nebo [from] Israel,' so I proceeded by night and I fought with it from the crack of dawn to midday and I took it and I slew all of them, seven thousand men and boys and women and girls and maidens because I had dedicated it to Ashtar-Kemosh and I took the vessels of Yahweh and I dragged them before (presented them to?) Kemosh" ("The Mesha Inscription." Shmuel Ahituv, *Echoes from the Past: Hebrew and Cognate Inscriptions from the Biblical Period* (Jerusalem: Carta, 2008), 394).

16   Many understand the Bible to portray a date for the Exodus at 1446 BC. This comes primarily from 1 Kings 6:1, which states that Solomon began building the temple in the fourth year of his reign (966 BC), 480 years after the Exodus. Assuming that number is straightforward, 480 years before 966 BC brings one to 1446 BC. The later statement of Jephthah in Judges 11:26 (perhaps dated to ca. 1100 BC) that Israel had inhabited the Transjordan for 300 years seems to support a date of the Exodus ca. 1446 and a conquest that began forty years later ca. 1406 BC. However, others argue that these numbers may be rounded or figurative, and that the Exodus and conquest under Joshua actually occurred some 200 years later, during the 13th century BC. In support, a good deal of archaeological evidence in Israel reflecting the emergence of the Israelites seems to better fit the latter date. At this time, then, the textual and physical evidence do not line up neatly to give a clear date for the Exodus and conquest of Canaan.

ISRAEL:
THE ARMY OF THE KINGDOM OF GOD—PART 2

2

MILITARY ORGANIZATION

As described in the last chapter, the nation of Israel went through a number of dramatic changes during a history that stretched for nearly a millennium. Israel's military organization went through a similar series of drastic changes as the nation's fortunes rose and fell. Israel struggled through its birth and early history, rose quickly to regional dominance under kings David and Solomon, then experienced division and subsequent periods of strength and weakness before each of the separate kingdoms fell victim to different international powers.

Many other powerful ancient Near Eastern nations experienced similar histories with ascendancy and decline, but Israel stands out because the Bible preserves a relatively clear record of its military as the nation developed into a strong power. Typically, one finds good military records from nations only after they attained great strength. Surprisingly, some of the best information from Israel comes from when it was struggling for birth and survival. The Bible's emphasis on God's aid to his young nation is evident in the stories of how the military operated through its successive phases; this presents a fascinating window into the military development of what became a major regional power.

Israel's military developed as Israelite society changed throughout its history, and conversely, the military helped drive some of the societal changes. The army of the kingdom of God began as a collection of part-time soldiers drawn from a loose federation of related tribes fighting to establish and then maintain living space. After Israel transitioned to a monarchy, the army grew to a meaningful force of professional soldiers that was supplemented by a continuing militia. The central government supported this expanding force by increasing taxation and through several types of major restructuring that changed the fabric of Israelite society. A people whose loyalties had long been tied to tribal and family lines found their society reconfigured in order to better serve the crown and its enormous financial needs—including the military.

Though the price was high, the rewards were also high—at times. Effective kings and their increasingly sophisticated militaries sometimes repaid their people with additional land, wealth, and glory. At other times, less effective kings or unfavorable international circumstances led to greatly reduced benefits. Ultimately, failed leadership and an increasingly difficult international political situation combined to bring about the end of Israel's kingdoms, a fate from which no military could rescue.

Recruitment and Organization

Early Israel apparently obtained its soldiers through a general levy of all able-bodied men twenty years and older (Num. 1:2–3, 45; 26:2, 4; 1 Chron. 27:23; 2 Chron. 25:5). Such a militia served as the only or later the primary part of the army during the conquest, the period of the judges, and into the early monarchy. The militia would have served continuously during the conquest under Joshua, and then transitioned to temporary, occasional service as needed during the judges and monarchy. At the time of need, a charismatic leader called a judge, or later the king, would issue a call for troops from the entire nation (Judg. 20:1–2; 1 Sam. 11:6–8) or just some of the tribes (for a localized threat— Judg. 4:6–10; 6:35; 7:23) and lead them into battle. The men would leave their farms or other occupations, take up their meager arms, and fight until the end of the crisis. Afterwards they would be dismissed "every man to his own tent (home)" (Judg. 7:8*; 1 Sam. 4:10*).

Such a system worked well sometimes, but at other times, it led to problems. Some of those who were called refused to come or provide requested support (Judg. 5:23; 8:5–9). Others not called or who chose not to take part got angry at being excluded (Judg. 5:16–17; 8:1; 12:1). In addition, such levied troops were typically lightly armed and poorly trained, and would have found themselves outmatched by more established armies. For example, in one engagement when Saul and Jonathan led the Israelite militia against the Philistines, only the king and crown prince had metal weapons (1 Sam. 13:19–22). Such problems were likely part of the impetus for the later call for a king, rather than judges, to govern and "go out before us and fight our battles" (1 Sam 8:20).

After Israel made the transition to a monarchy, the militia continued. Israel's first king, Saul, responded to military threats by summoning the militia (1 Sam 11:6–8; 13:3–4), though he apparently began to establish the nucleus of a permanent army early on. Shortly after the prophet Samuel publicly proclaimed Saul king, the Bible notes that a band of soldiers stayed with Saul, apparently the core of a permanent military force (1 Sam. 10:26). Saul made a practice of taking suitable men for military service (1 Sam. 14:52; in 16:21–22 Saul takes David), and apparently paid them with gifts such as land and military rank (1 Sam 22:7; cf. 8:11–15).

While Saul was struggling to build a national army, his rival David built a private army. David's early military successes fostered Saul's jealousy of him, forcing David to flee to the wilderness. There he organized a band of followers that functioned as an independent military force. Such unofficial groups appear repeatedly in the biblical texts, as with Abimelech (Judg. 9:4), Jephthah (Judg. 11:3), Rezon (1 Kings 11:23–24), and perhaps Jeroboam (2 Chron. 13:6–7). These groups would be made up of men wanted by the authorities or men without property who gathered around a strong leader like David. They would raid others' property and hire themselves out as mercenaries. David's personal army grew from four hundred to six hundred (1 Sam 22:2; 23:13; 27:2–3) and included families (1 Chron. 12:1–22), a priest with an ephod (a sacred garment—1 Sam 23:6), and a hierarchy of officers that later made up part of the corps of officers in David's official army (1 Chron. 12: 4, 9–13).

Once he became king, David integrated the men from his private force into the national army and continued developing both it and the militia. Each branch had its own commanders and organization. David used the standing army whenever a smaller force would suffice or speed was essential, but he also called upon the levies as needed (2 Sam. 10:7–17; 2 Sam. 11:1; 12:26–29). The victory of David's smaller, professional army over rebellious Absalom with the levied troops (2 Sam. 17:11; 18:1–8) perhaps demonstrates the relative strength of the two forces. David also had contingents of foreign mercenaries (including

Philistines[1]) in his pay as bodyguards, undoubtedly to increase the likelihood of their loyalty and to protect himself from local power struggles and potential revolt.

Expanding military needs required reorganization of the army and of the nation itself. By the end of David's reign, he had reorganized the militia into twelve different divisions (1 Chron. 27:1–24) rather than along tribal lines. Each division consisted of 24,000 men (24 'eleph אֶלֶף—see discussion under "Size of Army"), with each division serving one month every year. Every division had its corps of officers, including some which utilized old familial ties. The army used officers that commanded family units and tribes (1 Chron. 27:1, 16–22), but these were apparently incorporated into the larger divisional structure, probably to avoid many of the problems inherent in tribal organization. Solomon continued with reorganization of the nation and its military, dividing Israel into twelve districts (1 Kings 4:7–19), rather than the historic tribal divisions (Josh. 13–18), in order to better supply the expanding royal needs, including the extensive military.

Officers

The army needed a corps of officers that would have developed as the army grew. The earliest Israelite military had an overall commander, apparently supported by tribal leadership. Joshua led the army that invaded Canaan, and likely commanded units mustered from clans led by clan leaders (see story at the beginning of chap. 1). Joshua 23:2 mentions Israel's "elders, leaders, judges, and officials," an unclear and perhaps fluid organization of leadership over various functions in society, probably including the military. During the more settled time of judges, tribal leadership remained in place, and various charismatic leaders rose to take temporary overall command. Likely this arrangement led to significant problems, as the levied troops may well have resisted authority of leaders not from their own tribes.

After Israel transitioned to a monarchy, either the king or an officer appointed by him led the army, usually called "commander of the army" (שַׂר הַצָּבָא—śar haṣṣābā'). Abner, Joab, and Beniah filled this role under Saul, David, and Solomon, respectively (1 Sam. 14:50; 1 Kings 1:19; 4:4). Saul led the army during his reign, and crown prince Jonathan also led a division (1 Sam. 13:2). David likewise led troops before and after he became king, but he also appointed Abner and later Joab as commander of the army. Separate officers served as commanders of the militia (2 Sam. 20:4–5) and of the royal bodyguard (2 Sam. 20:23).

The commander of the regular army clearly held a position of great power, playing major roles in the political affairs of the kingdom. The Bible records them involved in matters such as affairs of the royal family (bringing Absalom back to the capital—2 Sam. 14), making treaties (2 Sam. 3:12), scheming to establish or crowning a new king (1 Kings 1:5–7; 2 Sam. 2:8–9), killing for the king (2 Sam. 11:14–25), and becoming king themselves (1 Kings 16:9–10, 16).

The Bible also mentions a number of lesser officers under this commander of the army, though the organization is often not clear and probably changed fairly often over time. One finds commanders over units of thousands, hundreds, and fifties (1 Sam. 22:7; 8:12), with thousands and hundreds appearing most frequently. Many other titles ("leader," "captain," etc.) also appear, but the information is not clear enough to determine an organizational structure. In addition to their military duties, officers also took part in other functions, including religious processions (1 Chron. 15:25) and royal coups (2 Chron. 23:9–11).

Military Branches

In contrast to the more abundant but still incomplete information about the corps of officers that led Israel's developing military, the information available for the organization of the different military branches is quite sketchy.

Infantry

Since Israel perhaps used a navy only for trade (see below under "Navy") and arguably developed a chariot force only around the time of Solomon, the infantry comprised the entire army early on, as well as the bulk of the army throughout the nation's history. The infantry (רַגְלִי—*raglî* or אִישׁ רַגְלִי—*'îš raglî*) was probably organized along tribal lines much of the time (1 Chron. 12:23–37), and sometimes the different groups specialized in different types of weaponry. Most soldiers seem to have carried spear and shield (1 Chron. 12:24; 2 Chron. 14:8; Fig. 2.1—right[2]). Others "drew the sword" (2 Sam. 24:9, ESV), some used the bow (Fig. 2.1—center) or bow and shield (2 Chron. 14:8), and still others fought using slings (Judg. 20:16; 2 Kings 3:25; Fig. 2.1—left). Some were all-around fighters proficient with "every type of weapon" (1 Chron. 12:33, 37).

Chariotry (and Cavalry)

Although chariots begin to appear in the Bible as far back as the time of Joseph in the book of Genesis (41:43), Israelite chariots do not appear until the time of David. The earliest biblical texts about these horse-drawn vehicles all refer to Egyptian chariots—used for ceremony and transportation by Joseph, or by the Egyptian troops at the Sea of Reeds. The Egyptians mastered the building and military use of this light, fast machine early on (see discussion in chap. 4), and the Egyptian connections continue for the Israelites at least through the time of Solomon.

Fig. 2.1—Israelite slinger, archer, spearman. Based on reliefs from ca. 700 BC.

Early biblical texts usually reflect Israelite fear of chariots and an aversion to using them. "When you go to war . . . and see horses and chariots and an army greater than yours, do not be afraid" (Deut. 20:1). The emerging nation of Israel first faced Egyptian, then Canaanite and later Philistine chariots, and when they captured these machines in battle, the early Israelites obeyed God's command to burn the chariots and hamstring the horses (cripple by cutting the hamstring in the back of the leg, rendering it unsuitable for military use—see Josh. 11:6, 9).[3]

This aversion to using chariots seemingly changed by the time of David, and clearly had changed by the time of Solomon. During his conquests in the north, David captured one thousand chariots and hamstrung all but one hundred horses (2 Sam. 8:4), perhaps to begin building a force of chariots to help conquer and rule his expanding empire. David's son Adonijah used chariots (1 Kings 1:5), though apparently for prestige rather than military purposes. When Solomon ruled after David, he clearly built a major chariot force, with 1,400 chariots in chariot cities as well as in the capital (1 Kings 10:26). Solomon traded extensively in chariots and horses (1 Kings 10:28–29), an understandable economic and political move, but in direct violation of God's expressed command (Deut. 17:16).

The later kings of divided Israel and Judah continued using chariots, both for transportation and in battle (2 Chron. 10:18; 35:24; 2 Kings 9:25). The expense and prestige associated with these vehicles perhaps limited their use to kings, generals, and the two nations' respective chariot forces (1 Kings 16:9; 2 Kings 8:21). The northern kingdom of Israel built a particularly effective chariotry. King Ahab of Israel fielded two thousand chariots, the largest number in the coalition of nations that opposed Assyria at the Battle of Qarqar in Syria in 853 BC,[4] an event known from Assyrian annals but not mentioned in the Bible. After the northern kingdom fell to Assyria in the 8th century, charioteers from that nation earned the unique honor of having an entire unit of Assyrian chariotry named for their former capital of Samaria (see opening story in chap. 6).

Though the Bible and other records include a number of references to Israel's chariots, they tell us little about who made them or what they looked like. Solomon clearly imported Egyptian chariots, but it remains unclear whether he or any subsequent Israelite king also developed an Israelite infrastructure to produce these machines rather than import them. Numerous references to Canaanite chariots (Josh. 17:18; Judg. 4:3[5]) suggest at least the possibility of local manufacturing.[6] At least some of Solomon's chariots would have looked like Egypt's chariots (described and depicted in chapter 4), and kings who ruled after the rise of Assyria likely imported chariots from Assyria or whoever supplied chariots to them. The only known picture of an Israelite or Judean chariot (Fig. 2.2) comes from the same Assyrian reliefs that contained the imagery used in Fig. 2.1. This Judean chariot is pictured among the spoils taken from the governor's palace in Lachish, so it likely depicts the governor's ceremonial chariot rather than a typical military chariot of the time. The large, eight-spoked wheels, quiver mounted vertically at the front of the box, and higher rear of the box are all characteristic of Assyrian ceremonial chariots of the time.[7]

Along with chariots, the Israelites may well have used cavalry, though if or when they developed this capability remains unclear. By comparison, the Assyrians were still using chariots at the end of the 8th century, but they had largely switched to cavalry for their mounted troops (see chap. 7). The

information in the Bible is frustratingly unclear about the use of equestrian troops. The Bible typically uses the same elastic term "horse" (פָּרָשִׁים/
פָּרָשׁ—pārāš/pārāšîm) for horses (1 Kings 10:26), chariots (2 Sam. 1:6), chariot riders (Ex. 14:9), and apparently cavalry (1 Kings 9:19; 2 Kings 9:17). Perhaps the biblical authors used it to indicate horse-related troops of all types, making it often difficult or impossible for the modern reader to discern which is meant. Though cavalry would seem much more useful than wheeled chariots in the hills of Judah and Israel, these two kingdoms seem to have preferred chariots. For example, in the Battle of Qarqar mentioned earlier, King Ahab supplied 2,000 chariots but no cavalry, unlike the other nations that supplied a large numbers of chariots.

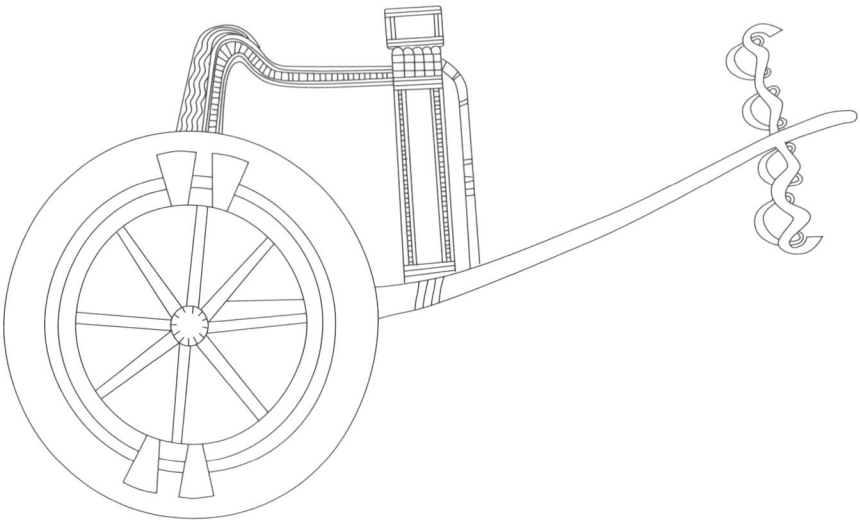

Fig. 2.2—Judean ceremonial chariot, ca. 700 BC. Note large wheel(s), vertically mounted quiver, and 4-horse yoke. Compare Assyrian chariot in Fig. 7.2.

Navy

In contrast to the more common infantry and dramatic chariotry, the biblical accounts mention an Israelite navy only in the context of merchant ships built for trade (1 Kings 9:26–28; 10:22; 22:48). None of these passages connect the ships to warfare, though chapter 3 describes how merchant ships could be and often were conscripted for military purposes.[8] Israelite kings may also have used merchant ships in that way when the need arose.

General Information

Along with describing the different branches of the Israelite military, the Bible also includes information about other aspects of that part of their culture. These include the size of the Israelite army and the key roles of Israel's kings and God in military activity.

In contrast to the texts of other ancient Near Eastern cultures which typically provide relatively little information about the size of their armies, the Bible includes a great deal of information about the numbers of Israelite troops. Unfortunately, much of that information is problematic.[9] The numbers of troops typically appear with the word *ʾeleph* (אֶלֶף, usually translated "thousand(s)"). If *ʾeleph* in these passages carries its normal meaning of "thousand," then many of the numbers appear extremely large. For example, at the time of the Exodus, Israel twice counted its men available for military service and tallied over 600,000 each time (Num. 1, 26). During the conquest, Joshua sent 30,000 men to move into position behind a hill for an ambush at Ai (Josh. 8:3–8). At the time of the judges, Samson killed 1,000 men by himself using only an animal's jawbone (Judg. 15:14–15). In his first act as king, Saul led a force of 330,000 to respond to the Ammonite attack on the Israelite city of Jabesh Gilead (1 Sam. 11). When David took his census of fighting men, the total came to 1,300,000 (2 Sam. 24:9; the parallel 1 Chron. 21:5 gives 1,570,000).

Size of Army

These numbers appear quite high, especially considering the apparent size of the armies of other, better established contemporary nations. For example, the Egyptians and Hittites met at the Battle of Kadesh in 1275 BC, during the time of Judges. At this battle between the two greatest ancient Near Eastern kingdoms of that time, the Egyptians and Hittites apparently assembled approximately 20,000 troops each (see chap. 3, "Size of Army"). Logically, the much smaller and less populous nation of emerging Israel would likely have been able to muster a smaller number.

This difficulty has led many to discount the biblical numbers altogether, or consider them to be intentional exaggerations. Clearly, the Bible does include exaggerations, as in the song of the Israelite women after David defeated Goliath: "Saul has slain his thousands, and David his tens of thousands" (1 Sam. 18:7). Surely David had not yet killed tens of thousands of enemies, and Saul probably hadn't killed thousands either. Much more likely, the women were using poetic exaggeration to declare that Saul was a great warrior, and David even greater. Thus, some argue that the biblical numbers often also exaggerate to make certain points, such as glorifying the God of Israel.

Others seek to understand the numbers more literally, but differently than usually translated.[10] The discussion hinges on the understanding of the term 'eleph (אֶלֶף). Though 'eleph usually meant "thousand(s)," the word clearly could also mean a part of a tribe (perhaps best translated "clan") that was smaller than the tribe but larger than an extended family ("father's house" בֵית אָב—bêt 'āb—Josh. 22:14). For example, Gideon protested to the divine messenger who had called him to leadership, saying, "my clan ['eleph] is the weakest in (the tribe of) Manasseh, and I am the least in my family" ("father's house"—Judg. 6:15). In a later event, Saul sought the fugitive David among all the "clans of Judah" (אַלְפֵי יְהוּדָה—1 Sam. 23:23).

Given that 'eleph can mean "clan" and that Israelite soldiers may well have mustered and fought by clans, then 'eleph might stand for the soldiers who mustered from a particular clan. If correct, this suggests that the Bible may often refer to numbers of tribal units rather than total numbers of troops. Since Israelite society was traditionally organized along familial lines, the biblical writers might well have expressed numbers in terms of tribal units rather than individuals. This would also better fit the wider cultural context, where the frequent lack of numbers in the records suggest that ancient Near Easterners were not as interested in total numbers as are modern Westerners.

Understanding 'eleph as a unit rather than "thousand" seems to solve many of the problems of large numbers associated with the Israelite military. Most of the large numbers that appear too large shrink down to a more believable but indefinite size if 'eleph means "clan" or the unit of troops drawn from the clan. It is perhaps more likely that Saul mustered 330 units of soldiers to rescue Jabesh Gilead rather than 330,000 soldiers. If the Hebrew writers also used the same term to describe enemy troops, then Samson may have killed an entire Philistine unit, rather than one thousand men, with an animal's jawbone.

If one uses this line of understanding, how large would Israel's army have been at the time of the Exodus? They wouldn't have had just over 600,000 troops; they would have had 5,550. Rather than the tribe of Reuben mustering 46,500 troops, it mustered 46 clans *containing* 500 soldiers (Num. 1:21). Applied to the numbers for all twelve tribes, this leads to 5,550 soldiers (in 598 clans) in the first census and 5,750 (in 596 clans) in the second (Num. 26). How many Israelites, then, left Egypt? If one can assume roughly the same number of adult females as adult males, then Israel may have had about 10,000 adults. If one can assume about the same number of youth as adults, then Israel may have had approximately 20,000 people making the journey from Egypt to Canaan. Though this smaller number is much less dramatic than 2,000,000-3,000,000, keeping 20,000 people alive and organized for forty years in the desert would still represent an enormous challenge.

Additionally, an Exodus and invasion force of roughly 20,000 better matches with the apparent numbers of early Israelites as estimated from the archaeological records. These put the numbers of Israelites at about 21,000 for the time of the judges, 55,000 during the early monarchy,[11] and 150,000 for the later Old Testament.[12] Likewise, one must also take into account Moses' statement that unconquered Canaan contained "seven nations more numerous and stronger than [Israel]" (Deut. 7:1*). Even allowing for poetic exaggeration, multiplying 2,000,000-3,000,000 times any number for the total population of Canaan in the 2nd millennium BC seems completely out of line with the physical evidence, whereas a multiple of 20,000 better fits with archaeological data.

Although this understanding of 'eleph helps resolve many problems, it also presents issues. The census totals given in Numbers 1:46 and 26:51 are correct only if 'eleph means "thousand." Additionally, understanding 'eleph as "clan" leads to difficulties understanding the titles of officers. As described earlier, the Bible often mentions officers over units of thousands (ălāphîm— אֲלָפִים), hundreds, and fifties, which sound like literal numbers, or at least some descending sequence. If "thousands" here means "clans," what do the other two terms mean? In summary, understanding 'eleph as "clan" shrinks the apparently large numbers of troops to a more realistic but vague size, but it doesn't resolve all the associated problems.

Regardless of how one understands the numbers associated with 'eleph, the biblical texts often give the size of Israelite forces. The numbers for Israel at the time of the conquest and judges range from 36 soldiers killed in one battle (Josh. 7.5) to 400 'eleph for the entire army (Judg. 20:2). During the early monarchy, Saul had as many as 330 'eleph soldiers (1 Sam. 13:2; 11:8). David began with a personal army of 400 when he was an outlaw (1 Sam. 22:2), but ended with 1,570 'eleph when king (1 Chron. 21:5). Solomon accumulated 1,400 chariots (1 Kings 10:26—here "thousand" works well for 'eleph) and 4 'eleph stalls for 12 'eleph horses (2 Chron. 9:25). Later numbers range as high as 400 'eleph soldiers in Judah and 800 'eleph in Israel (2 Chron. 13:3).

Role of King

As they commanded these various numbers of troops, Joshua, the judges, and later the kings demonstrated the key role that military leaders played in leading Israel. Joshua and the judges led the nation primarily because of the need for military leadership at their time. While the kings also led in civil and religious affairs, the biblical texts sometimes portray military effectiveness as their most important task. One sees this in the initial demand for a king (1 Sam. 8:20), in the public recognition of Saul as king after he led the rescue of Jabesh Gilead (1 Sam. 11), and when David overshadowed Saul through his military exploits (1 Sam. 17–18, esp. 18:16).

Israel's kings often took personal command of their armies. The accounts of Saul's battles always portray him at the head of his troops. In at least one case, he wore a crown and armband (2 Sam. 1:10), much as later kings typically wore royal robes to identify themselves (1 Kings 22:30). David rose to power largely because of his effective military leadership, but then shared that responsibility with designated commanders (see "Officers" above). Later in his career, David's troops insisted that he stay behind to avoid danger (2 Sam. 18:3–4; 21:17), undoubtedly to avoid the problem of losing the commander in chief in a culture where power was highly concentrated at the top (as in 1 Kings 22:34–36).

Along with leading the military, the king also filled numerous other roles related to the army. When faced with military dilemmas, the king sought divine counsel and aid, either through prophets or directly from God (2 Chron. 18; 14:11–15). He could request aid from foreign powers (2 Chron. 28:16–21) or decide on joint military ventures (2 Chron. 18:1–3). Ultimately, he bore responsibility for his nation and often earned prophetic rebuke for ungodly decisions, however well intentioned.

Role of Israel's God

As the kings carried out these functions connecting Israel and its military to God, they helped demonstrate the vital role that God played in the military and all major parts of society. The Israelites believed their God controlled their world, including warfare. In this respect, Israelite beliefs resembled those of other contemporary societies. Ancient Near Easterners in general thought that only a fool would say in his heart, "There is no God" (Ps. 14:1). They believed in gods and understood them to be intimately involved in life, especially warfare.

Such was certainly the case with Yahweh and Israel. He chose and empowered Joshua, the judges, and the early kings to lead their nation and their nation's army. Prophets and priests anointed the kings (1 Sam.

9–10; 16:1–13; 1 Kings 1:29–39), but were often ready to rebuke them to indicate God's disapproval or even rejection (2 Sam. 12).

Yahweh played an active part in Israel's military campaigns as well. He sometimes commanded warfare (1 Sam. 15:1–3) and predicted victory or defeat (2 Chron. 20:15–17). He encouraged Israel and caused its enemies to fear (Josh. 2:8–11; 5:1). Occasionally, God gave specific instructions for battles either verbally or with the lot (Josh. 6:2–5; Judg. 20:8–9), acted through nature or battle to aid Israel (Josh. 3; Judg. 4:14–15), and showed his presence with the troops through promises or by the presence of the priests (1 Sam. 14:2–3). He frequently punished the nation of Israel or its rebellious kings through military defeat (2 Chron. 21).

For their part, the leaders of Israel looked to Yahweh for victory (1 Sam. 7:7–9), and sought his direction before battle through dreams, Urim and Thummin (perhaps sacred lots cast in times of national crisis), and prophets (1 Sam. 28:6, 15). They made offerings and vows before battle (Judg. 11:30–40; 1 Sam. 13:8–9), dedicated cities and plunder to him (see later discussion), and commemorated divinely enabled victories (1 Sam. 7:12).

Like other ancient armies, Israel had to maintain ritual purity and obedience in order to prevent offending its God, who could and did punish them. Nocturnal emissions made soldiers unclean, so they had to restore their ritual purity. God even gave specific instructions on how to deal with bodily waste so that he wouldn't see any indecency and abandon them (Deut. 23:9–14). The army had to consecrate itself before beginning a campaign (Josh. 3:5). Disobedience led to defeat at Ai (Josh. 7), during the continued conquest and time of the judges (Judg. 2:1–5; 6:1), and into the monarchy (2 Chron. 12:1–4). Sin caused Saul to lose his crown (1 Sam. 15), David, the peace in his household and in his kingdom (2 Sam. 12–20), and Solomon, his undivided heritage (1 Kings 11).

WEAPONS

Although the Bible emphasizes the major role played by God in Israel's military, it also reflects the physical realities that Israel used to conduct its military activities, including different types of weapons. The earlier discussion of the Israelite infantry mentioned the major weapons used by Israel and most other armies of the time. These include short-range weapons like the spear and sword for hand-to-hand fighting, medium-range weapons like the javelin that could be hurled a moderate distance, and long-range weapons like the bow and sling that could launch projectiles the greatest distance and still effectively engage the enemy.

Short-Range Weapons

Unlike most modern combat, which is conducted from much greater distances, most ancient fighting took place at close range. As in most other armies of their time, Israelite soldiers typically used swords or spears for short-range fighting, and sometimes other weapons such as daggers, clubs, and axes.

Sword   Based on the number of occurrences in the Old Testament, one would think the sword was the most frequently used weapon of the time. "Sword" often appears in general or poetic references to warfare, indicating that it was commonly known and used. Israelites often "put to the sword" people or even entire cities (Josh. 11:10). Many passages refer to armies or military activity in general as "the sword" (2 Chron. 20:9). Those who die in battle "fall by the sword" (2 Sam. 1:12), and those who survive military attack "escape the sword" (1 Kings 19:17).

Likely the typical early Israelite sword was a sickle-sword, which had a handle attached to a straight shaft that continued into a curved blade (Fig. 4.2). The instrument was shaped somewhat like a harvesting sickle—thus the name—except that the sword was sharpened on the outside of the blade rather than the inside. A soldier used a sickle-sword to slash his enemy, giving rise to the expression strike with the "edge of the sword" (see Josh. 10:28, 30, ESV). Pictorial evidence from the region suggests that the dominant shape of the sword seems to have changed from the sickle-sword to the long, straight, double-edged sword (Fig. 4.2) after the arrival of the Philistines and the other Sea Peoples about the time of the judges (see chap. 5). The common Hebrew term for "sword" does not help differentiate between these shapes, so one often cannot tell which type the Israelites would have been using.

The Israelites also used variants of these two main styles of swords. They used shorter versions[13] of the straight, double-edged sword as well, perhaps best called "daggers." The judge Ehud famously killed a fat Moabite king in part because Ehud was left-handed and he could hide his dagger (one cubit (18")) long) on his right thigh, which the Moabite guards apparently did not search (Judg. 3:15–30). Daggers also appear in the hand-to-hand combat recorded in 2 Samuel 2. Curiously, the best picture of Hebrew

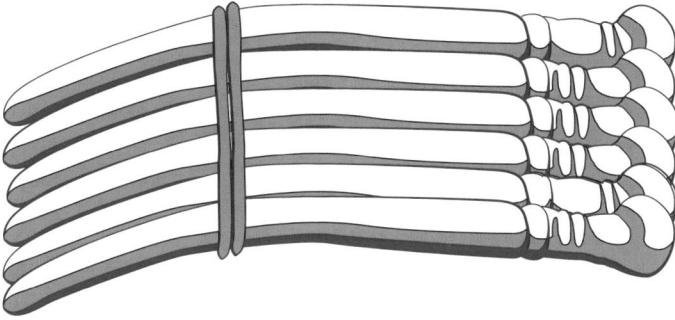

Fig. 2.3—Judean swords, ca. 700 BC. Part of plunder carried by Assyrian soldier. Note curved blades.

swords from the biblical period (Fig. 2.3) shows six long, curved swords that are neither of the main types—sickle-swords or long, straight swords. As with the Israelite chariot shown in Fig. 2.2, these swords apparently comprised part of the plunder from the governor's palace at Lachish, suggesting that they may have been ceremonial, and thus not necessarily the same style as normal swords. See also Fig. 2.4 for discussion and possible faint depiction of a straight sword from about the same time period.

Spear

Although the Bible mentions the sword more often, some of the frequent references to spears and shields (1 Chron. 12:8; 2 Chron. 14:8; 25:5) suggest that these were standard issue for Israelite troops during the monarchy. Spears were made with long, wooden shafts perhaps five feet long (Fig. 2.1—right) and pointed, sharpened metal heads of different types (Fig. 1.2).[14] Even the tail end of the spear could kill. Since soldiers often stuck their spears in the ground when not in use (1 Sam. 26:7), they probably sharpened the end or affixed a metal point to make this easier, thus enabling attack with the tail as well (2 Sam. 2:23).

Soldiers used spears as piercing weapons in hand-to-hand fighting. While one could throw a spear, as Saul seemed fond of doing (1 Sam. 18:10–11; 19:10; 20:33), it served primarily as a thrusting weapon for heavy infantry. Massed infantry arranged in battle lines often carried spears and large shields (or swords or possibly other close-range weapons as well). They often faced similarly armed enemy troops, and when the opposing lines closed, the spear-bearing soldiers would try to impale the enemy soldiers opposite them.

Although the spear appears frequently in texts from the later monarchy, it did not early on. Curiously, it does not appear at all in Joshua and only once in Judges (5:8—stating that Israel had none), perhaps suggesting the early Israelites did not have the blacksmiths to produce the metal heads. The spear does appear frequently in the stories of Saul (1 Sam. 22:6; 2 Sam. 1:6), as well in stories of hand-to-hand fighting during the time of David (1 Chron. 11:20, 23), and then most frequently in general references during the later monarchy.

Other Short-Range Weapons The Bible also mentions a few other short-range weapons such as axes and darts. Ancient Near Eastern peoples often used axes for cutting wood or even stone (1 Kings 6:7), and their armies sometimes used them as slashing weapons, especially in Egypt (see chap. 4 for discussion and images). When the Bible mentions axes in warfare, it usually refers to their use by other nations. However, in Judges 9:48 Abimelech and his troops use axes to cut branches during battle to burn a tower at Shechem.[15] One also finds another short-range wooden weapon in a few passages, such as when Beniah attacks an Egyptian with his *šēbeṭ* (שֵׁבֶט—"staff" or "dart"—2 Sam. 23:21). In 2 Samuel 18:14, Joab took three of these weapons in his hand and stabbed Absalom in the heart, suggesting some sort of wooden stick perhaps with a sharpened end or metal point that could penetrate easily.[16] Whatever this weapon was, Beniah and Joab used it for hand-to-hand combat.

Medium-Range Weapons

The Bible mentions only one weapon that Israelites could throw a moderate distance—the javelin. The javelin resembled a smaller version of the spear with a wooden shaft and a metal point usually somewhat smaller than a spearhead. The javelin served as a popular weapon for charioteers and cavalrymen throughout the ancient Near East, usually supplementing the long-range bow. Ancient soldiers may have been able to throw a javelin approximately sixty-five feet (twenty meters), though some added an attached looped cord to spin the javelin and add extra force, thereby increasing the distance up to fourfold.[17]

If Israelite equestrian troops used the javelin like other contemporary armies, we find little evidence of it in the Bible. The only Israelite with a javelin in the Bible is Joshua, and he used it for signaling to the troops in ambush behind Ai (Josh. 8:18, 26). The Bible also notes that Goliath had a javelin when he faced David (1 Sam. 17:6, 45), though he apparently did not get a chance to use either this medium-range weapon or his short-range spear or sword. David engaged first in that famous battle, using his only weapon—his long-range sling.

Long-Range Weapons

David's skillful use of his sling against Goliath represents just one instance of Israelites using this simple, but effective, long-range weapon. Some of David's followers were also skilled slingers (1 Chron. 12:2), as were the 700 men from the tribe of Benjamin who could "sling a stone at a hair and not miss" (Judg. 20:16). Slingers played an important role in the Israelite attack on Moab in the 9th century (2 Kings 3:25), and by the time of King Uzziah in the 8th century, the crown supplied slingstones for the army (2 Chron. 26:14). Even a poetic description of God aiding Israel included slingstones (Zech. 9:15).

Sling

The men from Saul's tribe of Benjamin seemed to have had a particular affinity for the sling, as well as for left-handedness. Some Benjamites could sling (or shoot the bow) with either hand (1 Chron. 12:2). Others were both left-handed and famed for their great accuracy with the sling, noted above. The judge Ehud mentioned earlier was also left-handed and from the tribe of Benjamin, all of which may suggest that this tribe had some genetic and/or cultural disposition toward left-handedness, a point given at least some support by modern genetic understanding.[18] Though left-handedness could be advantageous in certain military contexts (as with Ehud), it is more difficult to find any advantage when using long-range weapons like slings or bows.

Ease of production undoubtedly contributed to the popularity of the sling, also called "the poor man's bow." A sling can be as simple as a strap some three feet in length and one inch in width, though it is often made with two narrow cords attached to a wider pouch in the center (Fig. 4.5). Often the sling is woven from wool or some other type of flexible material from an animal or a plant. One end is looped or knotted to attach to one of the fingers of the thrower's hand, and the other end knotted for the thumb and forefinger to grip until the moment of release. The Bible gives no indication of how the Israelites made their slings, though the shepherd David likely would have woven his from readily accessible wool. David used water-worn stones to attack Goliath (1 Sam. 17:40). Stone would have served as a common raw material for Israelite slingstones, either in their natural shape or else rounded to fly straighter. Rounded slingstones were typically two to three inches in diameter. Armies also used clay and later lead to make sling pellets, both denser materials that allow for smaller pellets.[19]

After placing the slingstone or pellet in the sling's pouch, the slinger apparently used one of two techniques. He could spin it horizontally over his head (like the Egyptian slinger in the crow's nest in Fig. 3.10) or vertically at his side, somewhat like pitching a softball underhanded (see Assyrian slinger in Fig. 7.1). Our only images of Israelite slingers (see Fig. 2.5, 2.1 for adaptation) seem to depict vertical rotation.[20] Slingers apparently used three to four revolutions, generating enough force to launch the projectile at speeds up to sixty miles per hour. At this rate, the projectile could easily penetrate the body or inflict deadly wounds even without penetrating.[21]

How accurate were ancient slingers, and at what range? The Roman historian Livy (59 BC–AD 17) wrote of Greek slingers who "would wound not merely the heads of their enemies but any part of the face at which they might have aimed."[22] David's skill against Goliath appears to reflect equal accuracy, but the Benjamites' hair-width aim may suggest poetic exaggeration. The range of slingers would depend in part on the size of their projectiles. The Roman writer Vegetius (4th to 5th centuries AD) wrote that archers should practice with targets six hundred feet away, and competent slingers could outrange archers.[23]

Bow   In addition to the sling, Israelites obviously used bows extensively. Just a few of the dozens of biblical references to the weapon involve hunting (Gen. 21:20; 27:3), whereas most describe it as an instrument of war. Like we saw with "sword" earlier, some references to "bow" are poetic[24] or refer to military might in general (Josh. 24:12; 2 Sam. 1:22), suggesting widespread use and knowledge of this long-range weapon. A large portion of the Israelite army consisted of long-range archers (2 Chron. 17:17) who complemented the heavy infantry carrying spear and shield for close-range fighting (2 Chron. 14:8).

Ancient bows were made of either a long, single piece of wood, or else a composite of multiple pieces of wood, sinew, horn, and strips of bone, glued together to provide maximum strength (see also discussion of Egyptian bows in chap. 4). The simple bows, much like slings, offered ease of manufacture and low cost, but composite bows delivered the greatest strength and distance, if a nation had the skill and

Fig. 2.4—Archer on seal found in Jerusalem, 7th century

resources to produce them. Unfortunately, the Bible gives little indication about the types of bows it refers to, though one might assume that Israel produced and used composite bows at least by the time of the later monarchy.

Imagery from the biblical period provides a bit more information. The Assyrian reliefs portraying the fall of the Judean city of Lachish ca. 700 BC show several Judean archers (Fig. 2.5),[25] though none clearly

Fig. 2.5—Israelite defenders at Lachish ca. 700 BC. Note helmeted archer and slinger, round shields on wall.

enough to determine the types of bows they are using. The composite image of the archer in Fig. 2.1 is based on these reliefs. A seal uncovered recently in Jerusalem[26] may offer more help (Fig. 2.4). The seal depicts an archer, possibly Judean. He is barefoot, with head covering and clothing similar to the 8th century Judeans portrayed in the Assyrian reliefs of Lachish. A quiver hangs on his back, and a straight sword apparently projects back and downward from his waist on the left side, where a right-handed man would place it. The archer draws his bow, curved at each end like a high-quality composite bow, and aims slightly upward. The inscription on the seal reads, "Belonging to Hagab [grasshopper[27]]."

Defensive Equipment

Along with these different types of short-, medium-, and long-range weapons, the Israelite army also had to provide their soldiers with defensive equipment. Soldiers in all armies needed protection in battle, and the Israelites used physical protection typical of the time, as well as trusting their God as their shield, rock, and fortress—all terms of military defense (Ps. 18:2, 30, 35).

Shield

The Bible typically uses two different words for shields, apparently designating large (צִנָּה—ṣinnâ) and small shields (מָגֵן—māgēn). Heavy infantry carrying spears used large shields, whereas archers had small shields (2 Chron. 14:8). Solomon made ceremonial large (200) and small (300) shields of (probably overlaid with) gold for display in his palace (2 Chron. 9:15–16). After Solomon's death, the Egyptians invaded and took these shields, so Solomon's son Rehoboam replaced them with shields of bronze. Palace guards used these when on duty (2 Chron. 12:9–11) and during a later coup (2 Chron. 23:9).

As so often is the case, one finds the best imagery of Israelite shields on the Assyrian reliefs of Lachish. They show an Assyrian carrying one round shield as part of the plunder from the Judean palace (used in Fig. 2.1). The battlements of Lachish also appear to be protected and decorated with numerous similar round shields (see Fig. 2.5 as well as 6.6, where one is also shown falling from the crumbling defenses[28]).

Helmets

Although helmets would seem to make up an obvious part of a soldier's equipment, the single reference to actual Israelite helmets comes from the list of military supplies provided by King Uzziah of Judah in the 8th century (2 Chron. 26:14). This may suggest that Israelite armies couldn't produce adequate helmets until the late monarchy. Other passages with the term refer to helmets of foreign soldiers (Goliath—1 Sam. 17:5) or armies (Egypt, Persia, etc.—Jer. 46:4; Ezek. 27:10), or of God donning the "helmet of salvation" to rescue humanity (Isa. 59:17; used by Paul in Eph. 6:17).

The Assyrian reliefs of Lachish show perhaps a third of the defenders on the city's walls wearing slightly different styles of conical helmets (Figs. 2.5, 2.1), probably made of bronze or iron. The Israelite helmets shown vary slightly in design, but all appear to be conical (cf. conical Assyrian helmets in Figs. 6.3, 7.1, 7.3, 7.9, etc.), probably to deflect overhand blows and to allow for heat to escape from the head. If the reliefs are accurate, they show that the Judeans did have helmets in the late 8th century, but not enough to protect the majority of their most exposed defenders at Lachish. The other defenders wore head-wraps (Figs. 2.1, 2.5, 6.7) apparently made of some type of cloth, which would have provided some, but clearly less, protection.

Armor, Armor-bearer

The available evidence presents largely the same information regarding body armor. The Philistine Goliath wore bronze scale armor (שִׁרְיוֹן קַשְׂקַשִּׂים—*širyôn qaśqaśśim*—see also chap. 4 and Fig. 4.7) to battle David early in the monarchy (1 Sam. 17:5). Uzziah produced armor for the Judean army late in the monarchy (2 Chron. 26:14), though the term "armor" (שִׁרְיוֹן—*širyôn*) is more general than for Goliath's scale armor, and could refer to plate armor instead (cf. the apparent Philistine armor in Figs. 5.4, 5.7). Neither biblical texts nor pictorial evidence tells us what Israelite armor may have looked like. In between the biblical references to Goliath and Uzziah, one finds Israelite armor only on kings Saul and Ahab (1 Sam. 17:38; 1 Kings 22:34; both use simply שִׁרְיוֹן—*širyôn*). Saul probably had the only set of armor in the young Israelite army, which he may have obtained as plunder; Ahab may have had one of a few sets in the more developed, later Israelite military. Saul offered his armor to David, who declined, possibly because of the weight characteristic of such metal protection.

Perhaps only kings and generals enjoyed the relative luxury of metal armor until Uzziah upgraded the equipment for his troops. Before Uzziah, Israelite soldiers likely wore leather armor at best (see opening story of chap. 1). Perhaps significantly, the Assyrian reliefs of Lachish show no armor among the plunder from the city, nor do the defenders appear to wear any, though their torsos are largely shielded from view by the walls on the ramparts. The reference to Ahab's armor also indicates a major drawback in such armor—vulnerability at the joints in the armor where the metal didn't overlap.[29]

In addition to armor, one also finds the compound term often translated "armor-bearer" (נֹשֵׂא כֵלִים—*nōśē' kēlîm*) in military texts that mention young men who served warriors like Abimelech (Judg. 9:54), Jonathan (1 Sam. 14:1–17), Saul (1 Sam. 16:21—David; 31:4–6), and Joab (1 Chron. 11:39). A general translation like "equipment-bearer" would probably be more accurate, since these men carried items such as weapons or baggage as well as armor. Joab had ten such helpers (2 Sam. 18:15), not all of whom would have carried his armor. The term for what these helpers bore (כֵּלִים—*kēlîm*) is used for weapons in some passages (1 Sam. 20:40; 21:8), further suggesting that these "armor-bearers" carried more than armor.

STRATEGY AND TACTICS

The final section of this chapter will explore the numerous biblical passages dealing with battles to describe Israel's strategy and tactics as thoroughly as possible. What strategies directed the Israelites' overall campaigns? What were their motivations for fighting? What did the Israelites do before, during, and after battle? What tactics did they use for individual battles? As with most other areas, the available information is rarely complete, but it helps paint an interesting picture nonetheless.

Overall Strategy

Throughout its long national history, Israel fought wars that fit into overall strategies that the careful reader can often discern. These strategies changed with the nation's fortunes, moving from carving out living space, to fighting for survival, to conquering others to being conquered by others.

At its birth, Israel fought to conquer the land that God had promised to Abraham centuries earlier. Israel succeeded in its battle for living space and used the simple strategy of divide-and-conquer. Joshua led the nation to attack at Jericho on the eastern side of central Canaan. After taking Jericho, the Israelites ascended into the center of Hill Country, into the region that would become the heart of their nation. They cut through this region from east to west by defeating Ai, accidentally gaining an ally in Gibeon, then pushing the coalition attacking Gibeon out of the hills into the western foothills. The Israelites then swung south to defeat the major cities left vulnerable by the victory at Gibeon. Finally, they turned north and defeated a coalition there. According to divine orders, they were to totally destroy all who lived within Canaan and subject those living outside Canaan. Israel only partially fulfilled the first part of that directive, but under David, it largely succeeded with the second part.

Before David would come, Israel had to struggle through several centuries of defensive wars. Weak Israelite tribes served as prey for stronger outside invaders, and military leaders the Bible calls judges led them in a series of defensive wars that did little more than rescue them from extinction. These struggles continued during the early monarchy under Saul. Like the judges, Saul fought a number of defensive actions, and he ultimately fell in a final, vain defensive action against one of Israel's greatest foes, the Philistines.

Under the skilled and blessed leadership of the new king David, Israel's fortunes quickly reversed. David not only withstood continued Philistine aggression, he turned and subdued this longstanding foe. He then shifted Israel from a defensive to an offensive posture, leading the Israelite army on a series of wars of conquest. Israel conquered most of its neighbors and subjected them to servitude and the obligation to pay tribute annually, making Israel fabulously wealthy for a frustratingly brief period of time.

Following the death of David's son Solomon, the nation divided and lost most of David's gains. The two kingdoms quickly found themselves fighting both a civil war and renewed defensive wars. They survived these early challenges and tried to go back on the offensive. Israel and Judah sought to re-conquer and hold as much foreign land as they could for as long as possible. When they succeeded, they received immediate plunder. When they maintained control, they received annual tribute like in the days of David and Solomon.

Throughout the rest of the divided kingdom, the two nations fought both offensive and defensive wars—reflecting their rising and falling fortunes—with the stronger northern kingdom of Israel better able to conquer and hold outlying regions. The two countries used various strategies to achieve their military goals. These included forming coalitions, hiring mercenaries, and offering bribes. Occasionally they bribed attackers to withdraw, or bribed a distant greater power like Assyria to attack an antagonistic neighbor. Though these strategies often succeeded, one reads of God voicing displeasure through prophetic messages to the offending king. Overall, the nations' general military strategies resembled those of their neighbors, with the important addition of a God who showed more concern with covenantal fidelity than national success, and who had the power to bring about good or bad for his people through military and other means.

As they worked through these overall strategies, what motivated the ancient Israelites to risk their lives in battle? As mentioned earlier, the Israelite army often fought at the command and with the blessing of Yahweh, whose support probably served as one of the soldiers' major motivations. The desire for honor and for material gain would have factored in as well.[30] The Israelites under Joshua fought to gain a homeland, homes, material

Motivation

goods, and perhaps wives (Deut. 21:10–14). The cry, "To the plunder" (2 Kings 3:23) probably reflects a sentiment that has motivated soldiers in most armies all throughout history. When David arrived at the battlefield where he would fight Goliath, he learned that whoever defeated the giant would receive great wealth, exemption from taxes for his family, the personal honor of marrying the king's daughter, plus honor for his nation by "remov(ing) this disgrace from Israel" (1 Sam 17:25–27).

Such motivations would have helped overcome one of the soldier's greatest enemies—fear. God needed to tell the early, overmatched Israelite military, "When you go to war against your enemies and see horses and chariots and an army greater than yours, do not be afraid of them, because the LORD your God . . . will be with you" (Deut. 20:1). Fear appears often in military texts throughout the Old Testament, even providing one of the reasons for exemption from service (Deut. 20:8). Though the fearful soldier may have been allowed to return home, he probably would have had little honor in a society that highly valued it.

Season for War Like other armies of the time, the Israelites probably campaigned between the spring and fall harvests, the two times when the men were most needed in the fields. The regular campaigning season began "in the spring, at the time when kings go off to war" (2 Sam. 11:1; cf. 1 Kings 20:26). At that point, one's own harvest would have been done and the enemy harvest would be available to plunder, as when the Midianites came to take Israel's grain in the story of Gideon (Judg. 6:1–11). Armies would fight through the dry summer months and return before the fall harvest and the advent of winter rains that made travel difficult, if not impossible.

The March, Camp The clearest information about the campaigning Israelite military on the march comes from their time in the wilderness as the entire nation moved toward their future homeland. One finds specific instructions for moving and camping in military formations (Num. 2, 10), with trumpets for signaling, and the leadership and Tabernacle moving and camping in the center, flanked by groups of tribes on each side. Such formations would have allowed for the shortest and clearest lines of communication between the leadership and each group, as well as protecting the leadership and valuable articles of worship.

Although Israel's military probably assumed that God was always leading it, sometimes God had them clearly portray this with priests carrying the Ark of the Covenant, marching in front of the army. One finds this both in the approach to the Jordan River at the beginning of the conquest (Josh. 3–4), as well as at Jericho and perhaps later at Ebenezer (Josh. 6; 1 Sam. 4). Contemporary armies such as those from Egypt, Assyria, and Persia frequently followed similar practices (see Figs. 3.8 and 7.4 and accompanying discussions).

The Israelites would also have used military camps like their contemporaries, though one rarely finds them mentioned after the beginning of the conquest. At the beginning of the book of Joshua, the Israelites camped across the Jordan River as they prepared to invade, then left their families and possessions in the camp when the army entered Canaan (Josh. 1). Once across the Jordan, they established another camp at Gilgal near Jericho, and used that as their base for their actions against Jericho, Ai, Gibeon, and the campaign in the south (Josh. 4–10). Israel's camps were undoubtedly full of soldiers, tents, and pack animals, plus horses if the army had begun to use chariots (cf. 2 Kings 7:7, 10).

Food and Logistics

As the Israelites marched and camped, they obviously needed to supply their troops with food and other provisions. Such a support system would have developed over time, like so much of their military. Israelite troops at the time of the tribal levies would have depended heavily on plunder from the enemy (Josh. 5:11–12; 1 Sam. 14:30) or support from their family or tribal unit (Judg. 20:9–10). In such a system, the soldiers probably carried what they could, then relied on relatives to resupply them or managed as best they could as they went along. David was on such a resupply mission with roasted grain, bread, and cheese for his brothers and their commander when he arrived at the battle where he would face Goliath (1 Sam. 17:17–22).

Undoubtedly, the system for supplying the army grew more sophisticated as the monarchy developed. Samuel's warning that the king would take the people's best cattle and donkeys and 10% of their flocks probably included the procurement of food and pack animals for armies (1 Sam. 8:16–17). Donkeys, camels, mules, and oxen carried military supplies (1 Chron. 12:40). Leaders and other troops rode on donkeys, mules, and occasionally chariots, as noted earlier (2 Sam. 13:29; 18:9). Solomon's organization of twelve districts to supply provisions for the crown certainly would have included the needs of the military (1 Kings 4). Solomon's son Rehoboam built fortresses and supplied them with food, oil, wine, shields, and spears (2 Chron. 11:5–12). Along with the foods already mentioned, one also finds Israelite soldiers eating cakes of raisins and figs, wheat, barley, flour, beans, lentils, honey, curds, cattle, sheep, and water,[31] though certainly not all at the same time.

Intelligence

The biblical texts also describe some of the effort the Israelite troops ex-
erted to obtain intelligence about their enemies. They gathered military
and political information, as well as data about topography, productivity,
ecological factors, and ethnic makeup of target populations. The nation
sent twelve spies into Canaan who reported to the entire nation before its
fateful decision not to invade as directed (Num. 13), but Joshua apparently
learned from that episode and privately sent just two spies to Jericho, who
reported directly to him (Josh. 2). Joshua likewise sent men to spy out
Ai, the next objective. In addition to reporting what they saw, these spies
advised on strategy, which helped lead to Israel's first defeat (Josh. 7:1–5).

Indications of gathering military intelligence continue into the time
of Judges and the monarchy. The tribes of Ephraim and Manasseh sent
spies to Bethel, and like with Rahab at Jericho, the spies promised safety to
one inhabitant in exchange for information on how to enter the city (Judg.
1:22–25). King Saul frequently requested and received reports about the locations and actions of his enemies (1 Sam. 22:9–10; 23:27). David likewise
sent out scouts, received reports, and gathered information on the battlefield (1 Sam. 26:4; 30:11–16). Diplomatic contacts served as opportunities
for intelligence-gathering missions (2 Sam. 3:24–25; 10:1–3).

Battle Tactics

All of this preparation led up to various military engagements. The numerous biblical passages describing these engagements sometimes include details about the tactics used for individual battles and strategies
for overall campaigns. Perhaps surprisingly, one finds more such information from Israel's early history before it had a strong, well-established
army. For example, the Bible takes six chapters at the beginning of the
book of Joshua to describe how the invaders approached and conquered
Jericho. By contrast, the Bible devotes only a single chapter to David's
campaigns that conquered a large part of the ancient Near East (2 Sam.
8). Why is this? Apparently to show that Israel's God helped them to
win when they were clearly outmatched, whereas victories with superior
forces gave less glory to God. While such an emphasis makes for good
devotional reading, it offers the reader less information about how the
more capable Israelite armies operated during the monarchy.

One also finds that Israelite tactics changed with their increasing capabilities. Since early Israel often faced foes with superior forces, their
early tactics reflect those of guerilla forces—moving at night, making

surprise attacks, etc. Later on, one finds the Israelite military maneuvering like a major force—forming phalanxes of massed infantry to engage similarly grouped enemy troops, or using chariotry against enemy chariotry before the infantry engaged.

Pitched battles in the ancient Near East between relatively evenly matched forces probably resulted in short but decisive engagements. Armies would arrange themselves for combat with phalanxes or rows of massed heavy infantry carrying shields and short-range weapons in front, and archers (and slingers if they used them) in the rear. If the armies had chariots and/or cavalry, these may have assembled on the wings. As the two armies began to close, equestrian troops from both sides likely skirmished with one another using bows and javelins, plus firing on the opposing infantry, probing for weaknesses. The archers would commence firing as soon as the enemy was within range, shooting over their own troops into the massed enemy. When the sides got too close, the equestrian troops would withdraw, the archers would have to stop to avoid hitting their own men, and the two phalanxes of massed infantry would collide.

Battles in the Open

The fighting must have been intense. The heavy infantry fought shoulder-to-shoulder with their comrades, with additional rows of troops pressing from behind to try to force their side forward. The later Greek historian Xenophon described such fighting by saying, "Shoving their shields together, they shoved, fought, slew, and died." If the troops had no way to rotate to the rear, a tactic the Romans later perfected, such fighting probably couldn't last more than half an hour before physical and emotional exhaustion would take over.[32] (Note the biblical references to such fatigue, such as a warrior's hand growing so tired it froze to his weapon—2 Sam. 23:10.) Eventually, troops either gained the upper hand or else lost through death or injury, surrender, retreat, or panic and flight.

Once the momentum clearly swung in one direction, the winners typically won decisively. Fleeing troops usually discarded their shields, and perhaps weapons and armor as well. This allowed them to flee more quickly, but also made them inviting targets to the victorious side. Pursuing infantry, mounted troops, and reengaging archers could now slaughter the largely unprotected enemy. Battles often ended in massacre.[33] Three times in the summary of David's victories in 2 Samuel 8, the dead and captured enemies number in the thousands.

The early Israelite armies apparently tried to avoid such direct attacks in the open, probably because they lacked the military strength. They positioned their troops in the hills to keep them safe from stronger enemies who often had chariots that operated better on the plains. For example, one sees Deborah and Barak with their troops on Mt. Tabor, out of reach of Sisera's chariots until the time of the battle. When they did attack, the outmatched Israelites engaged in a wetter area to neutralize the Canaanite chariots (Judg. 4–5). Likewise, the Israelites during the time of Samuel assembled at Ebenezer at the edge of the Hill Country, as compared to the Philistines who rendezvoused at the major site of Aphek on the Coastal Plain (1 Sam. 4). Gideon, and later Saul, both gathered their troops at Mt. Gilboa to face superior Midianites and Philistines spread out in the Jezreel Valley (Judg. 6:33; 7:1; 1 Sam. 28:4). Camping at the edge of the hills would have prevented the enemy from advancing into Israelite territory in the hills, and it allowed the Israelites uninterrupted lines of supply and communication with their population base, also offering an easy route of escape if necessary.

As already noted, the early Israelites often used guerilla tactics in battle. These included moving troops at night, sometimes in grueling marches.[34] This got their outnumbered forces into position for surprise attacks the following day, as with Joshua's ambushes at Ai and Gibeon (Josh. 8, 10), and Abimelech's attack at Shechem (Judg. 9:34). Gideon did the same, and launched his famously successful attack with torches at the beginning of the middle watch, just after the changing of the guard (Judg. 7:19). Most of the Midianites would have been fast asleep at this time, and the new guards would probably not have had time to adjust to the dark conditions. The Israelites would also have had plenty of time to press their deceptively undermanned attack before daylight revealed their true numbers.[35] In a similar fashion, Saul attacked the Ammonite camp at Jabesh Gilead during the last watch of the night (1 Sam. 11:11).

The biblical texts also include examples of representative warfare, where a single person or some limited number from each army would do battle, with the army of the loser promising to surrender to the victors. David and Goliath represented their nations in such combat, as did the twelve from each side in the battle between the houses of David and Saul at Gibeon (2 Sam. 2:12–28). Armies agreed to such a strategy primarily to reduce the amount of bloodshed. Often a fallen soldier meant a new widow, fatherless children, and a farm without its chief worker, so fewer deaths meant less overall loss to their societies. Unfortunately, representative warfare typically didn't work. The battle produced a champion, like David, but the losing side would flee rather than surrendering (1 Sam. 17:15–52), or the two armies would engage anyway (2 Sam. 2:17–28).

The biblical texts that describe general engagements occasionally mention the arrangement of battle lines or the disposition of troops. Joab arranged his troops into a battle line, but had to divide them into two forces with separate commanders when caught between the battle lines of Ammon and Aram (2 Sam. 10:7–14). In another battle, David sent his battle lines against those of the Arameans (1 Chron. 19:17). More often, the texts mention dividing troops into groups, often three, for multi-pronged attacks. Thus, Gideon attacked the Midianites (Judg. 7:16), as did Abimelech at Shechem (Judg. 9:43), Saul at Jabesh Gilead (1 Sam. 11:11), and David against Absalom (2 Sam. 18:2). A few passages give some indication of how long some battles lasted, perhaps because they continued unusually long. Saul's attack at Jabesh Gilead lasted from the last watch of the night until the heat of the day. David's band fought a group of Amalekites from dusk on one day to the evening of the next (1 Sam. 30:17).

The Israelites managed their battles in part by using messengers and trumpets to communicate before, during, and after battle. Messengers carried appeals for help and helped gather troops (1 Sam. 11:3–5; Judg. 6:35). On at least one occasion, a messenger also carried parts of a dismembered ox to get people's attention (1 Sam. 11:7). Messengers also relayed news and commands between the battlefield and the capital using letters and oral messages (2 Sam. 11:6–25). They delivered communiqués to the enemy (Judg. 11:12–28) and announced the outcome of battles (1 Sam. 4:12–17). The Israelites also used trumpets for various purposes: to signal for troops to assemble, to announce a rebellion, to attack, and to stop fighting (1 Sam. 13:3–4; 2 Sam. 15:10; Judg. 7:16–22; 2 Sam. 2:28).

As one might expect, early Israelite forces shied away from attacking fortified cities, probably due to inexperience and lack of equipment. The instructions in Deuteronomy 20:10–20 show that they were familiar with or perhaps were preparing for such tactics. Moses instructed them to first offer peace when attacking a city and subject the inhabitants to forced labor if they surrendered. If they refused, the army was to lay siege, then kill the men and take the women, children, and possessions as plunder when the city fell. *Attacks on Cities*

Until they developed that capability, the Israelites used covert approaches to infiltrate and bypass fortifications. One sees this at Bethel (Judg. 1:22–25) and with the water shaft at Jebus/Jerusalem (2 Sam. 5:6–8). At Ai, they lured the defenders away from the fortifications to fight in the fields.

The Bible indicates that over time Israel learned how to make direct attacks on cities. Several cities fell in Joshua's southern campaign after the army "took up positions…and attacked it" (Josh. 10:34). By the time of David, the texts reflect the type of attacks and siege tactics typical for that era. At Rabbah, the capital of Ammon, Joab and the standing army laid siege to the city and camped in tents. The Israelites made attacks on the city, and the defenders returned fire from atop the wall as well as making sorties out against the attackers. The attackers had to be careful of closing within range of archers and those throwing projectiles from the wall. At least once, a battle occurred at the city gate and several attackers died. Eventually Israel captured the city's water supply, and the fall of the city was imminent. Joab sent word to David, and the king mustered the militia and joined Joab for the final assault. When the city fell, the Israelites took plunder and subjected the inhabitants to forced labor (2 Sam. 11–12). Poetic references to scaling a wall (2 Sam. 22:30; Ps. 18:29) probably refer to such attacks on a city.

The Israelites must have subjected many cities to similar sieges, but few appear in the Bible. One finds a briefer account of a siege against the Israelite city of Abel Beth Maacah, where a rebel named Sheba had taken refuge. Joab built a siege ramp against the outer fortifications and battered the wall to breach it. The city's inhabitants delivered Sheba's head to the attackers to forestall the inevitable result (2 Sam. 20:15–22).

Though one rarely finds Israelite armies laying siege, warnings and descriptions of the terrible effects of a protracted siege appear fairly often, in part because Israelite cities were subjected to sieges by attacking armies. Israelite kings made extensive preparations to withstand enemy attacks, including constructing water systems and strengthening cities' defensive walls (2 Chron. 32). When the attackers arrived, most cities had adequate sources of water, but stores of food were limited and eventually would be exhausted. Famine and starvation resulted; food costs skyrocketed, and the people sometimes resorted to cannibalism (2 Kings 6:24–30). In addition, the inhabitants would have to bury the dead inside the city walls, leading to pollution of the water supply and widespread disease.

After the Battle

Following a successful battle on a city or in the open, the Israelite military armies collected spoils, rewarded their troops, and disposed of captured enemy leaders.

Plunder

The Bible recognizes that Israel's troops took plunder as a reward for military success. Israelite soldiers often enjoyed spoils including women, sheep, cattle, donkeys, camels, and clothing (Judg. 5:30; 1 Sam. 27:9), but one finds this emphasized less in the Bible than in the records of some other contemporary nations. The practice varies even in the Bible. In some cases, the Israelites killed the people and kept the plunder (Josh. 8:22–27), or killed the soldiers and kept the women, children, and other goods (Num. 31:7–12). Other times, by contrast, the Israelites killed all a city's inhabitants and totally destroyed its goods as a gift to God, like at Jericho. Joshua additionally pronounced a curse on anyone who would rebuild the city (Josh. 6:21–27).

Rewards

Israelite soldiers also could earn various rewards for great feats performed in battle, though this, too, varies. Caleb promised his daughter in marriage to the one who led the conquest of the city of Kiriath Sepher (Judg. 1:12–13). Saul also offered his daughter plus other rewards to the one who defeated Goliath, as discussed earlier. Joab received his position as commander of the army for leading the attack on Jebus/Jerusalem (1 Chron. 11:6). Joab later promised silver and a warrior's belt for killing an enemy leader (2 Sam. 18:11).

Like in other nations such as Egypt, Israelite soldiers cut off body parts from slain enemies to prove kills. David needed the foreskins[36] of dead Philistines to prove his success (1 Sam. 18:25–27). The inhabitants of two cities thought Gideon had in his possession the hands of two enemy leaders, indicating their deaths (Judg. 8:6–15). Often severed heads served as proof of death as well (1 Sam. 17:51–54; 1 Chron. 10:8–10).

Enemy Rulers

As did other contemporary armies, the Israelites gave special attention to enemy rulers after battles. Often the Israelites killed these leaders in some public manner, apparently intending to demonstrate superiority and humiliate them. Joshua hung the king of Ai on a tree (or impaled it on a pole) until sunset, then had the body buried under a pile of rocks at the city gate (Josh. 8:29). Joshua's forces trapped five Amorite kings in a cave during the battle over Gibeon. After the victory, Joshua and his commanders put their feet on the kings' necks to encourage the entire force that God would likewise help them defeat their other enemies. Then Joshua killed the five and had their bodies hung in trees (or impaled on poles) until sunset, after which the Israelites buried them under stones in the same cave (Josh. 10:16–27). Joab killed Absalom to end his rebellion, then threw his corpse into a pit and had stones piled over it (2 Sam. 18:14–17). Other rulers such as Samson and Saul were mutilated after being captured or killed.

All in all, the Israelite practice of warfare resembled that of neighboring nations. Israelites generally used the weaponry and tactics of other ancient Near Eastern nations, so studying the military of these other nations helps shed light on Israelite practices, and visa versa. To that end, the rest of this book will examine the military of five such contemporary nations: Egypt, Philistia, Assyria, Babylon, and Persia.

NOTES

1 David's bodyguard consisted of Kerethites (a term for Philistines—see Zeph. 2:5), Pelethites (2 Sam 8:18; 1 Kings 1:38; etc.), and sometimes Gittites (men from Gath—2 Sam. 15:18). Though the Israelites and Philistines were long-standing enemies, the Philistines had used David and his men as soldiers (perhaps out of respect for his ability—see 1 Sam. 27), an honor which David returned when he became king. Kings often used outside mercenaries as guards since they would more likely remain loyal to the one who paid them and be less susceptible to competing interests within the kingdom. Donald G. Schley calls such mercenaries "the Judean kings' permanent hedge against popular revolt" ("The *Shalishim*: Officer or Special Three-Man Squads?" *Vetus Testamentum* 40 (1990): 324). Compare the ongoing use of Swiss guards at the Vatican in Rome.

2 Images in Fig. 2.1 are composites of elements of Judean soldiers and exiles portrayed in the Assyrian reliefs celebrating the conquest of Lachish, a Judean city that fell to Sennacherib and the Assyrian army in 701 BC. These reliefs provide most of the best illustrations of Israelite military known from the biblical period. See excellent photographs and drawings of these reliefs in Ussishkin, *Conquest of Lachish*.

3 God clearly commanded Israel to destroy chariots captured in battle, probably to keep Israel from relying on their own military power (Josh. 11:6; Deut. 17:16). Likely the young military also had limited knowledge about how to use or service these vehicles, which had less value in the hills where the Israelites first settled. If so, it may have been better for the Israelites to destroy them rather than risk them falling back into the hands of their more capable enemies.

4 Hallo and Younger, *COS* 2.113A.

5 The multiple references to the Canaanites' iron chariots (Josh 17:16–18;

Judg. 1:19; 4:3, 13) is problematic, since chariots needed to be light and flexible and were made almost entirely of different types of wood. Chariots did use a few metal parts such as pins and fittings, and ceremonial chariots could be covered with thin sheets of decorative metals like gold or silver (see opening story in chap. 3, which notes that the chariots of the Egyptian pharaoh and the princes of Kadesh and Megiddo were decorated with gold and silver). Likewise, wooden shields could be covered with gold (2 Sam. 8:7) or bronze (1 Kings 14:27). Perhaps the Canaanites' iron chariots had fittings or even decorations made from iron, since iron could also be considered a precious metal when it was first introduced and was quite rare. Perhaps the Canaanites were using iron fittings in their chariots rather than the usual bronze, and this made them noteworthy. Or perhaps the mention of iron simply referred to skilled metalworking, still beyond the reach of Israelite craftsmen at this time, and thus another area where the new nation couldn't match their Canaanite neighbors.

6   See Yutaka Ikeda's helpful treatment of Solomon's chariotry, including his statement that "Israel in the time of Solomon surely had the capability of chariot production" ("Solomon's Trade in Horses and Chariots in Its International Setting," in *Studies in the Period of David and Solomon and Other Essays: Papers Read at the International Symposium for Biblical Studies, Tokyo, 5–7 December, 1979* (ed. Tomoo Ishida; Winona Lake, IN: Eisenbrauns, 1982), 218.

7   Compare Sennacherib's ceremonial chariot, pictured on pp. 88–89 in Ussishkin's *Conquest of Lachish*. Though it is quite possible that a Judean ceremonial chariot came from Assyria or resembled Assyrian ceremonial chariots of the time, one must also consider the possibility that the Assyrian artists were simply drawing a chariot using the forms they knew or had available when they completed the drawing.

8   This author witnessed a similar modern reality while working in Israel during the 1980s and 1990s. As the one responsible for the transportation in our manufacturing company, one of my duties involved sending the company driver to register the company's transport van with the army each year. In the event of a national emergency, the army had the right to conscript such vehicles for military use, perhaps like ancient Near Eastern governments often did with merchant ships.

9   For example, J. W. Wenham writes, "It is notorious that the Old Testament in many places records numbers which seem impossibly large" ("Large Numbers in the Old Testament," *Tyndale Bulletin* 18 (1967): 19). R. E. D. Clark states, "If we take them at their face value, the numbers that we find in the

Old Testament are sometimes so large that they are altogether unbelievable" ("The Large Numbers of the Old Testament—Especially in Connexion with the Exodus," *Journal of the Transactions of the Victoria Institute* 87 (1955): 82).

10 An additional possibility is to sometimes read the original, unpointed (vowel-less) אלף as אַלֻּף, with the meaning of "warrior" or "champion." Such an understanding better fits some situations. Joshua may well have sent thirty of his best troops to set an ambush behind Ai rather than thirty thousand or even thirty units. Unfortunately, this proposal often fails to resolve the numerical issues.

11 For these first two numbers, see Israel Finkelstein, *The Archaeology of the Israelite Settlement* (Jerusalem: Israel Exploration Society, 1988), 330–35.

12 Yigal Shiloh, "The Population of Iron Age Palestine in the Light of a Sample Analysis of Urban Plans, Areas, and Population Density," *BASOR* 239 (1980): 32.

13 See Rodriquez, "Arsenal," chap. 3 for helpful discussion of swords and daggers, as well as Appendix 1 for scores of examples found in the region.

14 See also Rodriquez, "Arsenal," 132–69, as well as Appendix 3.

15 See also Rodriquez, "Arsenal," 78–97, as well as Appendix 2.

16 See Rodriquez, "Arsenal," 98–100 for a helpful discussion.

17 Experiments conducted for Emperor Napoleon gave a distance of twenty meters for throwing a simple javelin, 80 meters for one with an added looped cord. A similar but different test yielded an increase from 25 to 65 meters (E. Norman Gardiner, "Throwing the Javelin," *Journal of Hellenic Studies* 27 (1907): 257–8). Gardiner also notes that spears sometimes also had a similar attachment as a handle, which may be in view in 1 Samuel 17:7. There, the author of 1 Samuel describes Goliath's spear as resembling "a weaver's rod," perhaps his way of describing such an attached loop— which the Israelites apparently didn't use. See also Rodriquez, "Arsenal," 134–6.

18 Since all the references in the Old Testament to left-handed people indicate they were from the tribe of Benjamin, I asked geneticist Joanna R. Klein, Ph.D., if a group of related people could have a genetic presupposition toward left-handedness. She responded in part:

". . . The factors that influence handedness have been studied for years, although there is still no clear understanding of all the determinants. Current research suggests that handedness is influenced by a complex interplay of both environmental and genetic factors. Studies of twins suggest that genetic effects account for 25% of the variation of handedness and unique environmental effects account for the remainder. Some proposed environmental effects on handedness are societal, such as modeling handedness, forced handedness and stigmatization.

"Other studies based on pre-natal ultrasounds show that handedness formation occurs prenatally, before societal influences on handedness are present. . . . Familial aggregation of handedness is also consistent with a genetic component. In one study, it was found that two left handed parents have a 26% chance of having a left-handed child, while the prevalence is 20% with one left handed and one right handed parent and 10% with two right handed parents. . . . Most recently, genetic mapping studies have provided support for a genetic basis of handedness. Several genes and chromosomal locations are associated with being left-handed (LRRTM1, 2p12, 12p21–23 and 10q26). . . . In summary, from my review of the literature, I believe there is a genetic component to handedness, but it is very complex interaction between multiple genes that is influenced heavily by environmental factors" (personal communication 21 Jan. 2011).

Perhaps the Benjamites had a genetic predisposition to left-handedness, and they may have also encouraged the trait as a point of tribal distinction and pride. This information also published as "Left-Handed Sons of Right-Handers." *Biblical Archaeological Review* 39:3 (May/June 2013): 26, 69-70.

19   See Manfred Korfmann, "The Sling as a Weapon," *Scientific Americana* 229:4 (Oct. 1973): 37–40; as well as Rodriquez, "Arsenal," 235–50 and Appendix 4. Lead sling pellets often date to the Roman period and were roughly the size and shape of almonds, though much heavier.

20   See Ussishkin, *Conquest of Lachish,* 80, 82, for pictures, which show several Israelite slingers, though none clearly. They appear to fire from behind chest-high walls. A vertical motion seems unlikely from such a position, since the stone would be launched at the bottom of the revolution. Perhaps the Assyrian artist simply portrayed the Israelite slingers like the Assyrian slingers, all shown using vertical rotation.

21   Korfmann, "Sling as a Weapon," 38–40.

22   Quoted in Korfmann, "Sling as a Weapon," 40.

23   Wallace McLeod, "The Range of the Ancient Bow," *Phoenix* 19 (1965): 7, 14.

24   David's claim that he "can bend a bow of bronze" (2 Sam. 22:35; Ps. 18:34) should probably be understood as a figurative expression of God enabling him to accomplish anything, given the figurative context and the lack of other references to such bows in Israel.

25   Ussishkin, *Conquest of Lachish,* 80–5.

26 Israel Antiquities Authority, "A Rare Hebrew Seal from the First Temple Period was Discovered in Archaeological Excavations in the Western Wall Plaza (10/30/08)," n.p. [cited 5 Mar 2011]. Online: http://www.antiquities.org.il/article_Item_eng.asp?sec_id=25&subj_id=240&id=1442&module_id=#as.

27 The agriculturally oriented Israelites often named their children after insects, animals, or plants. In addition to Hagab = grasshopper, one also finds Deborah = bee, Rachel = ewe, Zipporah = bird, Tamar = palm tree, and Hadassah = myrtle.

28 Also see Ussishkin, *Conquest of Lachish,* 80, 82, 84.

29 See clear illustration of this vulnerability in Yadin, *AWBL*, 196, where an arrow has pierced the scale armor of a Canaanite charioteer at the joint of his sleeve and his torso.

30 During one class discussion about the ancient Israelite military, this author asked a student who served in the military reserves why he served in the armed forces. He came from a family with a long tradition of military service, and he answered, "For honor, and for a paycheck." Basic motivations probably have changed much since the biblical period.

31 1 Sam. 25:18; 26:11–12; 30:11–12; 2 Sam 16:1–3; 17:27–29; 1 Chron. 12:39–40.

32 Artist Josh Seevers actively participates in modern recreations of medieval-style hand-to-hand combat. When asked whether thirty minutes seemed like a likely time limit for close-range combat, he wrote, "It depends on the physical fitness of the person and the tempo at which they are fighting. If a person was fit and trained in equipment and tactics, or the intensity of combat was low, I can see them going longer. However, I would guess on average, thirty minutes would be high. I also think the likelihood of someone staying on the front lines and fighting continuously for thirty minutes without getting hit, resting, or switching out, is low."

33 For helpful discussions of this reality, see Gabriel and Metz, *Sumer to Rome,* 47–110; and Hobbs, *Time for War,* 140–81. Gabriel and Metz write, "Wars were not so much exercises in strategy as they were exercises in political and military decapitation" (82). See opening story in chap. 5 of this book for a description of the Philistine decapitation of Saul and his Israelite kingdom.

34 The marches by Joshua and troops from Gilgal to Ai and Gilgal to Gibeon required marches of twelve and seventeen miles respectively, including ascents of 3,600 feet and 3,100 feet from the Rift Valley up into the central Hill Country.

35 Abraham Malamat, "The War of Gideon and Midian," *PEQ* 85 (1953): 61–65; Yadin, *AWBL*, 259.

36 "Foreskins" may be a euphemism for phalli. As discussed in chap. 4, the Egyptians used phalli from uncircumcised Libyans to prove kills; perhaps Saul wanted the same from his uncircumcised enemies. Additionally, it seems less likely that a warrior in battle would take the time to perform the somewhat delicate operation of circumcision rather than making what was probably a faster cut to sever the entire male organ.

EGYPT:
ARMIES OF THE PHARAOHS—PART 1

3

THE BIG DAY OF CHARIOT-WARRIOR
NAKT-HER-PERI: THE BATTLE OF MEGIDDO

It had been a big day for Nakt-her-Peri—in fact, the biggest day of his young life. Nakt-her-Peri was a chariot-warrior, in command of an Egyptian chariot, the greatest weapon of war in its day. No common recruit, Nakt-her-Peri served as a professional, a career military man in a long, proud family line of professional soldiers who had served bravely and faithfully under numerous pharaohs. Nakt-her-Peri was born to this life, had trained years for it, and had long yearned for a day like the day he just had. He had longed for the opportunity to gain glory for himself and for his military family, and he hadn't been disappointed. His first experience in a major battle had been challenging, exhilarating, rewarding, and if he were honest, a bit frightening. Nakt-her-Peri had just taken part in the Battle of Megiddo in north-central Canaan on May 12, 1468 BC.[1] The battle had secured Egypt's control over the Levant, the lands along the eastern Mediterranean, for the next 250 years. It had been a very big day indeed.

As Nakt-her-Peri lay on his mat in his tent that night, his mind returned to the events of the day and to the many events that had led up to it. He thought back to his early childhood, when he first became aware of his identity and the nature of his family. His name, Nakt-her-Peri, meant "Mighty-on-the-Battlefield," and he quickly learned that his parents had chosen it to help direct the course of their oldest son's life. Nakt-her-Peri had been born into a proud military family whose oldest sons had longed served as warriors for the pharaohs. They were more than common soldiers who were conscripted to fight for a particular campaign and afterward returned to their normal pastimes; they were professionals who served in the military full time. Several generations ago, their commitment to this service had earned for the family the property and fields that supported them well through the years. But the commitment also came with an obligation: at least one member of the family, normally the eldest son, must serve in the ranks of the pharaoh's armies. Often those sons had served as officers, and now even an officer in the chariotry, the best of the best of Egypt's forces. Their property and position had given the family wealth and prestige—plus pressure to live up to such status. "Mighty-on-the-Battlefield" had always secretly wondered if he would be able to live up to the pressure and to his name. Today he had.

Nakt-her-Peri also thought of the training and planning that had led up to the day's battle. His family lived near the military compound at Memphis in northern Egypt (Map 3.1), so when it came time to report, he didn't have far to go. He made it through the basic military training with little difficulty and won selection to the prestigious chariot corps as hoped. Then his training intensified. Egypt's chariots, like most of the time, carried two soldiers, a driver and a chariot-warrior (Fig. 3.1). Each chariot operated in conjunction with other chariots and supporting foot

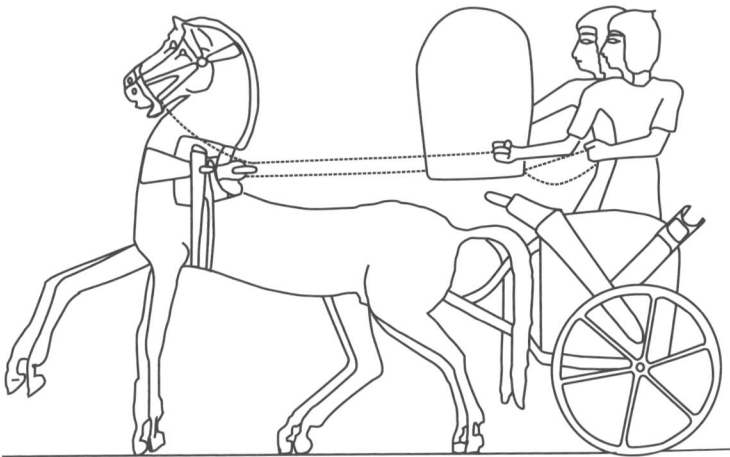

Fig. 3.1—Chariot with driver and warrior

soldiers called "runners." Nakt-her-Peri focused on the skills of the char-iot-warrior, of course, but he also had to learn the work of a driver. One never knew what could happen in battle and what a warrior might need to do. Thus he learned to handle horses and drive as well as how to fight with sword and spear. Nakt-her-Peri also became proficient with the powerful and effective composite bow, the weapon that made the chariot forces such a feared and formidable force. He also learned how to fight in concert with the runners who supported and protected these valuable and effective military machines (Figs. 3.2, 3.4)[2]. Much to his father's delight, Nakt-her-Peri even won acceptance to the officers' corps as one of the youngest men ever to earn that distinction at Mem-phis. Nakt-her-Peri took rather easily to the challenges and honor of the position of "First Charioteer," learning to command a unit of ten chariots and coordinate his unit with other units in their squadron.

The young officer's life had grown more intense in 1457 BC when the newly independent pharaoh, Thutmose III, announced plans for the first of what he promised would be numerous campaigns. Thutmose's former

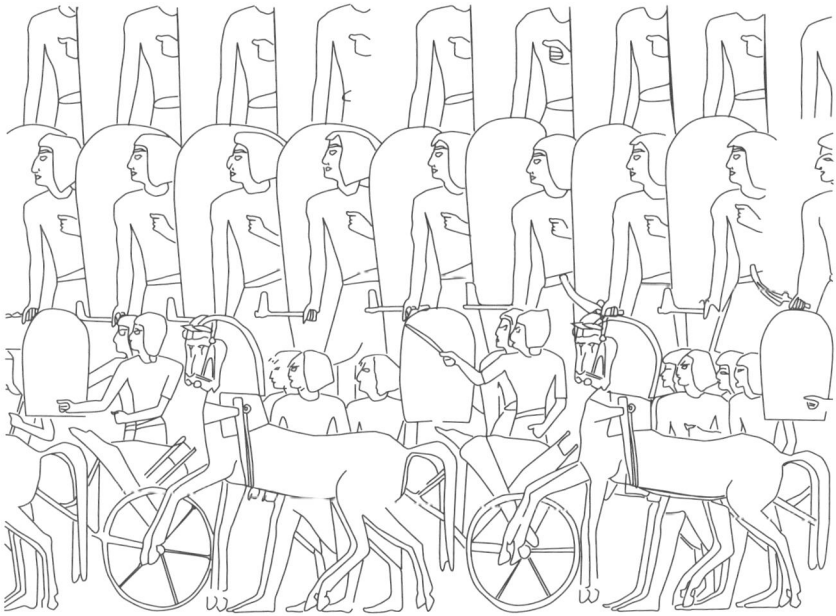

Fig. 3.2—Chariots and runners (apparently) below, with heavy infantry above

co-ruler, Hatshepsut, had not sent the military on many campaigns during the twenty-two years that she wielded final power. Indeed, there was little need to send out the army, as conquered nations sent in their annual tribute with little problem.

Military men chafed at the relative inactivity, and Nakt-her-Peri more than once heard his father praying to the family's gods for better opportunities for his son. Those prayers now seemed answered. After Hatshepsut's death, many subjected kings took advantage of the change

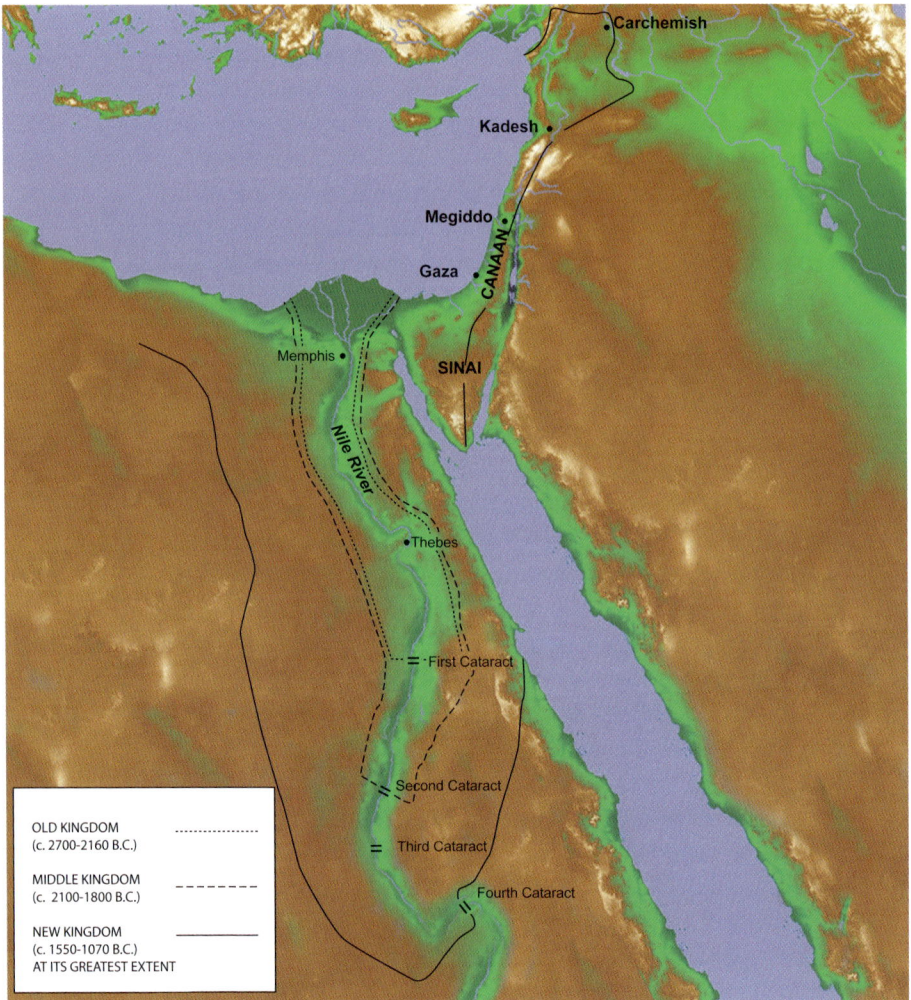

Map 3.1—Ancient Egypt during Old, Middle, New Kingdoms

in power and rebelled, refusing to send Egypt its expected tribute. Thutmose responded as the soldiers hoped, calling for the military to prepare. Thutmose would lead his army to put down the evil rebels and hopefully subjugate rulers and lands even farther north and south than what Egypt had previously controlled (Fig. 3.3). Success on the battlefield would mean riches and honor for the pharaoh, for Egypt, for its gods, and for the warriors who proved worthy. What a time to begin a military career!

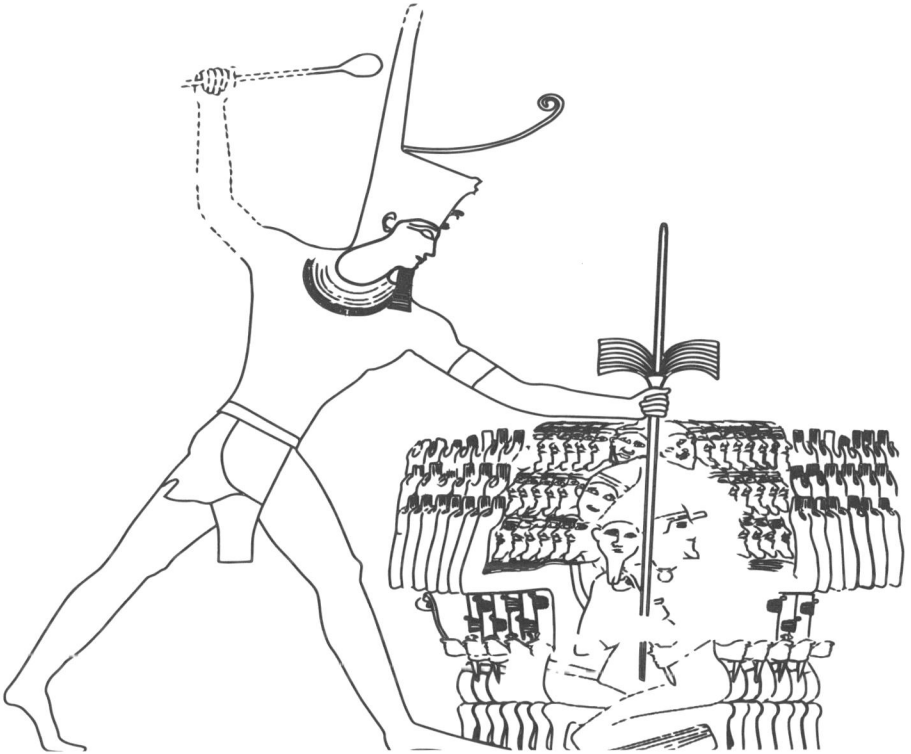

Fig. 3.3—Thutmose III striking enemies

Preparations had begun in earnest. Large numbers of new recruits were called and trained. The army also hired mercenaries, despite the distrust and disdain with which Nakt-her-Peri and other native professionals viewed them. Great quantities of food, clothing, weapons, and other supplies began to flow into the armories. The best materials went to the best troops. Nearly all the professional chariot forces received new chariots and weapons, and a number of chariot-warriors even received the expensive and effective scale armor instead of the traditional, cheaper, leather protective garments. Nakt-her-Peri and his fellow troops trained with their new equipment and looked forward to using it in battle against Egypt's foes.

Nakt-her-Peri remembered vividly the day the campaign began, which was, according to the Egyptian calendar, the twenty-fifth day of the fourth month of winter in Thutmose's twenty-second year (including the years of Hatshepsut's dominance). They joined with the other troops that had assembled at the fort of Tjaru on the border of Egypt (Map 3.2). He could not have felt more proud or excited. The young chariot officer rode at the head of his unit and with the rest of the large force, and the vast army started out across the northern Sinai Peninsula on the route known as the Way of Horus.

Their mission was clear. They were to enter Canaan from the south, then find and destroy the coalition of Canaanites and Syrians undoubtedly assembling to meet them. The vile prince of Kadesh in northern Syria had led the rebellion against Thutmose's rule, and would be assembling as many princes (rulers of city-states) and their armies as possible. Stakes were high: Egypt could either retain control over this large region along the eastern Mediterranean, or lose these lands and the wealth that such control promised. The gods would decide, and many mortals would die. Nakt-her-Peri knew that he could be among them, but he also knew not to dwell on the possibility.

Most of the journey toward the battlefield went smoothly, particularly the trip across the Sinai. After ten days of little but heat and sand, the Egyptian army arrived at Gaza, a stronghold that remained loyal at the southern edge of Canaan. The army had averaged approximately fifteen miles/per day to that point, but after leaving Gaza, the pace slowed significantly.[3] The loyalty of the local cities was unproven, and a surprise attack could happen at any time. Additional scouts went out in each direction, and Thutmose and his generals proceeded with caution. The farther the army traveled up the coastal plain of Canaan, the more apparent became the location of the upcoming battle. The major coastal road would turn inland, cut through one of several mountain passes, and then empty onto a great valley—large, flat, and open, eminently suitable for a major battle. Surely the prince of Kadesh and his allies would be waiting with their forces at the edge of this valley (later called the Jezreel Valley).

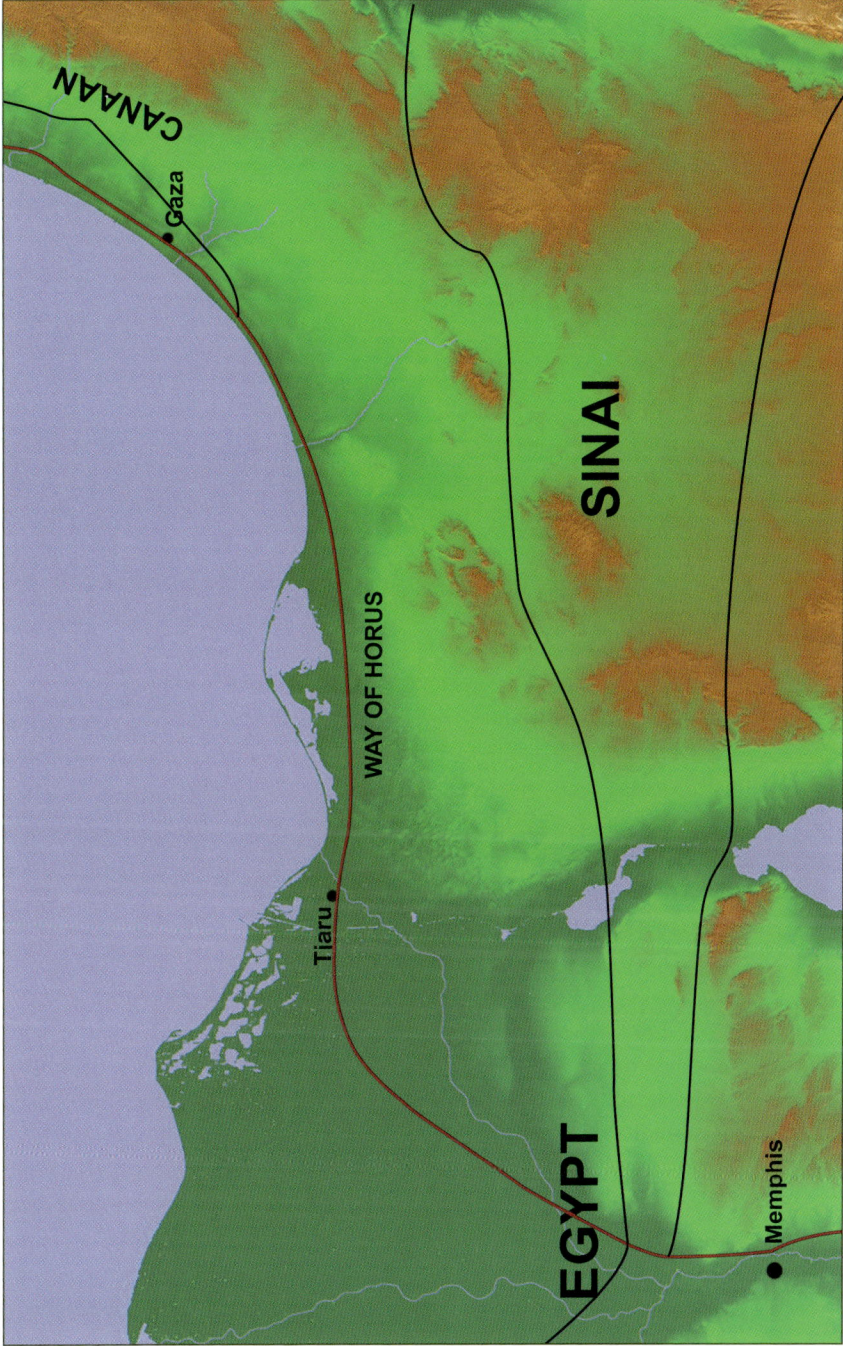

Map 3.2—Egypt to Canaan

Next, the Egyptians had to choose the best route to enter the valley. When they reached the village of Yaham (Map 3.3), their scouts reported on the three passes that cut through the long, low mountain that the locals called Mt. Carmel. The two outer routes had wider and better passages, offering the Egyptian forces the opportunity to stay in tighter marching formation and thus remain safer should the enemy launch a surprise attack. The tighter formation also meant it would take less time for the Egyptian army to traverse the pass and set up in battle formation once they reached the valley. But would they have time to assemble in the valley before the enemy attacked? The enemy coalition would probably expect the Egyptians to use one of the outer passes, and it would likely station its troops at the mouth of one or both of them. That would potentially set the stage for a quick attack on the pharaoh's troops as they began to empty out but before the rest of the army arrived and properly assembled.

By contrast, the middle pass presented the narrowest route and the highest risk. If the Egyptians took the center pass, they stood the best chance of surprising the Canaanites and their allies, but it would also increase the risk by stringing out their forces even more. As one general put it, "Will not horses have to go in single file, and the army and the people (support personnel) likewise? Will the lead troops be fighting there (in the valley) while those at the rear are standing around here in Aruna (before the pass), unable to fight?"[4] The center pass also exited just east of the Megiddo, the major city in the valley and undoubtedly the headquarters for the Canaanites as they prepared for the advancing Egyptians. If the Egyptians could successfully advance through this pass, they could set up near the Canaanite stronghold and force the enemy to come to them on their own terms. But would it work?

The decision fell to Thutmose, of course, and he chose the center pass. The army prepared and assembled, and the lead elements began the march shortly after dawn. Thutmose personally led the advance through the dangerous pass. After several nervous hours of cautious marching, Thutmose and the lead troops exited the pass about noon. Some seven more hours would pass before the rest of the army could arrive and assemble. Thutmose had chosen well. The Canaanites were indeed caught off guard. They had positioned their main forces near the outer passes and could not redeploy quickly enough to engage the Egyptians in battle before nightfall. Both armies selected their positions, set up camp, posted guards, distributed rations, and hunkered down for a restless night to await sunrise and the day of the great battle.

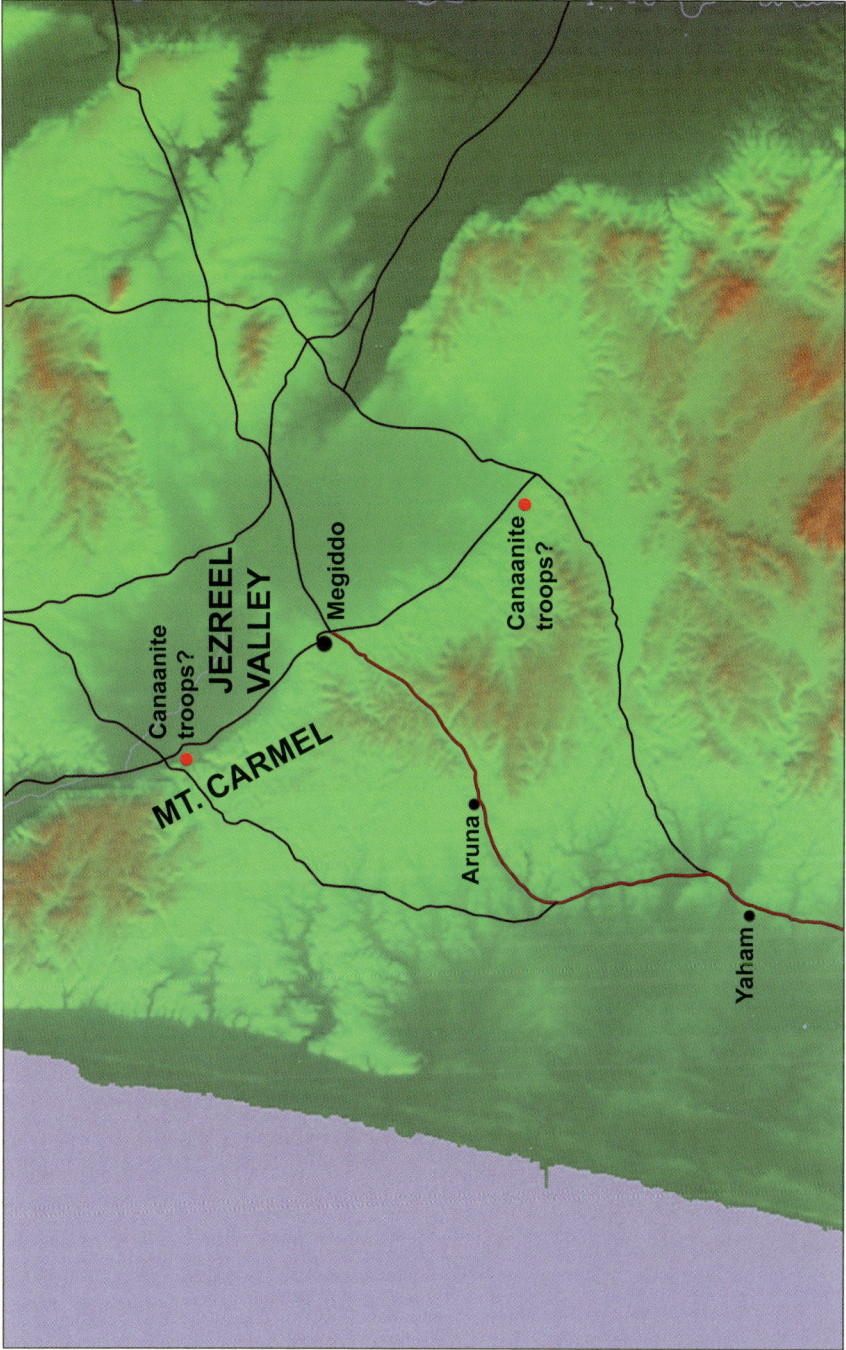

JEZREEL VALLEY

MT. CARMEL

Megiddo

Canaanite troops?

Canaanite troops?

Aruna

Yaham

Map 3.3—Approaches to Megiddo

Nakt-her-Peri's big day dawned bright and clear. Both the Egyptian and Canaanite troops assembled quickly, with noticeably less commotion and shouting than normal. The men fed, watered, and prepared their animals, and somberly made ready their own equipment and weapons. The air hung heavy and tense. Great uncertainty lay ahead, and each man knew that not everyone who had watched the sun rise would also see it set that night.

When the Egyptian army had finished preparations, Thutmose rode out to inspect his troops. He looked brilliant with the morning sun reflecting off his polished scale armor and his chariot decorated with gold. His troops had arrayed in three sections with their backs to the high ground, forming a rough semicircle around the enemy city. They clearly had superior position and were ready.

The coalition of Canaanites and their allies also assembled, but found themselves at a clear disadvantage, organized in response to the Egyptian position. The Canaanites had stationed themselves between the attackers and Megiddo as best they could, but they were out-positioned and appeared to be outnumbered as well. The allied forces had gathered a sizeable army that included thousands of foot soldiers and hundreds of chariots, but they looked and acted like a conglomeration of small armies that was clearly outmatched by a united and superior foe.

Suddenly, the battle began. Thutmose signaled and began the charge, and none of the Egyptians dared hang back. Nakt-her-Peri and his unit of chariots had been stationed in the Egyptian center in one of two groups of elite chariots flanking their pharaoh. The young chariot officer barked orders to his driver and runners, signaled to his other chariots, and they all joined the charge (Fig. 3.4). The chariots of each army sped ahead, with their infantry following in the rear. Amazingly, the enemy troops broke formation almost immediately. Their lead chariots had barely engaged the Egyptian chariots when they began to turn and flee, and some even collided with other allied chariots coming up behind. When the Canaanite infantry saw what was happening with their chariotry, they also broke and ran toward the safety of the walled city of Megiddo. *Cowards!*

For Nakt-her-Peri and the other Egyptians, their suppressed fear quickly evaporated and was replaced by courage and greed. The Battle of Megiddo would obviously become a smashing victory, and now they hungered to gain glory and loot. Nakt-her-Peri's chariot approached an overturned Canaanite chariot, and the two-man crew was desperately trying to right it. Nakt-her-Peri killed the bare-chested driver with a single arrow from his composite bow, but he needed three more to wound and down the leather-clad chariot-warrior[5] as he fled on foot. The driver stopped the chariot and Nakt-her-Peri leaped off with his sword to kill his opponent. Quickly accomplishing his task, he then leaned over, cut off the dead enemy's hand, and ran back to do the same to the dead Canaanite driver. He jumped back on his chariot and dumped the bloody body parts into a bag. Severed hands of slain enemy troops were proof of enemy killed,

Fig. 3.4—Chariot with driver and warrior, plus runner

and they guaranteed reward in the ceremony after a victorious battle. Nakt-her-Peri thus assured himself of receiving the coveted "Gold of Valor" from the pharaoh.[6] Though the battle had just begun, "Mighty-on-the-Battlefield" had already lived up to his name.

Unfortunately for the Egyptians, the great victory dissipated almost as quickly as it had materialized. As their troops pursued the Canaanites fleeing toward Megiddo, the Egyptians passed through the main enemy camp. Like Nakt-her-Peri, many of the Egyptians found themselves in their first major battle, and discipline broke down. Greed took over, and many stopped to plunder the Canaanite camp, allowing most of the enemy to reach Megiddo alive. The people in Megiddo had already closed and bolted the gate of the walled city, leaving the soldiers outside, frantically clamoring to be let in. Although the city's inhabitants refused to open the gate, they did rescue many by lowering improvised ropes made from articles of clothing tied together and pulling the troops up to safety. Far too many of the enemy escaped this way, including the prince of Kadesh and most of the other princes as well. The smashing Egyptian victory shrank to a clear victory as the Egyptians took possession of the battlefield and the plunder, but with the majority of the enemy troops alive in the temporary safety of the city. The Egyptian officers slowly restored order as their army surrounded Megiddo, and they began preparations for the long, arduous task of laying siege to the city.

Although the siege of Megiddo lasted a grueling seven months, the city had to be captured, given the site's strategic location and the importance of crushing the rebellion led by the princes who had taken refuge inside. In the words of Thutmose, "Every chieftain of all northern lands is bottled up within it…the capture of Megiddo is (like) the capture of a thousand cities." When the besieged enemy finally came out to surrender, Egypt had accomplished its goals of reasserting control over much of the Levant and capturing a great quantity of plunder. The victorious Egyptian army returned home with 3,400 prisoners-of-war, 2,041 horses, and 924 chariots, including those of the princes of Kadesh and Megiddo, which were decorated with gold. They also took 502 bows, 202 coats of mail, and livestock of various kinds, including 20,500 sheep. Curiously, the two hands Nakt-her-Peri had taken in battle came from two of just eighty-three enemy killed at the Battle of Megiddo. The low proportion of troops killed to chariots and prisoners captured apparently reflects the relative absence of heavy fighting, which was unnecessary due to the swiftness of Egypt's rout. Though it did not end exactly as the Egyptians could have wished, the Battle of Megiddo had indeed turned out to be a big day—for Nakt-her-Peri, for Pharaoh Thutmose III, and for all of Egypt.[7]

HISTORICAL SETTING AND BIBLICAL CONNECTIONS

As the preceding story suggests, Egypt had risen to a position of unprecedented greatness and power by the time of Thutmose III in the mid-15th century BC and would control a large part of the ancient Near East for another several hundred years. Historians call this period the Egyptian New Kingdom, one of three such times of dominance during ancient Egyptian history.

During the first of these periods, the Old Kingdom (ca. 2700–2160 BC[8]), Egyptians united the northern and southern parts of their land and built the pyramids at Giza. Egypt became the greatest power in the region, but it exercised direct control only along the Nile from the delta in the north to the first cataract in the south (Map 3.1). The six cataracts along the southern Nile each had sections of shallow water with boulders that sometimes produced rapids, creating barriers to boat travel and thus natural boundaries. When the Old Kingdom ended, a short period of civil war and relative weakness followed, which historians call the First Intermediate Period.

Egypt returned to power and dominance during the Middle Kingdom (ca. 2100–1800 BC; Map 3.1) when Egypt expanded its control southward to the second cataract and the pharaohs carried out large building projects and conducted significant international trade. During the Middle Kingdom, Egyptian history seems to intersect with biblical history for the first time. Egyptian records from both the First Intermediate Period and the Middle Kingdom contain multiple accounts of how the country struggled to deal with large numbers of nomads seeking entrance into the country to avoid starvation. For example, the "Prophecy of Neferti" (12th Dynasty, Middle Kingdom) states, "All happiness has gone away, the land is cast down in trouble because of those feeders, Asiatics (Semites) who are throughout the land. . . . Asiatics have come down to Egypt. . . . They beg for water . . . in order to let their flocks drink."[9] This description seems to fit well with many of the narratives from the middle and latter chapters of Genesis. In Genesis, one reads about the journeys of nomadic Abraham and his descendants, who were drawn to Egypt during times of famine. Thus the patriarchal narratives seem to fit the general picture known from Egypt during the Middle Kingdom, although direct connections still remain elusive.

The Middle Kingdom ended with another time of weakness called the Second Intermediate Period. During this time, Egypt lost control of its country to outsiders called "Hyksos" or "foreign rulers" and then regained it to start the New Kingdom. Scholars debate just how the biblical history in later Genesis and early Exodus might fit with these shifts in power. The latter part of Genesis describes the rise of Abraham's great-grandson Joseph to the position of Egyptian vizier. Many, including the author of this book, think this could well have occurred during the Middle Kingdom. If so, the Bible's later statement that "there arose a new king over Egypt, who did not know Joseph" (Ex. 1:8, ESV) could describe the Hyksos takeover, thus attributing the enslavement of the Israelites to the Hyksos. Another perspective puts the career of Joseph during the period of the Hyksos control, arguing that a foreigner like Joseph would more likely rise to such power when other foreigners controlled the country. With this understanding, the "new king" would likely have been a native Egyptian pharaoh at the beginning of the New Kingdom. Either way, the Israelites had become enslaved by the beginning of the book of Exodus and the early New Kingdom.

The New Kingdom (ca. 1550–1070 BC) saw Egypt reach its peak of power. The Egyptians successfully expelled the Hyksos and began a period of unparalleled dominance and prosperity. Thutmose III and other pharaohs expanded Egypt's domain southward to the fourth cataract of the Nile and northward all the way to Carchemish and the Euphrates River, a distance of some 1,250 miles (Map 3.1). Thus the book of Exodus opens with the Israelites enslaved to Egypt, the most powerful ancient Near Eastern kingdom of this era, making the prospects for gaining freedom rather bleak. How could a group of slaves gain freedom from the greatest power the ancient Near East had yet seen? What hope would those slaves have of defeating the military of such a nation? Little, unless the God of those slaves was indeed sovereign as he claimed, and fought on their behalf.

Regardless of how unlikely the Exodus might have seemed at such a time of Egyptian power, the Bible reports that it did happen, apparently during the New Kingdom. But exactly when it happened and under which pharaoh is not clear. For many, the Bible dates the Exodus to 1446 BC, squarely in the middle of the reigns of Thutmose III and Amenhotep II

(1479–1400 BC), when Egyptian military activity was at its peak. Others date the Exodus to the 13th century, as discussed in chapter 1. Regardless of whether one dates the Exodus and conquest to the 15th or 13th century, these events would have occurred with the backdrop of Egyptian dominance during the New Kingdom, and should be read against that backdrop.

The New Kingdom came to an end shortly after 1200 BC. Some great event (or events) apparently ushered in a dark age in the ancient Near East. Egypt and other great empires declined dramatically or collapsed altogether. Entire people groups migrated to new lands, adding to the general chaos and confusion of the time. Such is the framework for the period of the biblical Judges, which was also a dark time for Israel. One of the people groups migrating during this time was the Philistines, one of several groups that the Egyptians called "Sea Peoples." These Sea Peoples apparently left the area of the Aegean Sea between Greece and Asia Minor, made their way around the eastern Mediterranean, and tried to conquer Egypt. Pharaoh Ramesses III (1184–1153 BC) defeated them, and the reliefs and descriptions of this struggle provide much valuable military information. The Philistines subsequently settled along the southern part of the eastern Mediterranean coast. From there they would harass the emerging Israelite peoples up in the central Canaanite highlands, as recorded in the books of Judges and Samuel.

Although the Egyptians held off the invading Sea Peoples, Egypt's power declined dramatically around this time. For the next 800 years, Egypt would remain a moderate power, only occasionally able to reach beyond its homeland to take plunder and affect major events playing out in the politics of the time. For example, the Bible notes that, at the time of Solomon (10th century BC), Egypt had captured the important Canaanite city of Gezer on the western border of Israel (1 Kings 9:16). This implies Egyptian strength, but the same account also shows that Egypt was weak enough that it married one of its princesses to Solomon, king of the rising power of Israel. Such an arrangement would have been unthinkable during the earlier periods of Egyptian dominance. Then, shortly after Solomon's death ca. 930 BC, Pharaoh Shishak had enough power to venture north with his army to plunder both Judah and Israel (1 Kings 14:25–26), but he wasn't strong enough to maintain control of the area. Several centuries later, shortly before Judah's final collapse, Pharaoh Neco took his army all the way to Carchemish on the Euphrates River. He there joined up with the Assyrian army (2 Kings 23:29), but their combined forces couldn't defeat the Babylonian army under Nebuchadnezzar and prevent Babylon from taking control of the ancient Near East.

Although the Old Testament closes with Egypt having faded to the status of a second-rate power, the nation did play a meaningful role in the region's military and political events throughout most of Old Testament history. This is especially true from the time of the New Kingdom on, when the interplay between the Israelites and the Egyptian military was most significant. Thus, a description of the Egyptian military from this time should help readers of the Bible better understand a number of the events of the Old Testament in their context.

These chapters will describe the Egyptian military during this time by using information gleaned from written texts, artistic representations of war (some quite dramatic and informative), and surviving artifacts such as weapons and chariots. Relevant texts include royal inscriptions, official chronicles, personal accounts of individual soldiers from tombs, and the records of international correspondence. Some of these texts were originally written on perishable materials such as parchment or leather. Others were inscribed on the walls of temples throughout Egypt, often alongside pictorial reliefs of the pharaohs and the battles in which they invariably claimed victory. Still other relevant images decorated items such as the pharaohs' chariots.

The various reliefs from the walls of temples offer some of best information about warfare during this period, although curiously, most date from the 19th and 20th Dynasties rather than the more militaristic 18th Dynasty. The great pharaohs of the 18th Dynasty, like Thutmose III and Amenhotep II, left written records of their accomplishments, but apparently no great war scenes. One must use the later battle scenes to illustrate the earlier texts. When such scenes do appear, they seem to show how items such as weapons and chariots were actually used. They also portray artifacts that have not survived, both those made from perishable materials (leather, cloth, wood) as well as things like the tops of fortified city walls. The reliefs also illustrate to some degree military tactics and methods, and usually include the name of the pharaoh involved, thus dating the work.

Even though many of the witnesses to Egyptian warfare have survived, the combined evidence often does not present a clear portrayal of the art of war as practiced during this time. Some of the existing evidence is hard to interpret partly because the texts and pictures often served to glorify the pharaoh rather than supply accurate historical information. This can cause doubts about information such as numbers of troops or the role of the army, typically portrayed as merely mopping up after the pharaoh won the battle. Even the pictorial evidence can be confusing, with its stylized and possibly outdated portrayals. In addition to the interpretive problems, important information is often lacking in matters such as the size of armies, their organization and appearance, the time needed for troop movements or battles, and the roles of chariots and runners in battle. Despite these challenges, we now turn to describe the organization, weaponry, and tactics of the Egyptian military from the time of the New Kingdom to the close of the period of the Old Testament.

MILITARY ORGANIZATION

The armies of Egypt's New Kingdom differed dramatically from those of the Old and Middle Kingdoms.[10] Previously, the pharaohs had kept a small standing army and ordered local rulers to call up reserves in times of need. These reserves had little formal training and operated under the leadership of their local officials. This strategy changed dramatically during the New Kingdom, perhaps because of the disastrous defeats to the Hyksos. The standing army, comprised largely of professional soldiers like the fictitious Nakt-her-Peri, expanded considerably. Trained officers who operated within a well-organized chain of command led these professionals. Regular military service became a part of life for a large part of society. Like this author's modern Israeli boss, many Egyptians during the New Kingdom probably couldn't imagine life without the army.

Recruitment and Training

The pharaohs of the New Kingdom drafted large numbers of freeborn native Egyptians into military service. "They were drafted and taken away to the north (apparently the military compound at Memphis), it being said, 'They shall be infantrymen.'"[11] Little is known about how many were drafted other than the statement of Ramesses III in the 12th century that he did not take the usual one out of ten from those associated with the temples, implying a draft of ten percent of the available males. Volunteering also occurred but apparently was less common than conscription through the draft.

Inductees reported to reception centers at Memphis in the north or Thebes in the south, where they were registered, assigned to drill companies, and issued weapons and equipment. Training included daily drilling with arms on training grounds, accompanied by harsh, frequent beatings. If the soldier thought the treatment too severe and he ran away, his family could be imprisoned.[12]

Some young men entered military camps to begin their training at an early age, many of them coming from military families who lived in military colonies throughout the country. Each family had to make at least one member available for service at all times in exchange for tracts of land awarded to them earlier. Often they served as officers for the infantry or chariotry,[13] like Nakt-her-Peri.

Soldiers served in either the northern or southern divisions, headquartered at Memphis or Thebes. There, officers assigned them one of

Fig. 3.5 – Mercenaries. Note variety of helmets and weaponry (Missing parts of illustration also missing from original).

many roles, including serving on foreign campaign, garrisoning border stations, providing royal escorts and parade troops, suppressing riots and maintaining order, or providing labor companies that worked in quarries and built royal monuments. If the country was at peace and his services were not required, a soldier could even live at home until called up.[14]

As time passed and it became increasingly difficult to fill the armies with natives, pharaohs relied more and more on foreign mercenaries (Fig. 3.5) and prisoners of war. At the beginning of this period, most mercenaries came from nearby Nubia and Libya, but later on, one finds more and more Sherden and other Sea Peoples. Such mercenaries often appear in reliefs wearing native dress and carrying native weapons. By the end of the 18th Dynasty, the Egyptians also used prisoners captured in earlier campaigns. They were branded with the pharaoh's name[15] (Fig. 3.6), settled in military camps, assigned clothing and provisions, and conscripted into the army as auxiliary infantry. By the 19th Dynasty, mercenaries and auxiliaries may have outnumbered Egyptians in the army.[16]

Fig. 3.6—Branding POWs. Style of headdress suggests prisoners are Philistine

Military Branches

As noted in the preceding section, the Egyptian military had a well-developed but sometimes unclear structure, which undoubtedly changed over time. References to the different branches of the army usually just use general terms like "infantry," "chariotry," and later on, "Sherden"[17] (apparently a general reference to mercenaries), making it difficult to determine the exact structure at any given time. Nevertheless, the Egyptians' organizational ability and military structure clearly played an important part in their military successes during the New Kingdom.

Infantry   As with most armies throughout history, foot soldiers comprised the largest part of the Egyptian military. References sometimes distinguish between the less well-trained and more lightly armed "recruits" (draftees) and the "heavy-armed troops" (professionals), who often carried battle-axes along with shields and spears (Fig. 3.7—lower register). Professionals trained as archers made up another part of the infantry. Some records also refer to special crack troops called "elite troops," "braves of the king," or simply "braves," who spearheaded assaults. The accounts of the Battle of Kadesh in 1275 BC note the key role played by *na'arun,* or "youth," apparently a select unit. The *na'arun* were off to the west when the fighting at Kadesh started, but they arrived just in time to rescue Ramesses II and the Egyptian army from disaster.[18]

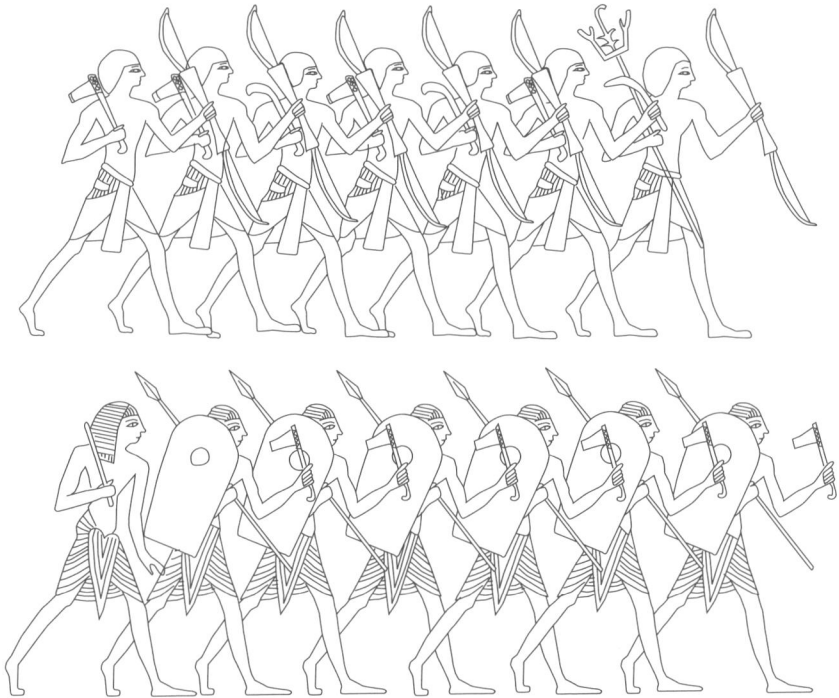

Fig. 3.7—Units of archers (top) and heavy infantry (bottom)

Often the infantry units were organized according to types of weapons. Infantrymen typically carried shields plus one or two of the following: spear, sword, battle-axe, throw-stick, mace, or metal rod (see Fig. 3.7 and further description under Weapons). The heavy infantry in the lower register of Fig. 3.7 carry the typical shields (with holes for better vision) and spears, plus battle-axes and one with a rod, (see chap. 4, "Short-Range Weapons"). The soldiers in the upper register all carry bows plus battle-axes or throw-sticks, and the officer in front bears a military standard (Fig. 3.8).

The basic organization of smaller to larger units may have been squad-platoon-company-battalion-division, though the information doesn't allow for certainty. Squads made up the basic fighting unit, perhaps comprised of ten men at full strength, including a commander and assistant. Some evidence suggests that five squads made up a platoon of fifty, and four to five platoons comprised a company of 200 or 250. The companies were organized by type of weapon and type of soldier (recruit, professional, garrison, etc.). Four or five companies made up a battalion of one thou-

Fig. 3.8—Egyptian god leading troops. Chariot with elevated standard of Amon-Re as ram's head with solar disk.

sand, with perhaps five battalions in a division.[19]

A well-defined officer corps supported this organizational structure, comprised of men drawn from the ranks of common soldiers, civil service, and members of the royal court. A commander called "captain of a troop" led each squad, and each platoon had "the greatest of the fifty." A "standard bearer" commanded the company and was supported by both a scribe and an "adjutant of the company" for matters of service and supply. A "commander of a host" led each battalion and was aided by an adjutant. Generals, often royal princes, led the divisions. The pharaoh served as commander in chief, either in fact or just in name. Thutmose III actually commanded the army at Megiddo, described earlier, as did Ramesses III at Kadesh. In other cases, the pharaohs delegated most of the military responsibilities to a "minister of war."[20]

As noted above, scribes provided administrative support for the army, as did quartermasters. Quartermasters oversaw the storage and issuing of food and supplies. Scribes registered recruits, handled rations, kept records on the battlefield, and registered kills and rewards after the battle. Scribes apparently had their own chain of command with a "chief scribe of the army" at the top.[21]

Each company bore a name like "Ramesses, strong of arm" as well as a standard, an identifying symbol at the top of a pole (Figs. 3.7, 3.8) that sometimes had streamers. The Egyptian army had used standards as far back as the Old Kingdom, but they rarely appear in battle scenes before the New Kingdom. The standards would have enabled commanders to keep track of the location and to gauge the condition of each unit, as well as serving as a rallying point for the members of the troop.[22]

Military divisions also carried standards and bore names, apparently taken from the principal gods of Egypt. Records from the 18th–20th Dynasties all list divisions named after Amon, Re, Ptah, or Seth, often accompanied by pious descriptors like "Beloved of Amon" or "Manifest in Justice." The reliefs of Ramesses III show such a standard mounted on a chariot driven ahead of the troops (Fig. 3.8). The standard clearly portrays the god Amon-Re going before the pharaoh and troops to grant them success.[23] Many ancient Near Eastern societies, including Israel, shared this concept of the god(s) leading their army. The Israelites, however, had to content themselves with a sacred chest (the Ark of the Covenant—Josh. 3; 1 Sam. 4) representing Yahweh, rather than the more graphic depictions allowed by Egyptian culture.

Chariotry
In the military records of this era, the more impressive branch of chariotry typically overshadows the infantry. Apparently introduced to chariots around the time of the Hyksos, the Egyptians developed great skill in producing and using the light, horse-drawn vehicles. The Egyptians likely used chariots for multiple military purposes: acting as a protective screen for the army while on the march, attacking opposing chariots and foot soldiers in battle, and chasing down and killing enemy infantry after they broke rank and ran.[24] Armed with powerful composite bows, Egyptian chariot-warriors could rain arrows on more stationary enemy forces from these light, highly maneuverable platforms, while

remaining protected by their own mobility and speed as well as their shield and body armor.

Egyptian chariots carried two soldiers, which was common for the time, whereas some other nations used three or more soldiers, as discussed in subsequent chapters. The Egyptians called their chariot drivers both "charioteers" and "shield-bearers," as they apparently drove and held the shield when in battle. The second soldier was the fighter, or "chariot-warrior." He primarily fought with the powerful and effective composite bow, though he also had available to him javelins, swords, and other weapons for close fighting on foot.[25]

Along with the two mounted chariot troops, texts also mention foot soldiers called "runners" apparently attached to the chariotry (note also 1 Sam. 8:11). They occasionally appear marching or running alongside chariots (Figs. 3.2, 3.4), and apparently fought with shield and javelin to support the chariots. Although their exact function is unclear, they may have acted to shield their own chariot troops and horses from enemy combatants while simultaneously attempting to disable enemy chariots. Such ground troops could have finished off wounded enemies or those stranded by an immobilized chariot. Chariots could become immobilized by a dead or wounded horse, or by a breakdown of the somewhat fragile wooden chariot.[26]

When chariots first came into use, they were apparently incorporated into the organization of the infantry. As time passed and the chariot corps grew in size and importance, it was separated from the infantry and given its own organization and chain of command. Separate ranks and titles for chariotry begin to appear early in the 15th century, suggesting a separation at that time. Subsequent requests from subject princes in Canaan and Byblos for Egyptian men (infantry) and chariots (or horses) in the 14th century seem to confirm this timing.[27]

Such requests always petition for chariots or horses in multiples of ten, suggesting that chariot units may have had ten each. These units bore names such as "Manifest in Justice" or "The Phoenix." Undoubtedly a number of units, apparently five, served together as a squadron, and a number of squadrons made up larger tactical units. The evidence, however, is scanty and may have changed as the number of chariots increased over time.[28]

A corresponding hierarchy of officers supplemented by support staff led the chariot corps. The charioteers in each unit apparently served under the "First Charioteer" or "Charioteer of the Residence," the company under the "Standard Bearer of Chariot-Warriors," and the largest unit perhaps under the "Commander of a Chariot Host." By the end of the

18th Dynasty, an officer with the title "Overseer of Horses" commanded the entire chariot corps.[29] These officers received help from a hierarchy of "Stablemasters" who were responsible for the feeding, upkeep, and training of the active and replacement horses. The lowest "Stablemaster" had charge over one or more teams of horses. Further support came from craftsmen who repaired the chariots.[30]

In addition to its military importance, the chariot also developed into a symbol of prestige and power. In the contemporary communication between nations, kings often wished one another that all would go well with "you . . . your household . . . *your horses, your chariots . . .*" (emphasis added).[31] Kings likewise traveled by chariot (cf. 1 Sam. 8:11; 1 Kings 12:18). Pharaohs learned to fight as chariot-warriors as part of their training, often fought at the head of a chariot division, and commonly had themselves portrayed shooting from a chariot in reliefs of battle and hunting scenes.

The chariot's prestige extended to non-royal chariot troops as well. Often chariot drivers and chariot-warriors were volunteers from the upper strata of Egyptian society and went through special training to learn archery, driving, and tactics. Their positions did not protect them from hardships, however. One scribal satire refers to the "miserable office, the chariot-warrior of the chariotry."[32] Chariot-warriors had to endure blows from superiors, suffer bites from horses, overcome the logistical challenges of getting the chariot through difficult terrain, and keep the sometimes-delicate machines in good repair.

Egyptian sources seem to reflect a growth in the numbers of chariots over time, although they tell more about the numbers of captured enemy chariots than about those belonging to Egypt. As noted earlier, Thutmose III captured 924 chariots at Megiddo in the mid-15th century. His successor, Amenhotep II, recorded plunder of 730 and 1,092 chariots from two Asiatic campaigns later the same century. In 1275 BC, Ramesses II faced 2,500 (or 3,500) chariots of the Hittites and their allies at Kadesh. Thus the numbers of large enemy chariot forces rose from approximately one thousand to a few thousand over this period of two centuries.

Navy

In addition to their infantry and chariotry, the Egyptians also had a navy, although warships and naval battles *per se* were largely unknown[33] until Ramesses III fought the Sea Peoples in 1179 BC. The Egyptians had long used boats for transportation on the Nile River, of course, but their military use was primarily confined to transporting troops who fought on land, as well as communicating and hauling freight. The pharaoh would ride on board ship when accompanying the army, while the land troops advanced on either side.[34]

The Egyptians also sailed beyond Egypt, and used ships for military transport northward to the Levantine coast. Thutmose III in the mid-18th Dynasty used maritime transport as part of a well-constructed strategy that ultimately extended the Egyptian empire to the Euphrates. In a series of conquests that lasted over eighteen years, the pharaoh steadily advanced northward. He secured the harbors of Phoenicia and seized ships to return to Egypt at the end of his fifth campaign. Beginning the following year, the army regularly sailed to Syria to avoid the tiring and time-consuming march through Palestine. Ships also brought prisoners and spoils back to Egypt.[35] On one campaign, Thutmose III built ships of cedar on the Phoenician coast, placed them on carts to be transported to the Euphrates, and used them to ferry his army across the river.

The Egyptians lacked most of the native woods necessary for building ships required for their campaigns, so they had to import lumber or entire finished ships from Nubia in the south and Phoenicia and Syria in the north. Eventually the Egyptians learned to do their own shipbuilding.[36] Although the location of their shipbuilding during this period is largely unknown, some records have been found referring to a naval dockyard

Fig. 3.9—Seagoing ship from 18th Dynasty. Modeled after relief of ships used on Red Sea. Powered by single large sail or oars (not shown), steered by pair of paddles. Deck beams pass through and secured on outside of hull

called Peru-nefer ("Good Departure") that was located on the Nile near Memphis. Beginning as a small dock, Thutmose III expanded it into an extensive installation that included shipyards, temples, and rest houses for receiving foreign envoys. Both Thutmose III and Amenhotep II used Peru-nefer as their base for transporting troops to Palestine and Syria. The worship of the Canaanite gods Baal and Astarte at Peru-nefer apparently reflects the importance of the Phoenician shipwrights and foreign craftsmen brought in by Thutmose III.[37]

These foreign shipwrights taught Egyptian craftsmen, who eventually built different styles of ships such as "Keftyew (perhaps Crete) ships," "Byblos ships," or "Sektu ships." Such names may indicate the boats' homeports, or where that style of ships was originally built, or the types of ships that typically travelled to those locations. Different styles served different uses. Those used along the Levantine coast only had to travel short distances between harbors, so they were designed for large carrying capacity rather than speed. They had no superstructure, and were broad with large storage areas for cargo, including chariots, and occasionally stalls for horses. Ships used along the Red

Fig. 3.10—Warship battling Sea Peoples 1179 BC. Fig. 4.10 gives color depiction

Sea (Fig. 3.9), by contrast, had to traverse great lengths of barren and waterless coastline, so they had the longer lines and larger sails of a fast-running galley. Ships built for travel on the Nile had to be light, with shallow drafts to navigate the river's many sandbars and the rocks of the cataracts. These had cabins with steps leading to the roof for lookouts to survey the countryside and the river ahead. Boats used on the Nile ranged from opulent royal flagships to ordinary merchant ships that transported the goods of the empire.[38] Pictures show ships of different kinds with crews of seven to seventeen, but the pictures may be stylized and the numbers not reliable. Like in the infantry and chariotry, naval units bore names like "Pacifier of the Atun" or "The Wild Bull."

As demonstrated in Ramesses III's portrayal of the naval battle with the Sea Peoples in 1179 BC, Egypt eventually did develop true warships with marine fighting units. In the relief, the prow of each Egyptian ship is shaped like the head of a lioness with the head of an Asiatic in its mouth, perhaps functioning as a ram (Figs. 3.10, 4.10). Raised bulwarks along the sides protected the rowers who helped power and maneuver the ships. The single sail was raised rather than lowered, apparently to allow more fighting room on deck. Raised gangways and square structures in the bow and stern provided places for marine warriors to fight, pictured with bow and arrow, spear, metal rod, javelin, and mace. A lone figure in each fighting top slings stones at the enemy. One Egyptian soldier throws a four-armed grappling hook. It grasps the rigging of an enemy ship, perhaps to overturn it or else to tear the sail and make the oar-less ship virtually non-maneuverable.[39]

General Information

As the preceding information suggests, a soldier in the Egyptian military could serve in a regular or professional unit in the infantry, chariotry, or navy and could do so at home in a garrison or abroad on a foreign campaign. During more peaceful periods, soldiers often served on work details, quarrying stone or transporting monuments. One scribal satire highlights the difficult plight of the soldier, constantly in demand for work projects, awakened at any hour, made to toil like a donkey, and worked past sunset.[40]

The importance of the military during this period and the financial rewards that came from meritorious service gave the growing military class an increasing amount of wealth and power. This culminated with the installation of military men as pharaohs beginning at the end of the 18th Dynasty. Haremhab, the last pharaoh of the dynasty, had served as

Military Class, Power

a general during the reign of Amenhotep IV (1352–1336 BC). Ramesses I, the first ruler in the 19th Dynasty, had been a military commander and perhaps vizier under Haremhab. Likewise, the rest of the pharaohs of the New Kingdom were either former military commanders or their descendants. (Compare events in Israel, where David became king after serving in the military, as did Jehu, Omri, and others in the north.)

The powerful military caste gained its wealth primarily from the rewards given during periods of service and at retirement. The pharaohs provided well for their valued military commanders. They gave the "Gold of Valor" (or "Gold of Praise")—gold ornaments, weapons, etc. to officers and men for deeds of bravery and skill during battle. In addition, all members of the armed forces shared in the plunder of slaves, animals, weapons, jewelry, clothing, and household items captured from enemy armies and citizens. In Egypt, troops and their families could live in military settlements established to maintain sources of manpower for the armed forces. Veterans received fields, servants, and animals from the royal holdings, which then stayed in the family as long as one of the males in the direct line of descent was available for military duty (as with Nakt-her-Peri). Thus the military profession passed from generation to generation and controlled a greater and greater amount of the nation's wealth and power.[41]

Size of Army

The number of men who served in the powerful military, like so many other aspects of Egyptian military history, cannot be determined with certainty. General statements ("a numerous army"), obvious exaggerations ("millions and hundred-thousands of men"), and especially incomplete data make it impossible to fix the size of the Egyptian army in most cases. This is typical for ancient Near Eastern cultures. With the significant exception of the Bible, ancient data about numbers of troops is typically fragmentary or nonexistent, perhaps reflecting a general disinterest in such information. While modern Western cultures often value statistics, ancient Near Easterners and modern Middle Easterners often do not. The Bible appears to be the exception to this rule, with its many large numbers of troops, as discussed in chapter 2.

Egyptian records rarely give precise numbers of troops, but at least on one occasion, they indicate a total of four divisions in the field for a major battle. Since a division apparently was comprised of 5,000 soldiers,[42] one can easily infer a total of 20,000 Egyptians at the Battle of Kadesh in 1275 BC. On that occasion, Ramesses II clearly had four divisions (named Amon—led by the pharaoh, Re, Ptah, and Sutekh) fighting against the Hittites. They faced an army of Hittites and their allies whose numbers are known only from Egyptian records, perhaps not the most reliable source. Egyptian accounts apparently state that the Hittites mustered 2,500 + 1,000 chariots (x 3 soldiers per Hittite chariot = 10,500) and another 8,000–9,000 infantry.[43] This suggests that the Hittites also had approximately 20,000 troops when these two superpowers fought for control of the northern Levant in the 13th century BC.

The records of Merenptah and Ramesses III fighting against Libyan invaders also furnish numbers of troops, but this time only of enemy killed. At these battles, which took place in the late 13th and early 12th centuries after Egyptian power had already begun to decline, they presumably could have mustered only a smaller army. The records state that in 1208 BC they killed 9,376 enemy and captured 9,111 swords (apparently from the slain). In 1182 BC they report 12,535 killed, plus more than 1,000 prisoners. In 1176 BC the Libyans suffered 2,175 dead and 2,052 taken captive.[44] Assuming these figures are correct, the Libyans fielded armies of at least 9,300 in the first attack, 13,500 in the second, and 4,200 in the third. How many more they could have had is unclear, as is the number of Egyptians they faced.

The other major battle involving Egypt during this period that gives some indication of numbers is the Battle of Megiddo, described earlier. The Egyptians captured 924 chariots, killed 83 enemy soldiers, and took another 3,400 captive. Based on his careful analysis of the terrain at Megiddo as well as the report of the battle, Nelson estimated the troop strength at 10,000–20,000 Egyptians and 10,000–15,000 in the Canaanite coalition.[45] Although the terrain may have allowed for such numbers, the relatively small number of enemy who were killed and taken prisoner may suggest lower numbers, at least for the coalition. Since Egypt routed the enemy in battle and subsequently captured the city of Megiddo, to which many had fled, it may have killed or captured the bulk of the enemy forces. The number of Egyptian troops is unclear, although their apparent rout of an army with almost one thousand chariots would suggest a substantial force. The Egyptians perhaps had at least as many chariots as their enemy and an infantry numbering possibly 10,000+. Overall, the information from this period suggests that Egypt could put an army into the field numbering up to the low ten thousands.

Role of Pharaoh

Though the size of his army is largely unknown, the pharaoh's role in the military was clear—commander in chief and often commander in fact. Many pharaohs planned and personally directed military campaigns, often leading chariot divisions in battle, as Thutmose III did at Megiddo. Some also installed their sons as generals to train them in leadership and in the art of war. Princes during the New Kingdom trained from youth to learn skills such as archery, chariotry, and ship handling, all expected of future kings. Pharaohs boasted about their extraordinary military skills as proof of their fitness to rule, as when Thutmose III recorded that he shot an arrow so deeply into a three-inch-thick target of copper that he had it placed in the temple of Amon. His son and successor, Amenhotep II, boasted that he rode a chariot full speed past four similar targets spaced thirty-five feet apart and shot an arrow clean through each one so that they "came out of it and dropped to the ground."[46]

Such boasting extended to reported feats on the battlefield as well. The pharaoh's very appearance supposedly inspired awe, as did his actions ("raging like a divine falcon, his horses flying like a star of heaven"). At times the kings indeed exhibited true bravery, such as when Thutmose III led his army through the narrow and dangerous pass leading to Megiddo or when Ramesses II personally led a counter charge six times with his chariot against the attacking Hittite chariots at Kadesh. Other stories sound more like propaganda than fact, as when Amenhotep II claimed to have guarded a group of prisoners alone all night, surrounded by ditches filled with fire.[47]

Role of the Gods

In leading the Egyptian army, the pharaoh was fulfilling one of his primary responsibilities as king. The pharaoh had to uphold truth, justice, and right order, in part by using the country's military to protect Egypt from the hostile barbarians of the world. The pharaoh also had to keep other nations from interfering with its territorial right, which happened to be rather extensive. Each pharaoh also felt pressure to equal or surpass the deeds of his predecessor in service to the gods and the benefit of Egypt. Thus each had to extend the boundaries of the empire, bring foreign spoils back to Egypt, and make sure that everyone understood the extent of his deeds. As descendants of the gods themselves, the pharaohs had divine mandate to rule and conquer, and their divine origin gave them supernatural power to inspire fear and awe in their enemies on the battlefield. Other ancient Near Eastern kingdoms, including Israel, shared in these concepts to some degree. Although Israel's kings were not gods, they had been chosen by

Yahweh to conquer and rule other nations in the divinely established order (see Psalm 2, as well as "Role of King" in chapter 2).

The pharaoh's service to the gods was part of a reciprocal relationship between royalty and deity. Egypt's chief gods blessed the different pharaohs, promising them strength, valor, protection, and victory over all enemies. The gods promised to bind foreign adversaries and establish fear of the king's glory in all lands. In return, the pharaoh pledged fidelity to the gods and promised to grant justice, protect the people, and enrich Egypt with temples and proper worship.[48]

Egypt's gods regularly promised Egypt success in battle and commissioned war in order to punish the crimes of Egypt's enemies. Records tell of the pharaoh consulting his god in the temple the morning after receiving report of revolt in some land. There, the god gave an oracle of success, apparently through a priest (compare Judah's King Hezekiah and the prophet Isaiah in 2 Kings 19:1–7). After the army had assembled and was ready to depart, it left via the temple where the gods came out to meet the king (perhaps through the priests bearing the god's image) and prepare him for battle. With assurance of divine aid, victory was a foregone conclusion.[49]

The pharaoh could then proceed under the god's protection, often portrayed in the reliefs through imagery and/or text. The god's presence and protection might be symbolized with the actual standard of the god, as described earlier (Fig. 3.8), or simply through imagery, as with the picture of Horus over the pharaoh's head (Fig. 3.11). Scribes wrote about divine protection and aid as well. An inscription above Ramesses III before his battle with the Libyans promises, "Utterance of Amon-Re, king of gods: 'Lo, I am before thee, my son. . . . I will open (for) thee the ways of the land of Temeh (Libya). I will trample them before thy horses."[50] Divine aid might manifest in some supernatural way, like a celestial event. Thutmose III mentions a miraculous (shooting?) star that spooked the horses, terrified the enemy, and led to a great victory for Egypt.[51] Compare the biblical story of Israel's God giving victory through a hailstorm and a supernaturally long day in Joshua 10:1–15.

After the subsequent victory won with the god's aid, the pharaoh would return to the temple to give thanks and to present captives and plunder to the god as an offering. Thus the pharaoh and his god(s) worked in concert to protect and bless Egypt through military victory. Other ancient Near Eastern cultures, including Israel, believed and acted in a similar fashion.

Fig. 3.11—Pharaoh with protecting god. Thutmose IV and Horus.

NOTES

1   Date per Wilson, "Asiatic Campaigns," 236, n. 35; Nelson has May 15, 1479
    (*The Battle of Megiddo,* 1). For accounts and commentaries on the Battle of
    Megiddo, see Nelson (dated but still helpful with photos and maps); Wilson,
    "Asiatic Campaigns"; Faulkner, "Battle of Megiddo;" Lichtheim, "First Cam-
    paign"; and Hoffmeier, "Annals of Thutmose III."

2   Egyptian texts mention runners along with chariots multiple times, as does
    the Bible (1 Sam. 8:11; 2 Sam. 15:1; 1 Kings 1:5), and some reliefs appear to
    show runners with chariots. Just how foot soldiers could operate in support
    of the much faster chariots is problematic.

3   For lengths and rates of march, see Wilson, "Asiatic Campaigns," 235, n. 16,
    18; as well as the discussion in Hans Goedicke, *The Battle of Megiddo* (Balti-
    more: Halgo, 2000), 22–23.

4   Translation taken from Hoffmeier, "Annals of Thutmose III", 9. Nelson de-
    scribes the center pass as "merely a rough mule-path" from his visits in 1909
    and 1912 (*Battle of Megiddo,* 12. See his Views III and IV for nice photo-
    graphs of the time). When this author first traversed the pass in 1981, it had
    a narrow two-lane highway, with tank barricades sitting to the side of the
    road at one point.

5   The quality and quantity of the Canaanites' (and Syrians') armor is uncer-
    tain, though the list of plunder from the end of the campaign gives some
    indication. It lists 924 chariots, 502 bows, and 202 coats of mail taken. If
    one can assume that the Canaanite chariots each carried a warrior armed
    with bow and arrow, the number of bows suggests that perhaps only up
    to half of the Canaanite chariot-warriors were captured (bows from ar-
    chers in the infantry may also have been taken). The number of coats
    of mail suggests that only a fraction of the chariot-warriors wore scale
    armor, and perhaps none of the chariot drivers. If the Canaanite chariot-
    warriors did not have scale armor, they may well have worn suits made
    from just leather, which was less expensive and less effective than suits of
    leather covered with overlaying bronze scales. Also possible is that many
    Canaanite charioteers escaped the battlefield altogether or found refuge in
    Megiddo, where they were able to hide their armor and weapons before
    the city surrendered.

6   Compare Napoleon Bonaparte's comment, "A soldier will fight long and
    hard for a bit of colored ribbon."

7   Nelson comments, "The importance of the fall of Megiddo cannot be overes-
    timated. It crushed once for all the rebellion. . . . It was a fitting introduction

to the wars of the greatest conqueror the world had then seen. . . . It is the first battle in history in which we can in any measure study the disposition of troops and as such forms the starting point for the history of military science" (*Battle of Megiddo*, 63).

8 Dates for Egyptian history and spelling of pharaohs' names taken from K. A. Kitchen, "Egypt, History of (Chronology)," *ABD* 2:321–31.

9 To help keep out the unwanted nomads, Egypt established forts, dug a seventy-meter-wide canal, and made preemptive military strikes against the "sand-dwellers." James K. Hoffmeier, *Israel in Egypt: The Evidence for the Authenticity of the Exodus Tradition* (NY: Oxford, 1997), 56–68; quote on 58–59.

10 For helpful general descriptions of the Egyptian military during the Old and Middle Kingdoms, see Faulkner, "Egyptian Military Organization," 32–41; Schulman, "Military Organization in Pharaonic Egypt," 289–90; and William C. Hayes, "Egypt: Internal Affairs from Tuthmosis I to the Death of Amenophis III," in *The Cambridge Ancient History* (3d ed.; Cambridge: Cambridge University Press, 1973), 2:313. For the various aspects of the military during the New Kingdom, see Faulkner, 41–47; Schulman, 290–300; and Hayes, 2:363–72.

11 Schulman, *MRTO*, ¶ 114. Also see 229 for subsequent reference to 10% draft, as well as 100, 112.

12 For induction process, see Harold. H. Nelson, "The Naval Battle Pictured at Medinet Habu," *JNES* 2, no. 1 (1943): 40; and Hayes, "Egypt: Internal Affairs," 365. For descriptions of the harsh conditions, see Schulman, *MRTO*, ¶ 94, 99, 113, 124, 126, 128, 137. *MRTO* ¶ 123 reads in part, "The infantryman is brought as a child. . . . He is beaten with exertions. He awakes in the morning to receive beatings until he is split open with wounds. . . . A painful blow . . . a doubling blow . . . a turning upside-down blow . . . a falling-down blow. . . . He is pummeled with beatings. . . ." In addition, the very interesting picture of Ramesses III's camp at Kadesh shows perhaps nineteen Egyptian soldiers with rods apparently beating either fellow Egyptians, enemy Hittites, or a donkey (or child). James H. Breasted, *The Battle of Kadesh: A Study in the Earliest Known Military Strategy* (Chicago: University of Chicago, 1903), pl. 1; for a smaller, colored version, see Yadin, *AWBL*, 1:236–37.

13 Hayes, "Egypt: Internal Affairs," 366–67, 371.

14 Breasted, *ARE*, 3: ¶ 56; 4: ¶ 410; Schulman, *MRTO*, ¶ 124, 129, 159, 196, 235.

15 Harold H. Nelson, *Medinet Habu Reports I: The Epigraphic Survey 1928–31* (Oriental Institute Communications, No. 10; Chicago: University of Chicago Press, 1931), 34.

16   Schulman, *MRTO,* ¶ 236, 293–303.

17   Ibid., ¶ 151, 213, 231.

18   Ibid., ¶ 29, 168; Faulkner, "Egyptian Military Organization," 43–45.

19   Schulman, *MRTO,* ¶ 142, 149, 240. Also see Seevers, "Practice of Ancient Near Eastern Warfare," pp. 20–22.

20   Schulman, *MRTO,* ¶ 237–38, 305–72, 400–25, 491–510, pp. 82–86; Hayes, "Egypt: Internal Affairs," 364–65.

21   The Hammamat Stele lists twenty scribes and twenty quartermasters for a division of 5000, apparently indicating one each per company of 250. See Schulman, *MRTO,* ¶ 380, 442–71, pp. 82–86.

22   R. O. Faulkner, "Egyptian Military Standards," *JEA* 27 (1941): 12.

23   Ibid., ¶ 148, 152; Faulkner, "Egyptian Military Standards," 17–18.

24   Schulman, *MRTO,* ¶ 276–92.

25   Faulkner, "Egyptian Military Organization," 43; Schulman, *MRTO,* ¶ 162, 281, 433–41, 477–90.

26   Schulman, *MRTO,* ¶ 265, 275, 286–87.

27   Ibid., ¶ 242–58; Schulman, "Military Organization in Pharaonic Egypt," 290.

28   See Schulman, *MRTO,* ¶ 441 and especially ¶ 240, which notes a "charioteer of the Residence" and fifty charioteers in a work detail, suggesting fifty chariots in a squadron. See also Schulman, "The Egyptian Chariotry: a Reexamination," *Journal of the American Research Center in Egypt* 2 (1963), 83–84, esp. n. 44. Faulkner ("Egyptian Military Organization," 43) agrees with this number.

29   For a discussion of the title "Overseer of Horses" reflecting the growing importance of the chariot corps during the 18th Dynasty, see Charles Aling, "The Title 'Overseer of Horses' in the Egyptian Eighteenth Dynasty," *NEASB* 38 (1993): 53–60.

30   Schulman, *MRTO,* ¶ 135, 373–79, 382, 390–99, 430, 479–490; also Schulman, "The Egyptian Chariotry: a Reexamination," *Journal of the American Research Center in Egypt* 2 (1963), 82.

31   See, for example, William L. Moran, *The Amarna Letters* (Baltimore: Johns Hopkins, 1992), EA 1:2–3; 2:4–5; 3:1–3.

32   Schulman, *MRTO,* ¶ 96.

33   Texts describing the Egyptian expulsion of the Hyksos at the end of the Second Intermediate Period give some indications of ships being used for military activity. See Pritchard, *ANET,* 232–34.

34   Lichtheim, *AEL,* 2:13–14; Schulman, *MRTO,* ¶ 87–88, 95–97.

35   Torgny Säve-Söderbergh, *The Navy of the Eighteenth Egyptian Dynasty* (Uppsala: A.-B. Lundequistska, 1946), 34, 39.

36   Ibid., 5–6, 43–44.

37   S. R. K. Glanville, "Records of a Royal Dockyard of the Time of Tuthmosis III: Papyrus British Museum 10056: Part 1," ZÄS 66 (1931): 105–20. "Part 2: Commentary." ZÄS 68 (1932): 7–41.

38   Säve-Söderbergh, *The Navy*, 16, 44–53; Hayes, "Egypt: Internal Affairs," 367–68; R. O. Faulkner, "Egyptian Seagoing Ships." *JEA* 26 (1940): 7–9.

39   Harold H. Nelson, "The Naval Battle Pictured at Medinet Habu," *Journal of Near Eastern Studies* 2 (1943): 42–55; Faulkner, "Egyptian Seagoing Ships," 9.

40   Lichtheim, *AEL,* 2:172.

41   Hayes, "Egypt: Internal Affairs," 2:363–64, 371.

42   Two sources seem to indicate 5,000 soldiers per division. The Hammamat Stele (12th century) lists a work detail including 5,000 soldiers (Schulman, *MRTO,* ¶ 240), and a scribe's logistical problem (late 13th century), possibly hypothetical, involves the parts of a division that total 5,000 troops (*MRTO,* ¶ 87). Both sources are late but consistent, and square with much of the other available evidence.

43   The text gives 2,500 Hittite chariots and later mentions another(?) 1,000 for an apparent total of 3,500. Schulman dismisses the number of even 2,500 Hittite chariots as "rhetorical hyperbole" since it implies a total of 7,500–10,000 horses (two to pull, plus one or two in reserve for each chariot), "and this would have presented insurmountable logistical problems, particularly in the matter of forage" ("Military Organization in Pharaonic Egypt," 297). However, the similar numbers of chariots by arguably lesser coalitions, discussed earlier, argue against such a position.

44   Breasted, *ARE 3:* ¶ 571, 588–89; 4:¶ 52, 54, 83.

45   Nelson, *Battle of Megiddo,* 6.

46   Pritchard, *ANET,* 243–44, 247.

47   Quote from Pritchard, *ANET,* 246. For Ramesses at Kadesh, see *COS* 2:36. Story of Amenhotep II in Pritchard, *ANET,* 247.

48   Pritchard, *ANET,* 23, 240, 246, 247, 373–75, 377.

49   Breasted, *ARE* 2: ¶ 823, 119; Nelson, *Medinet Habu Reports I,* 14.

50   Breasted, *ARE* 4: ¶ 49.

51   *COS,* 2:14.

EGYPT:
ARMIES OF THE PHARAOHS—PART 2

4

WEAPONS

Although the Egyptians ascribed their victories to divine aid, they accomplished them through physical means that included weaponry. The military success during the New Kingdom was due, at least in part, to advances in Egyptian weaponry, vastly improved over what the Egyptians had used before the time of the Hyksos. During the Old and Middle Kingdoms, the Egyptians had relied on maces (clubs with heavy stone balls at the end, used to crush an opponent—see Fig. 3.3), spears, battle-axes with broad blades, simple bows made from a single long piece of wood, and, for defense, leather-covered wooden shields. Such weaponry had proven effective against contemporary enemies who, like themselves, had little or no armor. But the subsequent losses to the Hyksos apparently convinced the Egyptians that they needed to upgrade their weaponry.[1] Beginning in the 18th Dynasty, they added to their weaponry implements such as composite bows, chariots, armor-penetrating axes (Fig. 4.1—lower right), helmets, and eventually metal body armor.

Such military implements can be classified as either offensive weapons, like swords, bows, and chariots, or defensive equipment, like shields and armor. Offensive weapons might be further broken down into short-range weapons used for hand-to-hand fighting, medium-range weapons thrown a moderate distance, and long-range weapons that shot projectiles a long distance. Each will be discussed in turn.

Short-Range Weapons

Mace

Infantrymen and others who fought hand-to-hand needed weapons like the mace that would function well at close range. The mace had long been a popular close-range weapon and even came to represent pharaonic authority, with the pharaoh often pictured striking his enemies with a mace (Fig. 3.3). But by the time of the New Kingdom, it had largely gone out of use, perhaps due to the increased use of helmets. However, some soldiers did continue fighting with maces (see soldier on bow of ship in Fig. 3.10), and Pharaoh Amenhotep II used one to slay seven enemy princes as late as the mid-15th century.[2]

Spear,
Battle-axe

Reliefs suggest that the spear and battle-axe may have become the most popular short-range weapons by the time of the New Kingdom. Similar to other contemporary armies, Egyptian infantrymen are frequently pictured with shields and spears or battle-axes (Figs. 3.2 and 3.7). They protected themselves with shields and used long thrusting spears or sharp penetrating axes to attack their opponents. Earlier battle-axes tended to have broader blades that could effectively cut unprotected or lightly protected opponents (Fig. 4.1—top). As time went on and armies began to use more and heavier defensive equipment like leather and later scaled armor, the blades of the battle-axes got narrower and longer (Fig. 4.1—bottom, as well as 3.7) to produce a more powerful force that could penetrate the protective gear.

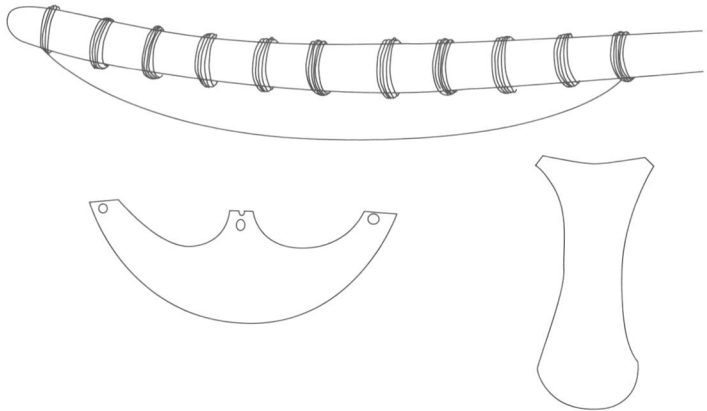

Fig. 4.1—Progression of battle-axes. Oldest on top, with handle. Newest and narrowest on lower right.

Sword

The sword went through a somewhat similar evolution over time. Earlier on, swords were shaped rather like a harvesting sickle (Fig. 4.2—left) and thus were called "sickle-swords." Unlike harvesting sickles with the sharp edge on the inside for cutting grain, sickle-swords had their sharp edge on the outside for slashing an opponent. The biblical expression of striking "with the edge of the sword" (Josh. 6:21, ESV; etc.) probably comes from the use of this type of sword. Sickle-swords started with a relatively long shaft and shorter cutting blade but changed to a much shorter shaft and a relatively long cutting blade (Fig. 4.2—left). Reliefs during the New Kingdom often portray the pharaoh with a sickle-sword, suggesting that it had replaced the mace as the pharaoh's weapon of authority. Toward the end of the New Kingdom, Egyptians began using straight, tapered swords as well (Fig. 4.2, 4.3, 4.11—on ladder). The straight swords first appear in reliefs in the hands of Sea Peoples (Figs. 5.7, 5.11), suggesting that the Philistines and related peoples may well have brought this design to the region.[3]

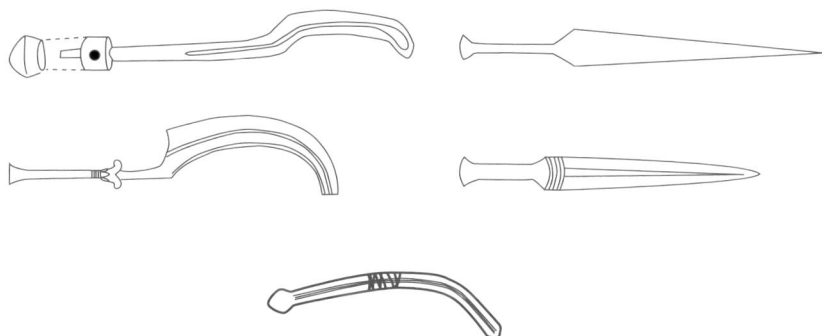

Fig. 4.2—Sickle swords (left), straight swords (right), throw-stick (bottom).

Metal Rod

The Egyptians also used a bronze metal rod as a short-range weapon, apparently for beating their enemies in combat as well as beating their own troops for discipline, as discussed earlier (see Fig. 4.3 and soldier just behind the mast in 3.10). Approximately one inch in diameter and three to four feet long, the rod appears as a common Egyptian instrument in reliefs of this period. It had a projection near the base to protect the combatant's fingers (as in Fig. 3.10), but users are also shown grasping the rod above the protruding piece, perhaps for a better grip. By the time of Ramesses III's land battle with the Sea Peoples in 1179 BC, some Sherden mercenaries had also adopted the metal rod as a weapon.[4]

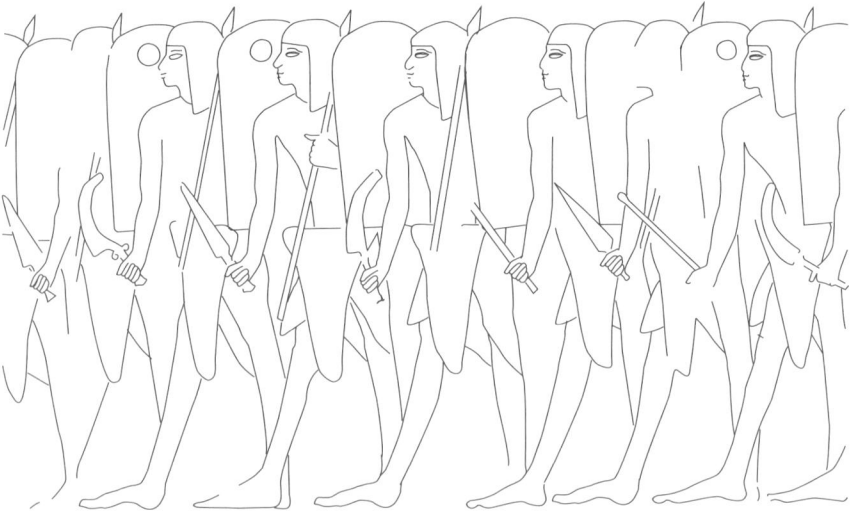

Fig. 4.3—Infantry with various weapons. Note straight swords, sickle swords, and rods, plus spears and shields.

Medium-Range Weapons

Javelin

Egyptian soldiers also had at least two weapons that they could throw a moderate distance—the javelin and the throw-stick. The javelin resembled a smaller version of the spear and apparently played an important role in chariot warfare. Charioteers carried two in a quiver on the side of their chariot, and runners probably used them as well (see Fig. 3.4 for both), apparently to kill or wound the horses of enemy chariots. One of the marine troops in Fig. 3.10 also prepares to hurl a javelin toward an enemy ship.

Egyptians also used, although perhaps less often, the throw-stick—a flat, curved, wooden implement (Fig. 4.2—bottom) similar to an Australian boomerang except that the throw-stick was not intended to return to the thrower. Egyptians apparently had used throw-sticks for hunting and in warfare more often during the Middle Kingdom, though its use continued during the New Kingdom.[5]

Long-Range Weapons

Bow

As with most other armies of the period, the Egyptians used the composite bow as their long-range weapon of choice. Earlier Egyptians had used the simple bow, which was made from a single piece of curved or double-curved wood, cut rather long to supply as much force as possible (Fig. 4.4—left). By the time of the New Kingdom, the Egyptians had adopted the composite bow from the Hyksos.[6] The composite bow was shorter but much more powerful (Fig. 4.4—right), with an effective range of at least 175 yards.[7] It was made by gluing together multiple pieces of various woods, horn, bark, and tendon.[8] Archers and chariot-warriors relied on this powerful but somewhat delicate weapon. Reliefs often portray bows carried in bow cases, suggesting that they needed to be protected from elements such as moisture. Reliefs of pharaohs sometimes depict them shooting composite bows, a further reflection of the weapon's importance.

Fig. 4.4—Archers training with simple (left) and composite (right) bows

Sling

The Egyptians also used, although perhaps only sparingly, the sling as a long-range weapon. The design of the woven Egyptian sling in Fig. 4.5[9] closely resembles slings still produced in the Middle East. Egyptians used the sling as a weapon during the New Kingdom, but apparently not as much as other ancient Near Eastern nations described later, even though the sling's effective range exceeded that of the bow.[10] In the New Kingdom reliefs, one finds Egyptian slingers only in the crows' nests of the ships in the naval battle against the Sea Peoples (Figs. 3.10, 4.10). The Egyptian slinger in Fig. 3.10 appears to whirl his weapon horizontally over his head, in contrast to the method used by Assyrian slingers discussed in chapter 7.

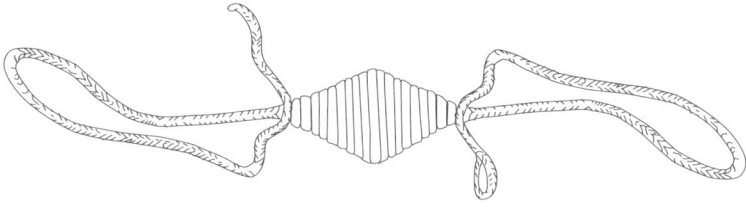

Fig. 4.5—Sling

Defensive Equipment

Along with offensive weaponry, the Egyptians also equipped their soldiers with defensive implements—helmets, shields, and, increasingly throughout the New Kingdom, scale armor.

Helmets   Helmets of fabric, leather, or metal (Fig. 4.6) apparently came into use in the Egyptian military only during the New Kingdom. Officers and royalty first wore helmets, but by the second half of this period, common soldiers had them as well.[11] Helmets helped protect soldiers from blows to the skull, the effects of which the Egyptian physicians developed great skill in treating.[12]

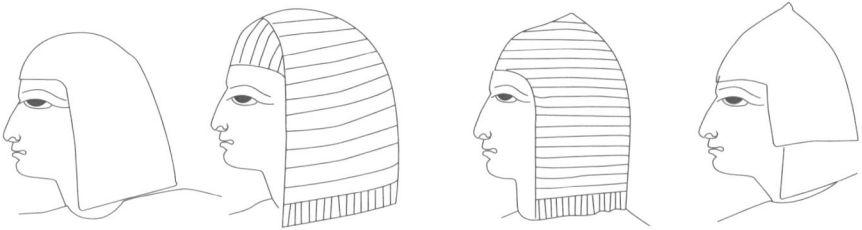

Fig. 4.6—Various styles of helmets

Shields   Arguably the most obvious defensive items, shields were made of wood covered with leather. Their shapes varied over time, and different shapes sometimes appear in the same reliefs. Most were rounded on top and tapered to a flat bottom (Figs. 3.2, 3.4, 3.7, 4.3), but the Sea Peoples used smaller round shields (Figs. 3.5—top left, 5.6). As one can see in Fig. 3.2, heavy infantry used large shields to protect most of their bodies, while the charioteers' shields were smaller. Some shields had a hole in the middle (Figs. 3.4—shown blocked, 3.7, 4.3), apparently for better visibility. Soldiers occasionally slung their shields over their backs when they needed both hands free for tasks like attacking a city gate or climbing a scaling ladder (Fig. 4.11).

As noted earlier, the Egyptians began to use body armor in various forms during the New Kingdom, though just when that began is not clear.[13] Garments of linen or leather offered some protection, but armor with added metal scales or metal strips sewn on top of leather or cloth were most effective (Fig. 4.7). Prior to ca. 1200 BC, the use of such body armor seems limited to a relatively small part of the military (pharaohs and perhaps charioteers), but afterward more and more infantry used it as well. By the time of the naval battle in 1179 BC, the majority of both the Egyptians and Sea Peoples appear to wear armor consisting of waist-length corselets with strips of metal as well as leather skirts that reached to mid-thigh (Fig. 3.10).[14]

Armor

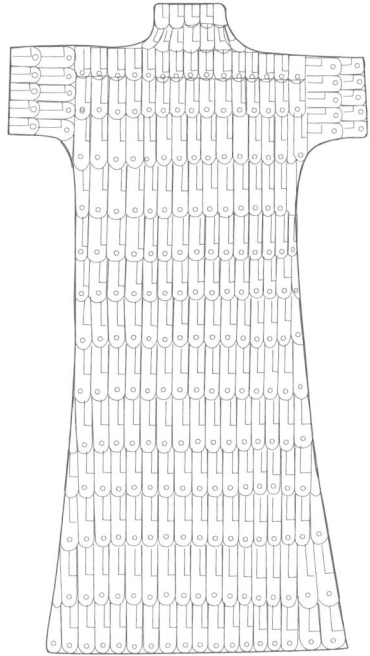

Fig. 4.7—Suit of scale armor from tomb of Ramesses III

Chariots

Along with weapons and defensive equipment, the army of New Kingdom Egypt also put great effort and expense into the construction and maintenance of horse-drawn chariots, the greatest military implement of the time. Egyptian texts of the early 16th century refer to chariots of the Hyksos, who may well have used the chariot to help conquer Egypt. After the Hyksos period, the Egyptians quickly adopted it as well, and by the mid-15th century, the chariot played a major role in military activities in Egypt and throughout the Levant. The Old Testament includes more than 170 references to the chariot, reflecting its importance in Israelite society (note, for example, 1 Sam. 8:11). Texts and reliefs also show pharaohs and other rulers using chariots for ceremonial and hunting purposes.

Pictorial evidence from numerous reliefs plus several actual chariots from Egyptian tombs present a reasonably clear picture of how these war machines were made (Fig. 4.8).[15] In contrast to wheeled wagons used earlier and heavier chariots used later in parts of the ancient Near East, most chariots during this period were light vehicles built to carry two men. They were made mostly of bent hardwood and leather, with a few metal parts and wrappings of birch bark to repel moisture. Earlier Egyptian chariots tended to have wheels with four spokes, and some later chariots had eight spokes, but the majority of the Egyptian chariots during the height of the New Kingdom had wheels with six spokes, each approximately three feet in diameter.[16] A long axle connected the wheels, giving the chariots a wide, stable wheelbase (about five to six feet). The axle was attached to the rear of the chariot body to allow for maximum speed, stability, and maneuverability.

The chariot bodies formed a wide and shallow D-shape (about 3.3 x 1.5 feet), with the round end to the front, allowing room for a driver and a warrior. The frame was again made from bent wood, filled with thigh-high siding of dressed leather or very thin wood extending around the front, sides, and sometimes halfway across the back. The floor was woven from rawhide thongs that helped hold the frame together and provide shock absorption for the riders. Several other war implements would have been attached to the body—a bow case was mounted diagonally and opened toward the front of the chariot, and at least one quiver for arrows and javelins pointed toward the rear.

Fig. 4.8—Chariot with six-spoked wheels from tomb of Tutankhamun

A pole connected the chariot body to the two horses that pulled it. The long (8–8.5 foot) pole curved into a shallow S-shape was lashed to the underside of the body and reached forward to a yoke approximately three feet long. From the yoke hung Y-shaped saddles (not pictured) that lay across the shoulders of the horses. The driver controlled the horses with blinkers and reins that attached to bitted bridles or perhaps bands around the horses' noses.

The Egyptians made their chariots from elm and tamarisk wood. The tamarisk grows in semi-arid regions around the Mediterranean and thus was native to Egypt. The elm, by contrast, had to be imported from perhaps as far away as Asia Minor, showing the lengths the Egyptians would go to obtain the materials to make their chariots or perhaps even the complete chariots themselves. The wood had to be steamed and heat-bent, and perhaps also trained to grow in the desired shapes as much as possible. Scenes of chariot workshops found in tombs illustrate some of the splitting, shaping, and bending of wood necessary to make chariots. Note in Fig. 4.9 the processes and chariot parts, as well as other items also made from wood and leather, including shields, quivers, and bow cases.[17]

Fig. 4.9—Tomb painting of chariot workshop.
Workers produce chariots and other items of wood and leather.

TACTICS

The final section of this chapter will describe the strategy and tactics that the Egyptians used during the period of the New Kingdom. What were their motivations for fighting? What strategies did they use for individual battles as well as the overall campaigns that made Egypt the greatest power of the day? What did the Egyptians do before, during, and after their battles? As before, the available information is rarely complete, but it helps paint an interesting picture nonetheless.

Motivation

The Egyptians undoubtedly had numerous and complex reasons for going to war. In the records of Thutmose III's first campaign, he lists several: "to kill the treacherous (rebellious) ones . . . and to give things to those who were loyal . . . to extend the frontiers of Egypt according to the command of his father, Amon-Re . . . that he should capture (plunder)."[18] Such statements provide theological support for actions that clearly served the pharaoh's self-interests as well. The reader is hard pressed to find examples of the pharaoh actually giving "things to those who were loyal," but the records often describe how he captured plunder to enrich himself and his nation.

As described earlier, the pharaoh was responsible to maintain order and return favors to the gods who supported him. The pharaoh needed to put down rebellions by those whom Egypt had the right to rule— which happened to be quite numerous. As the size of the empire grew throughout the New Kingdom, the opportunities for rebellion and the need to subdue them grew as well.

The pharaoh acted at the command and with the help of his gods, and in response he needed to build the gods' temples and enrich them with foreign plunder. For example, Thutmose II defended his rise to the throne by stating that Re had established him "that I might supply with food his altars upon earth; that I might make to flourish for him the sacred slaughtering-block with great slaughters in his temple, consisting of oxen and calves without limit . . . fill(ing) for him his granaries with barley and spelt without limit."[19] By comparison, note King Solomon's immense wealth, which resulted from ruling the vast Israelite empire that his father had secured (1 Kings 4:21–28), and how Solomon then used a portion of those resources to build the temple for his God (1 Kings 5–6).

Strategy

The records of several pharaohs demonstrate how they accomplished their goals by using carefully planned military strategies that stretched over many years and multiple campaigns. Thutmose III extended the Egyptian empire northward all the way to the Euphrates River in systematic, logical fashion. In his first campaign, Thutmose defeated the Canaanite coalition at Megiddo, reestablishing Egyptian authority in Canaan and Syria. In each subsequent year, he would travel farther north, consolidating earlier conquests and collecting tribute. He also established Egyptian garrisons at key points, ordering the local subjects to fill them with provisions for future operations. An earlier section described how he used ships as part of this strategy. The ships transported troops and supplies to the Phoenician coast in preparation for operations farther inland and then brought troops and plunder back to Egypt. Thutmose III's strategy and success over seventeen major campaigns helped make him arguably the most successful military leader of ancient Egypt.

More than two centuries later, Seti I followed a similar strategy, as did Ramesses II after him. Each moved north to regain control of the Phoenician coast, probably lost in earlier revolts. They then used ships to move men and supplies into position for further advances.

The Egyptian army typically set out on these campaigns during the spring and continued them during the dry summer months when roads were passable and food was available. Since the spring grain harvest occurred earlier in Egypt than in Canaan, the Egyptians would leave just after the Egyptian harvest and just before the harvest farther north so they could take what they needed as they passed through different areas. *Season for War*

The more complete record of Thutmose III's first campaign gives some of the best information about the dates and time involved. The Egyptian army left the frontier station of Tjaru on April 19 and returned to the capital at Thebes to celebrate on October 11. During those nearly six months, they approached and fought the battle at Megiddo, besieged and captured the city (during which time they foraged, then harvested the grain around the city), marched an additional seventy-five miles north, captured three cities, built a fortress, returned to the Nile delta, and voyaged upstream to Thebes.[20]

Several campaigns of other pharaohs followed similar patterns. Amenhotep II and Ramesses II both left Egypt in April or May on at least some of their campaigns to the north.[21] Amenhotep fought a successful battle in northern Palestine in May, crossed the Orontes River on May 12, and continued north. The records do not tell when he returned to Egypt.

Other ancient Near Eastern nations seem to follow this approximate schedule as well. The records of Merenptah show that Libya attacked Egypt in late March. In response, Merenptah gathered his forces and responded in mid-April.[22] Likewise, King David ordered an attack on Rabbah of Ammon "in the spring of the year, the time when kings to out to battle" (2 Sam. 11:1, ESV). See also 1 Kings 20:22, 26, where the same Hebrew expression describes the Aramean king going to war at that same time of year. *The March*

When the Egyptians began their campaigns, they often assembled and departed from the central military headquarters called the "Broad

Hall (of the Palace)." At this location, officers distributed weapons and supplies from a central depot and issued battle orders. Once everything was ready, a standard-bearer and trumpeter led the troops out while the king reviewed the army from a palace balcony.[23] Compare David reviewing the Israelite troops from the city gate as they departed to put down Absalom's rebellion in 2 Sam. 18:1–5.

The Egyptian army marched in columns, divided into their respective divisions. The account of the Battle of Kadesh notes that Ramesses II and his attendants led the march, followed closely by the first division. The other three divisions followed in order, separated by a distance of approximately 1.5 miles at one point. Such spacing lessened the chance that an enemy's surprise attack could destroy the whole army, but it also helped ensure that aid would not be too far away for any who might be caught off guard.[24]

Egypt's army could march approximately twelve to fifteen miles per day, though again, the evidence is scanty. Thutmose III and his forces apparently traveled about fifteen miles per day for much of their advance toward Megiddo, as noted earlier. Similarly, Ramesses II and his troops averaged about thirteen miles per day when approaching Kadesh.[25]

Soldiers on these marches often endured great hardship because of the loads they bore and the conditions in which they found themselves. Each soldier carried his weapons as well as a knapsack, supplies, garments, and staff or club. Scribal satires describe the plight of the common soldier—marching through the desert to Canaan, carrying food and water on his back like a donkey, drinking poor water and eating inferior food that were often in short supply, and marching long days with little or no rest. Even when the soldier could stop marching, he often had to stand guard. Secondary expeditions took some of the soldiers away from the protection of the main body. When the time came for entering battle, the soldier might be too exhausted, ill, or frightened to perform well.[26] Many died, were placed in a big sack, and were buried in a strange land, far from home and family.

If all went well during the day's march, the soldier had to help set up camp for the night and fortify it against possible enemy attack. Reliefs show Egyptian camps as rectangular enclosures, barricaded by shields. The royal tent occupied the center and was surrounded by smaller tents of the officers. Men cared for their equipment and animals. Craftsmen brought along portable workshops to service the equipment, especially the chariots.[27]

As mentioned earlier, Egyptian soldiers often did not enjoy good food while on campaign, especially compared with what they received back in their homeland. While stationed in garrison or on home work details, the soldier might get ground grain, bread, vegetables, meat, fowl, wine, oil, etc. On the march, however, he typically received bread and water, and had to supplement by foraging. Marching across the desert, he obtained water at fortified water stations along the road. Elsewhere, water was more plentiful, but often of poor quality.[28]

Food and Logistics

Food shortages were a constant problem. The army supplied some food, carried by pack animals or ox-drawn carts. Most came from the regions through which the army passed. Local rulers under Egyptian authority were responsible to lay up provisions in Egyptian garrisons. In hostile territory, the army took what it needed by force. Records often state that "(His majesty) arrived at (name of city), overthrew it, cut down its groves, harvested its grain." Nonetheless, scribal satires often describe the woes of the hungry soldiers and the challenges of trying to satisfy hungry troops with inadequate supplies.[29]

As mentioned above, the Egyptian army used animals and carts to haul supplies including food, water, spare weapons, etc. In earlier times they had used donkeys, but by the time of the 18th Dynasty, they added mules, and later, ox-drawn carts as well. Thutmose III even used ox-carts to carry boats inland from Byblos on the Mediterranean coast to the Euphrates River so his troops would be able to cross the Euphrates.

Such major military endeavors required an effective system of intelligence and communication. Mounted scouts were attached to units of chariotry under the "commander of horsemen," and sometimes appear in reliefs or on tombs. They supplied information about enemy troops (numbers of infantry and chariots, weapons, location, preparedness, and members of coalitions) as well as the terrain up ahead. Egyptian intelligence, for example, apparently advised Thutmose III that the Canaanite forces were not guarding the narrow central pass to Megiddo, allowing him to choose that route.[30]

Intelligence

The absence of proper intelligence could leave the army in serious trouble, as happened to Ramesses II at Kadesh. There, the Hittite king sent bedouin agents posing as deserters to purposely be captured by the Egyptians. They told Ramesses that the nearby Hittite army was 120 miles off to the north in order to lure the Egyptians into a trap. Just before the battle, the Egyptians captured two Hittite scouts and beat them with metal rods until they revealed their army's true location. Shortly thereafter, Hittite chariots attacked Ramesses' camp, and only his bravery and the opportune arrival of reinforcements averted a disaster.

The pharaohs and their senior officers discussed intelligence and other matters at war councils. The pharaoh chaired these meetings from his "throne of fine gold" that he brought along on the march. Officers could give their advice, but the pharaoh could overrule their recommendations and make the final decision, as Thutmose III did regarding which pass to take to Megiddo.

The Egyptians and others collected information and passed along orders through various forms of communication. As soon as he realized that his division was in trouble, Ramesses II sent messages by horseman and chariot to the trailing two divisions to speed their arrival. In an earlier campaign, the troops of Amenhotep II captured an enemy messenger carrying a letter of clay "at his throat," apparently a small clay tablet in a pouch hung around his neck.[31] The Egyptians and other armies of the time undoubtedly utilized other methods of communication as well.

Battle Tactics

As noted earlier, ancient records tell us surprisingly little about the tactics used in battles. From the information they do record, it seems that armies such as Egypt's used massed infantry armed primarily with spear and shield and arranged in rectangular formations called phalanxes, which engaged other enemy phalanxes. Infantry served alongside chariots that screened infantry on the march and acted in concert with them during battle. Chariots acted as mobile archery platforms to disrupt enemy formations and engage enemy chariots. Then at the close of battle, chariots would pursue and kill fleeing enemy troops. As the numbers of chariots increased, they likely played a greater and greater role in battles. Later battles seem to have consisted primarily of chariot engagements,[32] as at Kadesh.

Battle at Kadesh 1275 BC

The records of the battles at Megiddo in 1468 BC and Kadesh in 1275 BC offer the best information about tactics used. This chapter has already described in detail the action at Megiddo and mentioned numerous facets of the battle at Kadesh. The action at Kadesh (Map 3.1) resembled Megiddo in that the pharaoh and the Egyptian army marched north to do battle with a powerful enemy coalition to determine control of a major part of the Levant. During this battle, however, the Egyptians faced the Hittites and their allies from Asia Minor rather than Canaanites and Syrians, and this time Egypt had to overcome an enemy with clear tactical advantage to avoid disastrous defeat.

As noted earlier, Ramesses II led a force of 20,000 troops to Kadesh and was caught off guard by a Hittite ruse. The Hittite chariotry attacked and thoroughly scattered the second Egyptian division, Re, while it marched northward toward Kadesh. The Hittites then turned to attack Ramesses' lead division of Amon while it was setting up camp. Ramesses' division also scattered, and the Hittite chariotry surrounded Ramesses and his bodyguard. Ramesses quickly mounted his chariot and repeatedly led counterattacks against the enemy, driving it toward the Orontes River. This action left the Egyptian camp abandoned for the Hittites to plunder but also bought the Egyptians more time. Eventually the third division, Ptah, arrived from the south as well as the *na'arun*, mentioned earlier, from the west. The Egyptian troops now had the Hittite chariots caught between their lines, and the Hittites broke and fled to the safety of Kadesh.[33]

Despite the Hittites' clear advantage early on, as well as the bravery shown by Ramesses and the opportune arrival of Egyptian reinforcements later on in the battle, the outcome proved inconclusive in many respects. The fourth Egyptian division, Sutekh, could not reach the battlefield in time to take part, and the Hittite king kept his infantry force of 8,000–9,000 troops out of the action as well. Although Ramesses gained a great personal reputation and claimed victory, he took no further action to engage the Hittites or capture the city. He withdrew from the area immediately following the battle, raising serious questions about his claims of victory. The overall political situation remained largely unchanged, with the Hittites in control of Syria at least as far south as Kadesh.

As was the case with Megiddo, the Egyptian accounts of the battle at Kadesh leave many questions unanswered. How would the Hittites have described the action and results? Are the Egyptian numbers accurate for the enemy troop strength? How many were killed, injured, or taken captive? Casualties must have been heavy on both sides, but the Egyptians give no figures. The Egyptians apparently went into battle with 20,000 infantry in four divisions, but their chariot strength is completely unknown. The records seem to imply that the engagement consisted mostly of chariot battles, though this is uncertain. Since three Egyptian divisions were engaged, their infantry must have participated to some degree, though how much and in what way remains unclear.

Naval and Land Battles with Sea Peoples 1179 BC

The only known naval battle from this period occurred in the previously mentioned encounter between the Egyptians under Ramesses III and a coalition of enemy invaders whom the Egyptians called "Sea Peoples" in 1179 BC. The reliefs of the event apparently show only a selective representation of the naval battle, with just nine total ships, plus a land battle.

Evidently, the Egyptians knew about the advancing forces that had made their way from the Aegean Sea all the way around the eastern Mediterranean. The Egyptians prepared a trap, perhaps in the mouth of the Nile. The relief, if accurate, portrays major elements of the battle. Massed archers rained arrows from shore, while the Egyptian marine troops attacked with composite bows, javelins, swords, rods, and slings (Figs. 3.10, 4.10). Their long-range weapons would have outdistanced the enemy javelins and swords. The enemy boats are shown without oars, limiting their maneuverability and placing them at a severe disadvantage. The relief shows Egyptian marines hauling live enemy warriors from the water or capturing them when they reached shore so they could be used as slaves.

The corresponding land battle shows Egyptian infantry and chariotry attacking the Sea Peoples' infantry, chariotry and baggage train (see Fig. 5.11). The Egyptian troops outnumber the invaders in the relief, and seem to have caught them by surprise. The native Egyptian and mercenary Sherden (who would have been related to the invaders!) appear to kill the enemy soldiers and civilians with ease.

Other Battles

Although Egyptian records often mention other battles during this period, they do not give enough detail to determine the strategy used by either side. One does find elements of surprise, ambush, ruse, bribery, and extortion, as well as warfare against nomads, elephants, and confederations of foes. The records of Merenptah and Ramesses III fighting against Libyan attackers from 1208–1176 BC usually give the casualty figures for the Libyans, but not the numbers, composition, or arrangement of the Egyptian troops, or the events of the battles.

Attacks on Cities

In addition to the above-described battles in the open field, the Egyptians often attacked walled cities. When faced with such an attack, the cities' inhabitants had to choose to surrender or hold out and pray that their fortifications could withstand the attack. Egyptian reliefs sometimes depict such an assault on a fortified city, often shown elevated on a hill (as in Fig. 4.11) and surrounded by moats. In a typical attack on a fortified city, Egyptian archers provided heavy cover fire while assault troops protected by shields slung over their backs attacked the city gates with axes or climbed scaling ladders (all shown in Fig. 4.11). Egyptian attackers who reached the top of

Fig. 4.10—Naval battle against invading Sea Peoples. Egyptian warship in center, Sea Peoples' ship on right.

enemy walls would begin to slay defenders. One picture (not reproduced in this book) shows an Egyptian sounding his trumpet from the top of the wall, perhaps to signal the final charge or else to announce victory. Surprisingly, the reliefs and written sources during this period do not include battering rams, even though they were known since the 20th century BC.[34]

Fig. 4.11—Attack on fortified city. Troops of Ramesses II at Ashkelon in southern Canaan, 13th century BC.

If the Egyptians could not penetrate a city by direct assault, they had other alternatives. They might lay siege as they did at Megiddo, where they made an enclosure wall of timber and earth around the city to prevent the inhabitants from escaping. The siege of Megiddo lasted seven months; others took many years.[35] The attackers could also try to capture a city by ruse. During the reign of Thutmose III, Egypt captured the Canaanite city of Joppa by smuggling 200 soldiers into the city in baskets.[36] The final option would be for the attacking army to withdraw without capturing the city. Undoubtedly this also happened, but one is hard pressed to find passages that acknowledge it.

After the Battle

Following a successful battle on a city or in the open, the Egyptian armies collected plunder and prisoners, rewarded their troops, disposed of captured enemy leaders, celebrated their success, and made records of the victory.

Records of plunder captured during their campaigns probably make up the most extensive part of the Egyptian military records. Since the pharaohs promised to enrich the temples of their gods in return for aid in battle and since the temple personnel kept the records, those personnel were careful to list the items that they had or would receive.

Plunder, Prisoners, Rewards

Such records often list the numbers of enemy killed as well as the quantities of captured prisoners, livestock, weapons, suits of armor, chariots, tents, clothing, furniture and other household items, precious metals and stones, and various types of food. The quantities of captured goods range from a relatively modest eighteen prisoners and sixteen horses from one battle in Amenhotep II's first campaign to 89,600 captives in his second.[37]

The victorious pharaoh occasionally used some of these captives for display by having them bound and tied to his chariot and leading them back to camp in a triumphal procession. He then led the army in a ceremony, in which the army praised the god Amon and lauded the pharaoh, to celebrate the victory. The pharaoh then stood in a prominent place, like his chariot or the balcony of his palace if at home, while his troops presented him with prisoners and spoil and threw before him certain severed body parts of the slain.[38]

Soldiers who made captures or kills would present the person(s) or specified body part(s) to the pharaoh, who would commend the soldier and present him with rewards. Severed hands most often served as proof of enemy killed (Fig. 4.12). One text even proclaims, "How pleasant it is when you go to Thebes and your chariot is weighed down with hands."[39]

After their battles with the Libyans in the late 13th century, the Egyptians used the phalli of the uncircumcised Libyans instead of hands.[40] Compare in the Bible Saul's request to David for "foreskins" (perhaps a euphemism for phalli) from slain Philistines in 1 Sam 18:25–27 or the mention of apparently severed hands in Judg. 8:6, 15. For their kills, Egyptian soldiers often received as rewards items made of gold (the "Gold of Valor") like jewelry, golden lions, or golden flies used as decorations of honor.[41] If he captured prisoners, the successful soldier might get to keep those prisoners as his own slaves.

Oftentimes the pharaohs kept the plunder and prisoners as property of the crown. Such prisoners kept as slaves represented a significant source of labor for Egypt. Some were incorporated into the military, while others were settled in strongholds as farmers and taxed in clothing and grain. Many served as laborers in the temple complexes and the immense land holdings associated with them. By the time of Ramesses III, a listing of all temple property accounted for approximately two percent of the population, fifteen

Fig. 4.12—Pile of severed hands. From enemy troops at time of Ramesses III.

percent of all arable land, 160 towns, 90 ships, and nearly 500,000 animals, much of it coming from or made possible by war plunder.[42]

Captured sons of foreign rulers and officials often received special treatment. Like other nations of the time (cf. Dan. 1:3–7), the Egyptians often took foreign princes back to Egypt to educate them there and make these future leaders and officials more favorably disposed to Egypt. If such a captive was the son of a foreign ruler who died, the pharaoh could then send the son to replace the dead ruler and hopefully foster better relations between Egypt and that subject state.[43]

Not all enemy officials received such favorable treatment. The pharaohs often killed the leaders of rebellions in ceremonies and displayed their bodies as trophies of war (cf. Josh. 10:16–27). Pharaoh Ahmose in the 16th century hung a Nubian prince head downward at the bow of his royal barge as he returned from war. In the 15th century, Amenhotep II defeated and brought back seven Nubian princes hanging upside down on the prow of his barge while they were still alive. He then slew them himself with his mace in the temple of Amon and hung six of the bodies on the city wall of Thebes. He had the seventh hung on the walls of Napata upriver in Nubia as a warning to the Nubians. Later pharaohs such as Seti I, Ramesses II, and Ramesses III also slew kings in the temple as part of religious ceremonies demonstrating that power for victory came from Amon.[44]

Other Events after the Battle

The pharaohs also celebrated their victories by throwing great feasts and making records of their exploits in various temples. Together with their army, they celebrated by displaying plunder, making gifts to the gods, and giving elaborate "Feasts of Victory" with a variety of exotic foods. The campaign officially ended when the public records of the campaign were then inscribed on the walls of the temples. For example, Ramesses II had the record of his exploits at Kadesh engraved in temples at Abydos, Luxor, Karnak, Abu Simbel, and the Ramesseum, undoubtedly to proclaim his own glory as well as that of his god. During campaigns, scribes kept daily records on leather scrolls. These listed matters such as descriptions and details of strategic operations as well as individual sorties and names of commanders. These scrolls were then deposited in the temple of Amon after the campaign; they provided information for the general summaries that were chiseled onto monumental inscriptions in the temples or on stele.[45]

Once the campaign was over and the enemy defeated, conditions in Egypt reverted to those of peacetime. A text following Merenptah's defeat of Libyan invaders describes these changes as follows: the strongholds were left to themselves; the wells were reopened; messengers walked in the shade of city walls and waited for watchmen to wake up (in contrast to the urgency of wartime); soldiers slept; border scouts patrolled as they desired; and sentinels no longer cried warnings that foreign envoys were arriving.[46] Egypt's gods, pharaoh, and army had done their jobs, making Egypt prosperous and secure once again. Life was as it should be.

NOTES

1   Donald B. Redford and James M. Weinstein, "Hyksos," *ABD* 3:341–48.

2   Pritchard, *ANET,* 248 n. 59.

3   Though the straight sword worked well for hand-to-hand fighting with small shields, the reliefs suggest that the Egyptians did not use the straight sword as much as the sickle-sword. By contrast, the Libyans who attacked Egypt ca. 1200 BC and lost 9,111 swords (Breasted, *ARE* 3:588–89) are shown using straight swords (see Robert Drews, *The End of the Bronze Age: Changes in Warfare and the Catastrophe ca. 1200 BC* (Princeton: Princeton University, 1993), pl. 10).

4   For description (in German) of rod, see Wolf, *Bewaffnung,* 79; for use by Sherden, see Yadin *AWBL* 2:249, and illustration on 2:336–37.

5   For further discussion, see McDermott, *Warfare*, 82–83.

6   Ibid., 53–64, 150–57; Wallace E. McLeod, "An Unpublished Egyptian Composite Bow in the Brooklyn Museum," *American Journal of Archaeology* 62 (1958): 397.

7   Evidence from antiquity suggests that archers could shoot composite bows quite accurately up to sixty yards, with an effective range of at least 175 but less than 380 yards. See McLeod, "The Range of the Ancient Bow," *Phoenix* 19:1 (Spring, 1965): 8.

8   Wolf, *Bewaffnung,* 83–85; McLeod, "An Unpublished Egyptian Composite Bow," 399–400. Gad Rausing (*The Bow: Some Notes on Its Origin and Development* (Lund, Sweden: CWK Gleerups, 1967), 77) argues that materials like birchbark and birchwood used in making composite bows suggest that all were imported. See also Rodriquez, *Arsenal,* 207–15, 232–34 for helpful discussion and imagery of Egyptian bows and arrows.

9   The sling depicted survived with only the pouch and the cord with the looped end (Bonnet *Waffen,* Fig. 52). The second cord was added to the image for clarity. Two other Egyptian slings were found in the tomb of Tut-ankhamun. These were woven from linen, and were quite possibly of higher quality than the typical sling, which may have been made from leather. See Rodriquez, *Arsenal,* 244–45, for image and description.

10 The rather scanty evidence about the sling's range shows that its effective range exceeded 200 yards, compared to 175+ yards for the bow. See McLeod, "Range," 14.

11 McDermott, *Warfare,* 138–42.

12 See E. Stephen Gurdjian, M.D., "The Treatment of Penetrating Wounds of the Brain Sustained in Warfare: A Historical Review," *Journal of Neurosurgery* 39 (Feb. 1974): 157–67. Also see Gabriel and Metz, *Sumer to Rome,* 47–79 for information on the force soldiers could produce using different weapons and the ability of helmets and other defensive equipment to protect those who wore them.

13 The lack of clarity in the texts and the challenge of interpreting the reliefs contribute to this confusion. The reliefs are particularly hard to interpret given the possible loss of information because of detail that may have been originally portrayed in paint, now lost. For example, the reliefs clearly show some kind of garment on the upper torso of some of the chariot-warriors of Figs. 3.1 and 3.2 and the marines in 3.10, but the type of protection is unclear. The artists may be portraying simple linen or leather garments, or they may have chiseled into the stone the outline of the garment and used paint to portray scales or strips of metal. Some assume the absence of clear evidence means that even chariot-warriors like Nakt-her-Peri and his driver were probably bare-chested, or used only a linen or leather garment and a shield for protection in battle. Given the outline of the garment shown on the upper torso of Egyptian charioteers and the numerous coats of mail captured from the Canaanites at Megiddo, this book assumes that charioteers like Nakt-her-Peri may well have been mail-clad. If the Canaanite army could supply at least 200 coats of mail for their warriors, chances are that the Egyptians could have done at least that much for their charioteers. Note also discussion in Yadin, *AWBL* 1:85.

14 See drawings in Yadin, *AWBL* 2:251–52, and restored coloring on 2:340–41. Yadin (1:85) notes that scale armor could have large or small metal scales, ranging from ca. 400 to more than 1000 scales in a coat of mail. The higher the number, the better the quality. Hoffmeier ("Annals," p. 12, n. 64) notes that the Egyptian word "tunic" is written with a determinative for a leather hide, suggesting that the metal plates were sewn on leather garments.

15 For detailed descriptions and drawings of the six chariots found in the tomb of Tutankhamun and comparison with other extant chariots, see Littauer and Crouwel, *Chariots and Related Equipment,* esp. pp. 53–104. They note that the construction of these chariots "required great precision of workmanship. (T)his technique produced some of the finest examples of the

wheelwright's and carriage maker's craft ever known." They also point out that "such a construction, using glue and rawhide, would be completely un-practical in a damp climate" (p. 94).

16 The wheels' spokes were formed from six pieces of half-round wood, each bent at a 60° angle and glued to identical half-round adjacent pieces, thus forming six strong, round, connected, composite spokes. To further strengthen these joints, wheelwrights applied wet rawhide that shrank as it dried. They then joined the spokes to wooden tires made from several pieces of bent wood sections, again joined with glue and leather bindings, cov-ered in birch bark (Littauer and Crouwel, *Chariots and Related Equipment,* 76–78).

17 See also helpful descriptions of chariot maintenance in Yadin *AWBL* 1:89–90.

18 Pritchard, *ANET,* 234–35.

19 Breasted, *ARE,* 2:¶ 149.

20 Ibid., 2:¶ 409–10.

21 Ibid., 3: ¶ 298; Pritchard, *ANET,* 245. But note Amenhotep's campaign in year nine, which began in November (Pritchard, *ANET,* 246).

22 Breasted, *ARE,* 3: ¶ 570.

23 Lichtheim, *AEL,* 2:63; Breasted, *ARE,* 4:¶ 70–71. The modern American mil-itary still conducts a similar practice. The Marines call it "Pass and Review."

24 Breasted, *ARE,* 3:¶ 298.

25 Breasted, *The Battle of Kadesh,* 19, n. 76.

26 Schulman, *MRTO,* ¶ 94, 123, 128.

27 Yadin *AWBL* 1:108–09, 236–37; Breasted, *The Battle of Kadesh*, pl. 1.

28 Schulman, *MRTO,* ¶ 149; Breasted, *ARE,* 3:¶ 83.

29 One sarcastic and stressed scribe refers to the inadequate provisions as "peace offerings" (Pritchard, *ANET,* 476). Note the numerous references in the Amarna letters to local rulers in Canaan promising to follow the pha-raoh's instructions to prepare provisions for Egyptian troops (Moran, *The Amarna Letters*, EA 55:10–15; 324:10–15 ("I am indeed observing the or-ders of the king, my lord, the son of the Sun, and I have indeed prepared food, strong drink, oil, grain, oxen, sheep, and goats, before the arrival of the troops of the king, my lord. I have stored everything for the troops of the king, my lord."); 325:15–19; etc.).

30 Pritchard, *ANET,* 235. See also Schulman, "Military Organization in Phara-onic Egypt," 291; Yadin *AWBL* 1:110.

31 Pritchard, *ANET,* 246.

32   Note how military history has repeated itself more recently with the key roles played by tanks, planes, and aircraft carriers.

33   Lichtheim, *AEL,* 2:57–58; Breasted, *ARE,* 3:¶ 300–3, with diagrams.

34   For general information on attacks, see Yadin *AWBL* 1:228–29; 2:346–47; for discussion of battering rams, see 1:96–97 and illustrations on 1:17, 229.

35   See Breasted, *ARE,* 2:¶ 4 for descriptions of one siege lasting six years and another lasting "many years." Cf. 2:¶ 616.

36   Pritchard, *ANET,* 22–23.

37   Breasted, *ARE,* 2:¶ 783; Pritchard, *ANET,* 247.

38   Pritchard, *ANET,* 234–38, 245–46, etc.

39   Nelson, *Medinet Habu Reports I*, 24.

40   Breasted, *ARE,* 3:¶ 587 notes that the Egyptians used the typical severed hands for proof that a soldier had killed one of the Libyans' allies, but they required severed phalli for the uncircumcised Libyans. Perhaps this is due to the similarity in skin color between the circumcised Egyptians and the uncircumcised Libyans. More likely, the Libyans differed from the other peoples by not circumcising their males, so the Egyptians used the phalli as indisputable proof of a dead Libyan. One can imagine that an enemy might allow their Egyptian captor to remove their hand in a trade for their life, but not their phallus. Schulman, *MRTO,* ¶ 42 also records quantities of up to 250 heads in a list of plunder.

41   In Breasted, *ARE,* 2:¶ 21–24, one soldier boasts of receiving forty different items of gold from three different pharaohs. See also the long list of rewards won by the infantryman Amenemheb in Schulman, *MRTO,* ¶ 24.

42   Note, for example, the command to take the people of Joppa "as plunder, so that (the pharaoh) may fill the House of (his) father, Amon-Re, King of the Gods, with male and female slaves" (Pritchard, *ANET,* 23). See also *ANET,* 248, 260–62; Breasted, *ARE,* 4:¶ 151–412.

43   Pritchard, *ANET,* 239, 247; Breasted, *ARE,* 2:¶ 463.

44   Breasted, *ARE,* 2:¶ 780, 797; 3:¶ 113; 4:¶ 137.

45   Ibid., 2:¶ 541–73; 3:¶ 104–06, 348; Hoffmeier, "Annals of Thutmose III", 7–8.

46   Breasted, *ARE,* 3:¶ 616.

PHILISTIA:
ISRAEL'S NEIGHBOR AND ENEMY

5

EAT OR BE EATEN: THE PHILISTINES KILL KING SAUL

"Eat or be eaten." Dagarat[1] the Philistine warrior muttered the words aloud as he tossed aside the last bone from the wild dog that he and the other soldiers in his unit had just finished eating. Like most Philistines, Dagarat liked eating dogs occasionally,[2] but he figured he savored them more than most. Da garat also enjoyed observing dogs, and he appreciated their toughness and hunting instincts. They had to be tough to keep on the right side of the eat-or-be-eaten equation. Only the best stayed alive, and Dagarat admired that. He appreciated the way they tasted even more.

Eat or be eaten. It was the way of the dog. Whether working individually or in packs, stronger dogs killed and ate the weaker prey, including other dogs. Dagarat had witnessed the process play out again that day among the dogs that were following the army. He had often seen dogs moving along with the Philistine army, knowing that the soldiers would eventually provide them with a feast. Regardless of who won the battle, the dogs always enjoyed a good meal afterward (cf. 1 Kings 21:24; Jer. 15:3; 1 Sam. 17:44, 46). So they followed along, killing as needed while they waited for the big event. On this day, Dagarat had taken advantage of their preoccupation with their own hunt to get close enough to kill the biggest and strongest dog with his spear. Dogs were good hunters, but Dagarat was better. Sometimes even the best could get eaten.

Dagarat ran out of time for thoughtful reflection; it was time to finish setting up camp for the night. He knew the routine well from the dozens of military expeditions he had participated in over the last fifteen years. He was now an old man of thirty-five,[3] but he still had the strength to fight for his people and did his part proudly. He was getting old, however, and wondered if this would have to be his last campaign. He could tell he wasn't as quick as he had been—not a good thing in battle. He also grew tired more quickly and took longer to recover. Fortunately he wouldn't have to stand guard tonight, so he could get a good night's sleep. Tomorrow would be another long day of marching, probably the last before reaching the place of battle. Dagarat had long ago mastered the skill of shutting off his mind and resting,[4] and soon he fell fast asleep, renewing his energy for the next day's march.

Fig. 5.1—Head of Philistine warrior from Egyptian relief

The following morning the troops awoke early, broke camp, and resumed their march northward toward the Great Valley and the anticipated place of battle. Dagarat lived in the city of Ashdod near the coast, one of the five great Philistine cities. When the call came to assemble for war, the troops had gathered in each of those cities, marched the few miles north to the rendezvous point at Aphek (Map 5.1), and then continued north along the Great Coastal Road. He had often marched on this strategic route, as had many other armies before him. The Philistine forces were heading toward the Great Valley (which the Israelites called the Jezreel Valley) in north-central Canaan, hoping to draw King Saul and his weak Israelite army out of the hills into the open, where the stronger Philistine forces could destroy them. Dagarat and his fellow heavy infantrymen would probably play an important role in the battle, and he had plenty of time to ponder that and other thoughts as he marched through the day.

Once again, the refrain *eat or be eaten* filled his mind. It was the way of dogs; it was also the way of men. People had to help others, at least to some degree. But not all could thrive or even survive, so men also had to, in a sense, eat or be eaten. Men were stronger and smarter than animals, so men ate animals. Philistines were stronger and smarter than other men. They didn't eat other men, but they did kill others to take their land and possessions. Some may have thought this unjust, but Dagarat and his fellow Philistines simply used their strength to take what they needed, whether that meant land or crops or goods. *Eat or be eaten.* The tough and strong usually did the eating, and the Philistines fit that description. They got to eat, and the others' things got eaten; that's just the way the world worked.

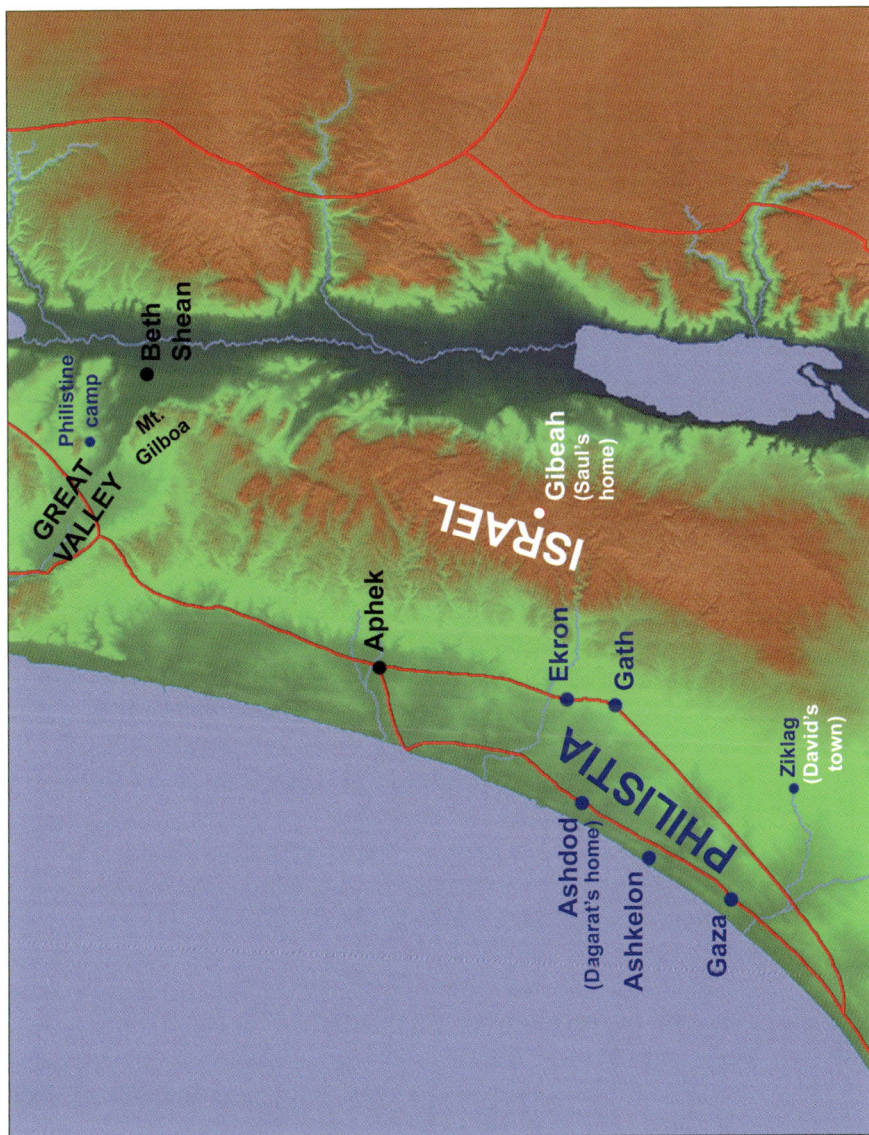

Map 5.1—Philistine and Israelite approaches to Saul's final battle

Dagarat was also thoughtful enough to realize that occasionally the weaker ended up eating the stronger—not often, but sometimes. He had observed weaker dogs gang up on a stronger dog and eat it. He had also seen weaker people occasionally overcome the stronger to kill them and take their things. Sometimes the weak used an advantage in tactics or terrain to kill the strong, and at times it seemed that the weak won without a clear human reason.

Did the gods will the weak to occasionally eat the strong? Perhaps. Perhaps that was the only way to explain victories by the weak. Dagarat considered himself as religious as most Philistines. They worshipped the gods Dagon, Ashtoreth, and Baal-zebub,[5] but Dagarat preferred Dagon because of his temple in Dagarat's city of Ashdod (1 Sam. 5:1–5). In all honesty, Dagarat wasn't always sure whether the Philistines flourished because their gods were stronger than other gods or because the Philistines themselves were stronger and better warriors. Maybe both. Who knew? The gods could be fickle, as demonstrated by the way events in life and the fortunes of one's people sometimes played out in history.

Some of Dagarat's earliest memories came from historical tales that his grandfather passed on about the Great Migration. In the time of Dagarat's grandfather's grandfather, the Philistines and their cousins among the Sea Peoples—the Tjekker, Sheklesh, Denyen, and Weshesh—had been forced to leave their ancient homeland across the Great Sea.[6] Their combined peoples made the Great Migration around the eastern end of the Great Sea all the way to Egypt (Map 5.2), defeating all who resisted during their search for a new home. They had eventually tried to conquer the fat, green land of Egypt in one final battle, but they lost to the weaker Egyptians. The stories said that the Philistines and their fellow Sea Peoples had been stronger, but the Egyptians had learned of the approaching conquerors and prepared their naval and land forces well (see "Battle Tactics" in chap. 4). The Egyptians caught the invaders off guard and overwhelmed them. Many died, and many more were captured. Had the two sides fought on equal footing, the invaders would certainly have won. But the weaker had the victory, and the stronger couldn't recover quickly enough to try again. They were forced to settle along the coast of Canaan instead and make that region their new home.

In the years following the Great Migration, the Philistines had established themselves and dominated most of the nearby peoples in Canaan, taking their land and possessions as needed. Their victims included the people who lived in the hills to the east and called themselves Israelites.

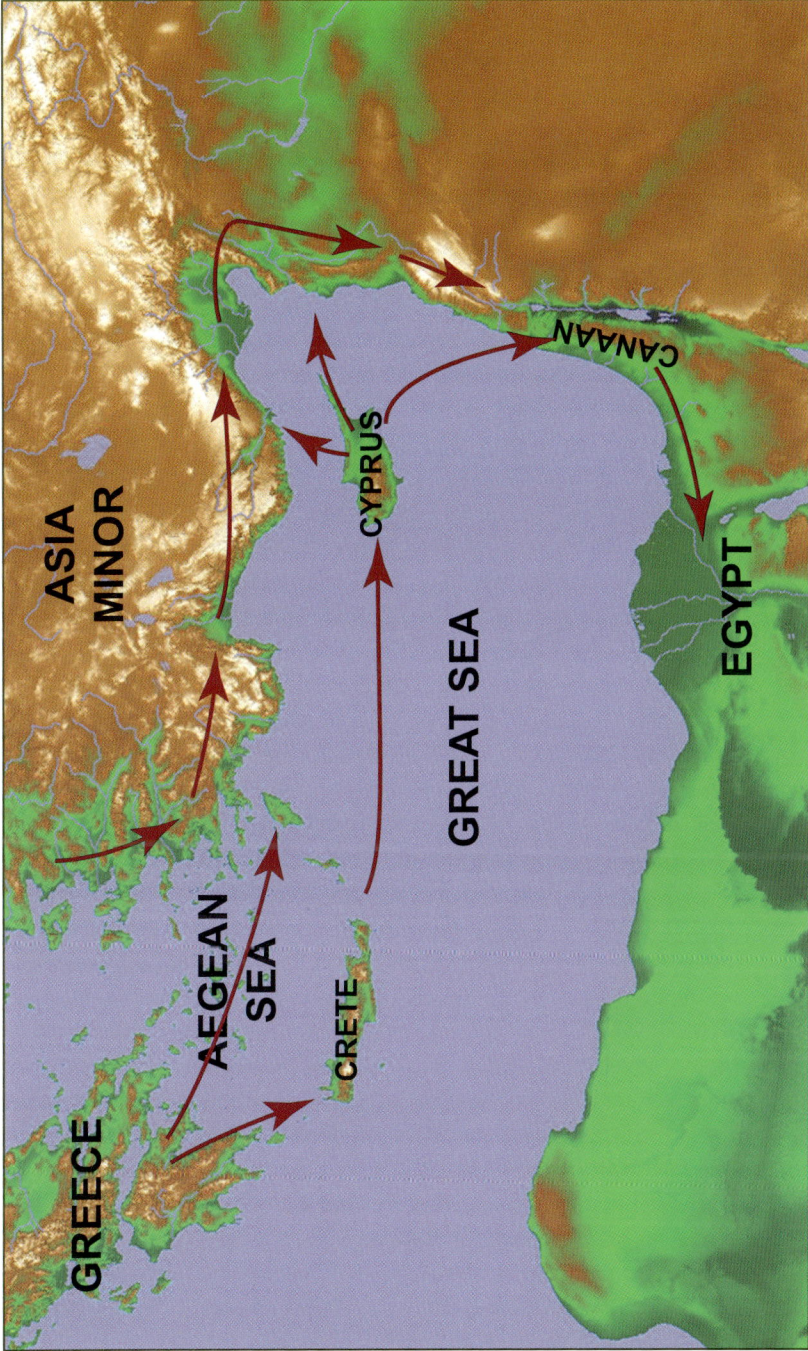

Map 5.2—Migration of the Sea Peoples

The Philistines had heard stories of the Israelites' history that included great acts by their one god in days gone by. *One god!*—Dagarat couldn't understand a people who worshipped only one god. No wonder they were so weak. Their god may have helped them earlier, but he didn't seem to do much in more recent days to protect and strengthen them. Occasionally the Israelites managed to defeat one of their neighbors, but more often the neighboring peoples proved stronger. This certainly included the Philistines, who had taken some of the Israelites' southern territory as well as much plunder (1 Sam. 4, 13). It was eat or be eaten, and the Philistines were doing most of the eating. Dagarat suspected that the upcoming battle with these Israelites would be no different.

Although the Philistines usually defeated the Israelites, Dagarat had also witnessed the weaker Israelites defeat the stronger in battle. He had been present in the border clash in the Elah Valley when the Philistine champion called Goliath had inexplicably lost to the Israelite pup named David (1 Sam. 17). Even after Goliath fell that day, Dagarat had wanted to stand and fight. But when the bulk of the army fled, he had little choice but to join them. That battle had shocked and humiliated the Philistines. Equally upsetting had been the earlier disaster up in the hills when the Israelite prince Jonathan had launched a victory that drove the advancing Philistines from the Israelite heartland (1 Sam. 14). That loss had been particularly painful for Dagarat, as his oldest son had fallen in that defeat. Dagarat had tried to warn him that the gods frowned on those who grew too confident and proud, but his son hadn't listened. The gods had apparently chosen that day to punish the proud Philistines and give the victory to Israel.

Will something similar happen in the upcoming battle? Dagarat wondered. It was possible, even though the Philistines clearly had all the advantages. They had a superior army in every respect, especially when one considered the excellent Philistine chariots (Fig. 5.2). The Israelites had no chariots at all, as far as Dagarat knew. If one fought up in the hills, the chariots were of little value. But out on open ground, the horse-drawn vehicles offered a tremendous advantage, and the Philistines were headed toward the Great Valley with plenty of open terrain. In addition to their advantage with chariots, the Philistine infantry was vastly better armed and trained than the Israelite troops. Only the gods could give Israel victory in this battle. But would they?

Dagarat thought that the presence of the Israelite David at the battle might actually cause the gods to give the victory to Israel. David had defied the odds and defeated Goliath, and David's god seemed to favor him often.

Fig. 5.2—Philistine chariots. Two chariots from relief of land battle with Egyptians under Ramesses III. Parts of image have worn away or are obscured by omitted elements.

David appeared to have a way of becoming stronger while avoiding danger. He had reportedly survived numerous attempts on his life by his own king, Saul (1 Sam. 18–26), and had gathered a private army of 400 men at the same time (1 Sam. 22:1–2).[7] The man was clearly a capable warrior and an effective leader. The threat from Saul had grown so great that David and his men had agreed to serve Achish, the Philistine king at Gath, in exchange for protection from Saul (1 Sam. 27). The Philistines had been glad to take advantage of the strife between David and his king to further weaken Saul and Israel. For their service to Achish, David and his men received their own little town, Ziklag, south of Gath on the edge of the desert (Map 5.1)— not much of a prize in Dagarat's opinion. In exchange for the town and sanctuary in Philistine territory, David and his private army had promised to serve and protect their Philistine overlord. Apparently they had kept their promise, and David had reportedly even carried out raids against his own people (1 Sam. 27:8–12).[8]

Now that the Philistines were going to battle against the Israelites, David found himself obligated to fight with his overlord against his own people (1 Sam. 28:1–2). Dagarat thought this an interesting and troubling prospect. Would David actually fight against his own king and his nation's army? Dagarat had his doubts, as did a number of other Philistine warriors and officers. David and his men had started out toward the battlefield with the troops from Gath, but they went no farther than the Philistine rendezvous at Aphek. In the war council there, the other Philistine kings had convinced Achish to send David and his army back home (1 Sam. 29). The Philistines gave up a fine leader and hundreds of proven troops, but they avoided a potential rebellion and perhaps lessened the chances of the gods working in Israel's favor.[9]

The Philistines had left their concerns for David behind them at Aphek, and now turned to face Saul and his army, weak as it was. The Philistines had chosen to push all the way to the Great Valley to try to force Saul out into the open. Although the Philistines had often defeated the weaker Israelites, so far they had been frustrated in their attempts to deliver the deathblow. Saul had wisely kept to the hills in the earlier engagements, taking advantage of the familiar, rougher terrain while neutralizing much of the Philistine military advantage.

The Philistines had now settled on the bold strategy of establishing themselves in the Great Valley. Taking the Valley would not only give them excellent farmland, it would also further weaken Israel by separating the majority of Israelites in the central hill country from their countrymen who lived in the hills of Galilee farther north. However, the Valley was a long way from the Philistine heartland, and they risked overextending themselves. They hoped to force Saul and his meager militia out of the hills to defend their holdings in the Great Valley. The region's fertility made it highly prized, and the Israelites would be reluctant to surrender it. Saul would have to come out, wouldn't he?[10] If he did, the Philistines could destroy the army, kill the king, and cut Israel in two—at least that was their plan. Dagarat knew he would do his part, as he knew the gods would do theirs. But what part would they play? One could never be sure, even after giving all the requisite offerings and prayers.

Dagarat and the Philistines set up camp near a village at the base of a hill on the eastern end of the Great Valley. They positioned themselves opposite the central Israelite hills that ended at Mt. Gilboa (1 Sam. 28:4; see Map 5.1), the place from which Saul and his troops would probably emerge—if they were brave enough to fight. Undoubtedly, Israelite scouts had reported the Philistines' movements to Saul. The Philistine scouts had much greater difficulty learning the movements of the hill-dwelling

Israelites and could only report that a number of them were making their way northward through the hills toward the Valley. So the Philistines waited and raided several Israelite villages in the Valley to take food and other supplies. Only a few offered resistance; it was the last thing they ever did.

While they waited, the Philistines held another war council to discuss strategy and pass along orders to all the troops. They first stressed the primary goal, which was not to decimate the enemy army or even to win. The primary goal was to kill King Saul[11] and any of his sons who might take part. If the Philistines could kill Israel's core leadership, these hill people might never recover enough to cause trouble for the Philistines again. Every Philistine had to target Saul and his sons above all else. The king should be easy enough to spot, with his crown and royal armband (2 Sam. 1:10). Identifying princes might prove more difficult.

Beyond deciding to target the royal family, the Philistines also settled on their battle plan. Each morning they would array in the usual formation with heavy infantry in a line in the center, light infantry behind them ready to fill gaps in the line or exploit breaks in the enemy line, archers and slingers in the rear, and chariots on the wings. First, some of the chariots would cross the narrow valley to probe and hopefully draw out the enemy. If and when the enemy came out from Gilboa and the forested hills, the chariots would return to the rest of the troops. The forces would hold their positions, giving the Israelite troops plenty of time to advance into the Valley.

Only when the Israelites got well out into the narrow valley would the Philistines move. On a signal from the Philistine commander, the chariots would advance and make a few passes in front of the enemy, firing several rounds with their bows. They were to look like they were attacking but do minimal damage, allowing the enemy to continue advancing. Then the Philistine commander would give a signal, and the chariots would head back toward their wings. By the time they returned, hopefully the Israelites would be about halfway across the Valley. Then the commander would signal again for the Philistine archers and slingers to begin firing and the infantry to charge, engaging and capturing the attention of the Israelites. Once the Israelites were occupied, the commander would signal yet again. The chariots would head back out, but this time, they would circle around the troops from both armies without engaging so they could get to the Israelite rear before attacking. If all went well, the Philistines would surround the Israelites and cut them to shreds. Dagarat thought the plan fit the situation well and had a reasonable chance of working, but as he knew from repeated experience, battles rarely went according to plan.

Surprisingly, this battle did. Although the Philistines knew that it could take many days or even weeks before the Israelites engaged (cf. 1 Sam. 17, esp. v. 16), they had to wait just a few days. Shortly after the Philistines drew up into battle formation one morning and the chariots made their initial sweeps, the charioteers signaled that they had spotted the enemy at the base of Mt. Gilboa. The horse-drawn vehicles returned as planned, and the Israelite forces emerged from the forested high ground as if on cue. The two armies had a clear view of one another. Dagarat scoffed at the enemy's small number and obvious lack of equipment and training, but he had to commend them for their bravery. The Israelites could see they were badly outmatched, but they continued their advance anyway. Were they brave or just stupid? Dagarat figured it was both, and thought that if the gods had not determined to help Israel, the enemy would have one fewer king and army by nightfall.

Dagarat was correct. The battle played out exactly according to the Philistine plan. When the Israelites got well into the valley, the Philistine commander signaled and the charioteers advanced to put down light fire with their bows. The commander signaled again, the horses returned, and the Philistines fired and charged. Their chariots then looped around as planned, enveloping the Israelites. Saul and his outmatched army fought bravely but in vain. The Philistines slowly but gradually cut them down until less than half their number remained.

Eventually Saul signaled for a retreat, and a part of his force broke through and began to flee back toward Mt. Gilboa and the safety of the hills. Those Israelites thought the move would save their lives, but as soon as they separated from the main Philistine force, the Philistine archers could begin firing again. The archers had stayed just behind their own lines with little to do for most of the battle. With the two sides so close together, they had to refrain from shooting lest they hit their own men. Now they could fire in earnest once more, and had the unprotected backs of the fleeing Israelites for targets. Many fell with the first volley, and the archers continued their deadly work (1 Sam. 31:3; 1 Chron. 10:3). Those who survived continued fleeing to and then up the lower slopes of Mt. Gilboa, out of the range of the archers. The Philistine chariots then took over, chasing down and finishing off most of them (2 Sam. 1:6). Dagarat heard several victorious cries from his fellow warriors and wondered if they had just downed Saul or perhaps one or more of his sons. Dagarat was too far away to see, but he knew he would hear before long. Everyone could see clearly that the victory had been overwhelming. Only a few Israelites escaped.

The battle concluded as successfully as it had begun. Nearly all the Israelites lay dead. The Philistines knew they had accomplished their second goal, but they would have to wait until the following day when they combed the battlefield to determine how well they had done with their first. When he finally had the chance to stop and rest, Dagarat noted that Israel's god had not helped his people this day, and the strong had once more eaten the weak.

That evening, after the Philistines had tended to their wounded and taken care to guard the bodies of their dead, they feasted around their fires back at their camp. Dagarat enjoyed the meal of tasty Israelite lamb, courtesy of one of the nearby villages, and he thought about the dogs that were probably feasting as well on the Israelite dead out on the battlefield.

The next morning, the victors enjoyed more of the spoils. They watched the last few Israelite farmers and their families abandoning their properties in the Great Valley, and word soon arrived that more Israelites in the nearby regions across the Jordan River to the east were departing as well. They all knew that Philistine settlers would arrive shortly to take over those lands and homes (1 Sam. 31:7).

The victorious Philistines also combed the battlefield, stripping the dead Israelites of anything of value. They found and collected the corpses of Saul and three of his sons, including Jonathan, the crown prince (1 Sam. 31:2). They gathered around the bodies for a brief celebration of thanksgiving to their gods (cf. Josh. 10:22–27). Then they removed both Saul's armor and head as trophies of war and sent them back to the Philistine cities in the south with messengers carrying news of the victory. The Philistines also took the bodies of Saul and his sons and fastened them on the walls of Beth Shean, a city at the far eastern end of the Great Valley (Map 5.1). This gruesome display announced to all in the area that the Israelite king and nation had just been decapitated, and that the Philistines now commanded the region.[12]

Dagarat and his countrymen continued to celebrate their great victory over Israel and its royal house as they marched back home, but the thoughtful veteran considered again the Israelite David. The Philistines had probably just imposed on the Israelites their most destructive and humiliating defeat ever, which might even threaten Israel's very survival. Could the nation continue without a king or capable princes to take his place? And what would David do? David had avoided death numerous times in the past; could he now help his nation avoid complete disintegration? Dagarat didn't know, and thought he would leave that for the gods to determine. The Philistines' gods seemed quite capable of defeating the god of Israel, didn't they? What were the chances that David and his one god could resurrect the Israelite nation to again trouble the mighty Philistines? *Probably very little*, thought Dagarat.

But this time the thoughtful Philistine warrior was wrong. The Bible tells how in the next years David and his God would indeed do that—and more (2 Sam. 5, 8). David and his God would help the weak become strong and turn Israel into the eaters rather than those getting eaten.

HISTORICAL BACKGROUND AND BIBLICAL CONNECTIONS

As the preceding story suggests, the Philistines established themselves along the southern coast of Canaan and dominated the Israelites and other nearby peoples for approximately 150 years before the reign of David. One finds colorful reports of their battles with the Israelites in the biblical books of Judges and 1 Samuel, as well as in scattered references throughout the Old Testament. Who were these uncircumcised foes of Israel? From where had they come, and what happened to them after they faded from the biblical record?[13]

A number of the earliest biblical references to Philistines appear in the patriarchal stories of Genesis, describing events that perhaps occurred ca. 2000 BC. Abraham and his son Isaac have dealings with "Philistines" in "the land of the Philistines" (Gen. 21, 26). Since the great migration of the Philistines and other Sea Peoples didn't take place until approximately 1200 BC, one might wonder why Philistines appear centuries earlier. Some simply call these early references anachronistic. Others allow that some Philistines or related peoples could have arrived earlier and settled in the same region that was later dominated by those who came in the great wave of immigration. If these earlier immigrants had come from among the Sea Peoples, later readers might naturally have associated them with the Philistines, and the name could have been updated for that audience, a practice found elsewhere in Genesis.[14]

Where did the Philistines originate at the outset of the "Great Migration" of Dagarat's ancestors? Apparently they came from the region of the Aegean Sea, perhaps from Crete or one or more of the other islands between Greece and Asia Minor (Map 5.2). Several of the Philistines' cultural characteristics such as their pottery and architecture, as well as Goliath's armor and weaponry (1 Sam. 17:5–7) have close parallels in Aegean culture. A number of textual references also seem to corroborate this connection. Egyptian records describe the Sea Peoples as invaders from islands in the north, and their list of places destroyed during the migration fits well with an origin in the Aegean.[15] Amos 9:7 and Jeremiah 47:4 state that the Philistines came from Caphtor (usually understood as Crete, though some[16] link it to the region of Cilicia in Asia Minor). In addition, Ezekiel 25:15–16 and Zephaniah 2:4–5 use the terms "Philistines" and "Kerethites" (Cretans) as poetic parallels, a pattern which typically denotes synonyms.

Until western scholars began studying Egyptian historical sources in the late 18th and 19th centuries, the biblical material represented nearly all of what the modern world knew about the Philistines. But beginning with Napoleon's expedition to Egypt in AD 1798–1803, French and other scholars began examining reliefs carved into the walls of ancient Egyptian temples and later deciphered the accompanying hieroglyphic texts and other materials. More recently, archaeology has uncovered Philistine remains from sites known from the Bible (Ashkelon, Ashdod, etc.) as well as some that are not (e.g. Tel Qasile just north of Tel Aviv). These pictures, descriptions, and remains have added a great deal of information to what one reads about the Philistines in the Bible.

The still-incomplete picture that has emerged shows the Philistines as one of a number of related people groups including Denyen, Tjekker, Weshesh, and Sherden, which had migrated to the southeastern Mediterranean, apparently from the area of the Aegean Sea in the region that is today Greece and western Turkey. The Egyptians called these invaders "Sea Peoples" since they came by sea as well as by land. Something, perhaps a cataclysm like a famine or volcanic eruption, apparently forced them to leave their homeland around 1200 BC. They began making their way around the eastern Mediterranean basin, conquering those who lay in their path. They took advantage of the general weakness of the contemporary ancient Near Eastern civilizations, including the formerly great powers of Egypt and the Hittites in Asia Minor. The Sea Peoples attacked Asia Minor, Syria, Canaan, and finally Egypt, contributing to the destruction and general turmoil of the time.

Pharaoh Ramesses III recorded that he repulsed the invaders at the edge of Egypt in naval and land battles in the early 12th century BC and afterward settled them along the southern coast of Canaan. Ramesses' magnificent reliefs of the two battles give us much of our best information about the Philistines' appearance and dress, their weaponry and naval forces, and the equipment they utilized for moving on land.

The archaeological record generally supports the Philistines' Aegean origins. The Philistines would have been Indo-Europeans, and they brought to Canaan a culture reflecting Aegean customs in a number of ways. They did not circumcise their males (Judg. 14:3, etc.), unlike the Semitic peoples such as Israel. When they arrived in Canaan, they apparently wrote in a linear script related to Linear A and B from Crete, although they later adopted the alphabet used in Canaan. Their earlier pottery closely resembles pottery known from Mycenae in Greece (Fig. 5.3), though the Philistine pottery subsequently evolved independently. Their architecture included at least one temple with an open hearth, a feature of buildings back in the Aegean. As noted earlier, even Goliath's armor and weaponry (1 Sam. 17:5–7) reflect what was worn and used in the Aegean.

About the same time[17] that the Philistines settled along the southern coast of Canaan with their distinct culture, the Israelites were beginning to establish themselves in Canaan, mostly in the hills in the central and northern parts of the country. The emerging Philistines and Israelites battled for land and supremacy, with the Philistines dominating from about the mid-12th to the end of the 11th centuries, the period of the latter biblical judges through the reign of Israel's first king, Saul. The biblical texts clearly reflect the Philistines' superiority— "At that time the Philistines ruled over Israel. . . . 'Do you not know that the Philistines are rulers over us?'" (Judg. 14:4; 15:11, ESV). The Philistines enjoyed a great technological advantage in metallurgy and thus weaponry, as reflected by both the biblical texts (1 Sam. 13:16–22) and by

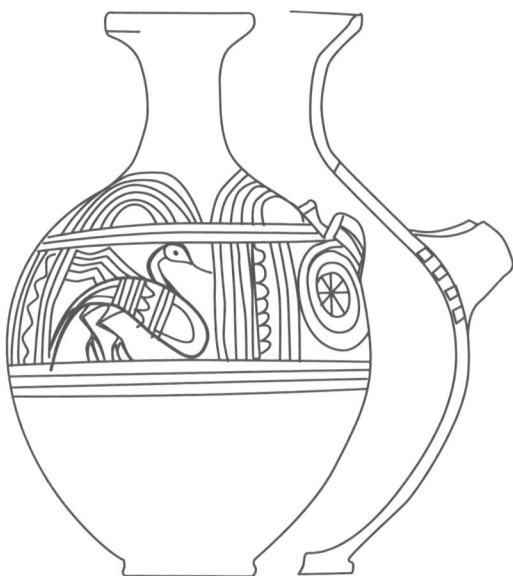

Fig. 5.3—Philistine "beer strainer" jug. Note perforations inside spout in cross-section on right, apparently for straining grain husks when dispensing beer. Also note typical stylized bird in decoration.

the numerous metal tools and furnaces—used for melting ore—uncovered at several Philistine sites.

One sees this Philistine dominance in the biblical texts describing the colorful and famous exploits of the judge Samson, who lived toward the end of the period of the judges (Judg. 13–16). Samson carried out what appear to be ultimately unsuccessful border skirmishes against Israel's more powerful neighbors to the west. Though Samson won a few battles, his greatest victory cost him his life, and after Samson's death the author of Judges can only say that he "had judged Israel twenty years" (Judg. 16:31, ESV) without establishing peace with the Philistines.

The Bible indicates that Philistine domination continued throughout the ministry of Samuel, Israel's last judge, and the reign of Saul, Israel's first king. Not surprisingly, the archaeological remains from Philistine sites during this time reflect prosperity and expansion. During the life of Samuel, the Philistines won a decisive battle at Ebenezer near Aphek on the coastal plain (Map 5.1) and captured the Ark of the Covenant, which led to the death of Eli the High Priest and his sons (1 Sam. 4). Although the Israelites subsequently got their Ark back, the best Samuel could manage against the Philistines was a single victory at Mizpah up in the heart of the Israelite hill country (1 Sam. 7; see Map 5.3).

The new king Saul had some military success against the neighboring Ammonites in the east (1 Sam. 11) and the Amalekites in the south (1 Sam. 15), but he could not decisively defeat the Philistines. At one point during Saul's reign, the Philistines penetrated and established themselves at Michmash, well past Saul's capital of Gibeah in the very heartland of his kingdom (Map 5.3), but it was Saul's son Jonathan, not Saul, who launched the victory that drove out the invaders. Saul squandered much of that victory's impact with his foolish vow during the battle that nearly cost crown prince Jonathan his life (1 Sam. 13–14). Likewise, when the Philistines moved to Azekah and Socoh to take Israelite land in the Elah Valley (Map 5.3), a shepherd named David famously led the victory rather than the king (1 Sam. 17). Conflict continued between the peoples throughout the rest of Saul's life (1 Sam. 18–23). Saul's largely ineffective reign ended when the Philistines killed him and most of his sons in battle, as told earlier in the story of the fictitious warrior Dagarat (1 Sam. 27–29, 31).

The death of Saul proved to be the high-water mark of Philistine power. In the following decades, David not only kept Israel alive but also made his nation into a force that dominated neighboring kingdoms including Philistia (2 Sam. 5, 8). Near the beginning of his reign, David moved his capital from the important but somewhat isolated Hebron in the southern hills to the more strategically located Jerusalem (Map 5.3). The Philistines apparently understood this as an effort to consolidate and expand, so they moved to weaken David. They made a surprise attack up a little-used route to reach a point in the Rephaim Valley south of Jerusalem. This cut off David in his new capital from his traditional bases of support in Bethlehem and Hebron farther south (Map 5.3).[18] David responded and defeated the Philistines rather decisively (2 Sam. 5). The only subsequent mention of battle with the Philistines during David's rise to greatness appears in summary form in 2 Samuel 8:1, which notes that David was by then conquering Philistine territory.[19] As one might expect, a number of Philistine sites show a layer of destruction from the early 10th century, evidently during the time of David's reign, perhaps done by David or even Egypt. The Egyptians seem to have taken advantage of this shifting power to conquer territory in southern Canaan as well (1 Kings 9:16). David appears to have finally given Israel superiority over these longtime foes.

Fighting would continue between the Israelites and the Philistines for some time (2 Sam. 21, 23; 1 Kings 15:27; 2 Kings 18:8; 1 Chron. 20:4–5; 2 Chron. 26:6–7), but only twice in the following centuries will the Bible note any Philistine advances into Israelite territory (2 Chron. 21:16–17; 28:18). The Philistines could never again threaten Israel's existence.

Following David's conquests, the Philistines gradually fade from the biblical record. Likewise, from the mid-10th century on, the Philistine archaeological sites reflect a decline in wealth and power, although the Philistine culture continued for some centuries after that. The Philistines continue to appear in the Bible and other historical records into the 6th century BC, after which they apparently lost their cultural identity and assimilated into the Canaanite population.

So, to return to our opening question—who were these uncircumcised Philistines, these longstanding enemies of Israel? They were part of a coalition of peoples who left their homeland in the Aegean, left a trail of destruction as they migrated through the eastern Mediterranean, and nearly conquered Egypt before settling along the southern coast of Canaan. They became a military and cultural force that challenged and nearly extinguished the emerging nation of Israel, only to be overcome when David led Israel to a height of power. With this backdrop in mind, we turn to describe the organization, weaponry, and tactics of the Philistine military as best the limited sources from Egypt, the Bible, and archaeology will allow.

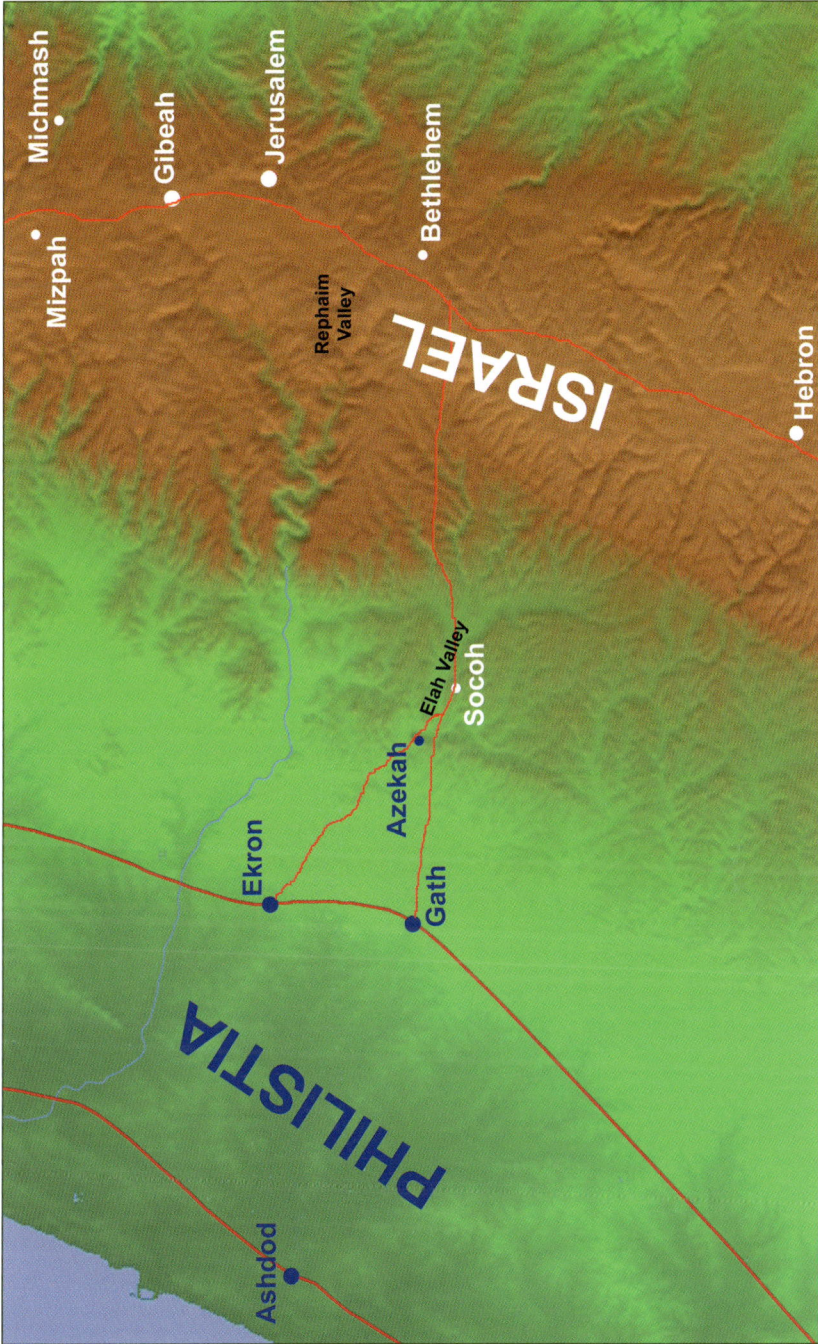

Map 5.3—Locations of Israelite-Philistine battles. Israelite victory at Mizpah; Philistine advance to Michmash; Battle in Elah Valley; David moves capital; Philistines attack via Rephaim Valley.

MILITARY ORGANIZATION

Like most armies of the time, the Philistines primarily utilized infantry and chariotry in their military. The Bible states that they also had archers, foreign troops, and possibly cavalry. As depicted in the reliefs of the naval battle between Ramesses III and the Sea Peoples, they also had some naval forces. The balance of this chapter will discuss each of these aspects along with other known elements of the Philistine military.

Structure

One finds surprisingly little information about the structure of the Philistine military in available sources, given the number of times it appears in the biblical texts and Egyptian reliefs. Clearly the Philistine military followed the general contemporary pattern of infantry complemented by chariotry, but most of the biblical references use terms too vague to describe the structures of these branches. The most complete description may be found in 1 Samuel 13:5, (ESV)—"And the Philistines mustered to fight with Israel, thirty thousand (number discussed below) chariots, and six thousand horsemen (identity discussed below), and troops like the sand on the seashore in multitude." The Bible clearly names the several branches, but supplies little detail about them. The reliefs offer some supplemental information but also raise matters of interpretation that lessen the reliefs' potential value.

For example, the effective Philistine military must have utilized an appropriate hierarchy of officers, but we know little about it. The Bible refers to their military leaders with the general term *śārîm* (שָׂרִים—"commanders" or "officers"—1 Sam. 29:3–4), but how many levels of organization they would have had or what units the officers would have commanded remain unclear. The Bible also uses the term *sĕrānîm* (סְרָנִים—"lords" or "rulers"—Judg. 16:30) for the supreme leaders of the five allied city-states. The term *seren* (סֶרֶן—singular), a non-Hebrew loan word, apparently came from the Aegean.[20] These "lords" governed their five respective city-states, led the nation against Israel in battle, and apparently commanded the troops from their respective cities and regions.[21] For example, Achish the "lord" of Gath marched with the Philistine army to the Jezreel Valley for Saul's final battle and took part in command decisions during that campaign (1 Sam. 29).

1 Samuel 29:2 gives additional information about Philistine military units as well. It describes the Philistines as being organized in units of "hundreds" and "thousands," each of which presumably would have

had officers. See the discussion under "Size of Army" in chapter 2 on the terms "hundreds" and "thousands"—which the Bible frequently uses to describe units in the Israelite military—for possible implications about the Philistine military.

The Bible mentions the Philistine infantry (1 Sam. 13–14, 17, etc.) much more frequently than its officer corps, but it does little to describe the infantry in any detail. Some biblical passages mention infantry units that were involved in tactical maneuvers. Other passages refer to Philistine infantry serving in garrisons stationed at strategic locations in conquered Israelite territory. For example, one finds Philistine infantry at Gibeah, apparently the home of Israel's newly anointed king Saul (1 Sam. 10:5), and at Michmash deep in the heart of the Israelite hill country (1 Sam. 13:23–14:46—see Map 5.3).

Infantry

The Bible also notes that Israelites served with the Philistine military on at least two occasions. The first, brief passage in 1 Samuel notes that an unknown number of Hebrews were serving with the Philistines and even went up with them into the central Israelite heartland to challenge Saul's young army. When Jonathan began the successful charge to drive out the Philistines, the Hebrews, possibly serving as mercenaries, defected to Israel (1 Sam. 14:21). Perhaps this experience helped lead to the Philistine concern and mistrust of the vassal David and his men potentially participating in the battle in the Jezreel Valley in which the Philistines killed Saul and his sons (see 1 Sam. 28:1–2 and 29:1–11, as well as the opening story of Dagarat, above).

Egyptian reliefs provide additional information about the Philistine infantry, offering details about their appearance, weaponry, and possibly their organization. The reliefs typically depict Philistine soldiers as beardless, wearing a distinctive "feathered" headdress (Figs. 5.1, 5.2, 5.4, etc.). The headdress had an

Fig. 5.4—Typical Philistine infantryman as portrayed in Egyptian reliefs

ornamented band that encircled what appears to be a crown of what seem to be feathers, spiked hair, or possibly reeds. It also included a neck-guard to protect the back of the head, and often a chinstrap to hold it in place.[22]

The reliefs further show the Philistines and other Sea Peoples wearing a paneled kilt with broad borders, falling to a point in front and frequently ornamented with three tassels (Figs. 5.4, 5.6, 5.7). On their upper torso the infantrymen usually wear a type of ribbed corselet, often shown with strips resembling ribs. Though the kind of material is not clear, the corselets may have been made from leather, or more likely, metal.

Curiously, the Bible's only detailed description of a Philistine soldier (Goliath in 1 Sam. 17:5–7) differs meaningfully from this rather consistent Egyptian portrayal. However, the Egyptian reliefs date to the early 12th century, and David apparently fought Goliath in the late 11th century. The Bible describes Goliath as wearing a bronze helmet rather than a feathered headdress, and bronze greaves on his lower legs (vs. 5–6) instead of bare legs as pictured in the reliefs. Goliath's helmet and greaves better match the portrayal of Mycenaean warriors on the Warrior Vase (Fig. 5.5) dating from the 12th century in Greece. The Bible also describes Goliath as wearing a coat of scale armor, different from both the ribbed corselet with paneled kilt in the Egyptian reliefs and the long-sleeved corselet with fringed and dotted kilt on the Warrior Vase. The Warrior Vase and the reliefs of Ramesses III date from approximately the same time, but they offer rather different pictures of Aegean warriors. Thus the differences between the Bible's description of Goliath's armor and the Egyptian reliefs nearly two centuries earlier may not be surprising.

Ramesses' reliefs also show the Philistines in battle, giving us some idea of their organization and weaponry, though, as mentioned earlier, the reliefs do present interpretive problems. For example, in the very busy relief of the land battle, the Philistine foot soldiers sometimes appear in units of four, leading some to understand that they normally fought in units of that size A careful examination of the relief, however, clouds that picture. The number of Philistine infantrymen in their "units" ranges from two to eight (see Fig. 5.6 which shows five), with four being the most common. In addition, the Egyptians appear frequently in the relief in groups of four, but they apparently organized their infantry in units of ten (see discussion in chap. 3). This suggests that the artist(s) may have used these groups to give an impression of soldiers fighting in battle rather than to denote the actual unit size.

Fig. 5.5—Mycenaean warrior from Warrior Vase, 12th century. Note bronze helmet instead of feathered headdress and greaves on lower legs, similar to the biblical description of Goliath.

As for weaponry, the Egyptians show Philistine infantrymen usually carrying small, circular shields and one or two spears, which will be discussed below. Instead of spears, a number of Philistines use the straight, double-edged sword characteristic of the Sea Peoples. Curiously, none carry bows, even in the three Philistine chariots shown in the relief. Did the Philistines not use archers in this battle, even in their chariots?

Again, a careful examination suggests that the absence of bows may be stylistic rather than factual. One Philistine chariot does appear to have

Fig. 5.6—Group of five Philistine infantrymen. Two carry spears and three have straight swords. One also carries the typical round shield.

the typical quiver mounted on the outside, pointed to the rear, allowing for easy access to arrows during battle (Fig. 5.2). Was the quiver included by mistake, or did the artist have a reason to omit Philistine bows? None of the Egyptian foot soldiers in the relief carry bows either. In fact, one sees bows only with the Egyptian chariots, including the oversized Ramesses III, who shoots one from his chariot. But from these Egyptians bows, only the pharaoh's numerous giant arrows appear in the relief, naturally causing tremendous damage to the enemy. The artist apparently omitted the arrows from the Egyptian chariots, and most Egyptian depictions of Hittite chariots also omit bows. Why? Perhaps it was meant to avoid showing enemy troops using bows and arrows that could clearly threaten Egyptian troops or even the pharaoh. All of this leaves open the possibility that the Philistines may have had bows in the battle, even though one only sees spears and swords in the relief.

Chariotry   As mentioned above, three Philistine chariots appear in the reliefs of Ramesses III, two of which appear in Fig. 5.2. All have wheels with six spokes and are drawn by two horses, like the contemporary Egyptian chariots. The axle appears attached at or near the rear of the Philistine chariot body, reflecting high-quality construction. As noted earlier, one Philistine chariot appears to carry the typical quiver that one would use for arrows. This quiver might hold the spears that most of the chariot riders are carrying, though the relative size of the spears to the case and the angle of mounting make this rather unlikely. Curiously, the Philistine chariots usually carry a driver plus *two* warriors, unlike the driver plus a single warrior of the contemporary Egyptian chariots. One of the Philistine chariot-warriors bears a round shield, typical of the Philistines, and three of the four carry pairs of spears much like the infantrymen's. Did the chariots function as troop carriers to move foot soldiers into place, or did the artist choose not to portray bows in the hands of the enemy, giving them the weapons of their infantrymen instead? One cannot be sure, but the latter may be more likely.[23]

The Bible adds just two references about Philistine chariots, and both prove difficult to understand. The first states that the Philistines assembled "thirty thousand chariots and six thousand horsemen and troops like the sand on the seashore in multitude" (1 Sam. 13:5, ESV), presenting a *very* high number of chariots.[24] The alternate reading of three thousand chariots (as in the NIV) better fits with the numbers of chariots known at the time. In addition, given the hilly, rocky terrain around Michmash, one wonders how even three thousand chariots could have maneuvered there. The term "thousand" may better be translated "units" instead.[25] A conjectured size of ten chariots per unit, as the Egyptians apparently had (see discussion in chapter 2), would mean that the Philistines may have taken approximately three hundred (or even just thirty) chariots into the hill country to confront the Israelites—still a substantial force considering the terrain and the opponent.

Next, we turn to the "six thousand horse(men)" of 1 Samuel 13:5. The term "horse" or "horsemen" (פָּרָשִׁים—*pārāšîm*) could mean charioteers—those who drove or rode in the chariots—arguably the most natural reading. If the Philistines were using two men per chariot by the time of their wars against Saul, then six thousand charioteers in three thousand chariots would fit nicely. The term could also mean simply "horses," with six thousand horses pulling three thousand chariots,[26] or the term might refer to men who rode horses, i.e. cavalry. If "cavalry" is the correct interpretation, the text would refer to chariots, cavalry, and infantry, with the numbers of the two types of equestrian troops dependent on how one understands the numbers and interpretation of the term "thousand/unit" (אֶלֶף—*'eleph*). However one understands the numbers and the meaning of "horse(men)," 1 Samuel 13:5 is clearly saying that the Philistines mustered a vast and formidable force that the Israelites could not match, and therefore needed God's help to win.

In the second biblical reference to Philistine chariots (2 Sam. 1:6), a fugitive gives a false report to David about Saul's death, apparently in order to gain favor with David. The fugitive reports that he killed the Israelite king when Saul was already mortally wounded and the Philistine "chariots and their drivers (בַּעֲלֵי הַפָּרָשִׁים—*ba'ălê happārāšîm*—lit. "masters of the horses") in hot pursuit." Although the man lied about killing Saul, his description about the Philistine forces may well be factual. If so, he uses a unique expression[27] to describe the men associated with the horses. As before, this term could refer to charioteers or cavalry troops, thus again suggesting that the Philistines may have had cavalry by this time.

Little archaeological evidence currently exists for Philistine chariotry apart from a two-faced linchpin uncovered at Ekron that was probably used to secure a chariot wheel to its axle.[28] This means that the Egyptian relief portraying three Philistine chariots gives our best information by far about what Philistine chariots may have looked like.

Navy

We turn from the Philistines' land forces to their navy, assuming they had one. Even though the Bible includes many references to this particular group of Sea Peoples, it makes no mention of Philistine ships or navy. The Egyptian reliefs and archaeological finds in Israel show that, in general, the Sea Peoples must have been skilled sailors, which presumably would have included the Philistines as well. As discussed in chapter 3, both the Egyptians and Sea Peoples used warships in their naval battle in 1179 BC. The Sea Peoples' ships (Figs. 4.10, 5.7) had a single, loose-footed sail (furled at the top) on a single mast with a crow's nest on top. The ships' hulls have projections resembling birds' heads fore and aft, as well as platforms on each end where troops stood to fight. The relief depicts the Sea Peoples' ships with rudders but no oars, suggesting that they

Fig. 5.7—Philistine ship from sea battle, 1179 BC. Note single mast with sail furled at top, crow's nest, birds' heads(?) on bow and stern, and absence of oars.

were powered by wind alone or may have been caught by surprise and did not have time to deploy their oars.[29]

Other sources suggest that the Philistines and the Sea Peoples in general may have brought about a number of advances in naval technology. The Egyptian ships portrayed in the naval battle against the Sea Peoples show a number of significant improvements over earlier Egyptian shipbuilding techniques, including the loose-footed sail and crow's nest. Since many of these improvements also appear on the ships of the Sea Peoples, the concepts may have originated in the Aegean. Archaeological finds also suggest that the Sea Peoples introduced other advances in naval technology, like the composite anchor (a stone anchor with holes for wooden staves to hold on to the mud on the bottom) and ashlar (square-cut stone) structures and quays.[30]

Role of the Gods

Although the evidence is somewhat sketchy, the Philistine gods appear to have played a meaningful role in the Philistines' military activities, much like in other nearby cultures of the time. The numerous statues of goddesses unearthed at Philistine sites suggest that the Philistines worshiped the Great Goddess, or Mother Goddess, of the Aegean world when they first came to Canaan.[31] By the time they emerged in the biblical record, however, the Philistines had apparently adopted Canaanite deities[32] and included these gods in their military activity. The Philistines seem to have interpreted certain events in nature as acts of some god, as when thunder caused them to panic and lose a battle to an overmatched Israelite force (1 Sam. 7:10). The Philistines carried their idols to the battlefield (2 Sam. 5:21), and their war trophies often ended up in the temples of their gods.[33] Philistine priests appear only in 1 Samuel 5–6, giving advice about what to do with the captured Israelite Ark, but they may well have played a significant role in military activity as well. The Philistines also practiced divination (1 Sam. 6:2; Isa. 2:6), which presumably would have dealt with military activity for such a militaristic people. The Philistines seem to have involved their gods in battle rather like the other peoples of their day.

WEAPONS

Our sources of knowledge about Philistine weaponry, like those that mention its military organization, are somewhat uneven. The Egyptian reliefs provide much information, as do archaeological finds. The biblical accounts are less helpful, the description of Goliath in 1 Samuel 17 notwithstanding.

The scriptural reference to the Philistines' monopoly on metalworking during the early Israelite monarchy has been understood to mean iron, but the text describes metalworking in general without mentioning either iron or bronze.[34] The Philistines apparently used their military superiority to prevent the Israelites from developing their own metalworking industry, gaining an economic advantage as well as preventing the Israelites from producing their own metal weapons. The archaeological record confirms that the Philistines indeed enjoyed a technological advantage during this time.[35]

Short-Range Weapons

Sword

The Philistines used their metalworking industry to produce swords, spears, and daggers for close fighting.

The Egyptian reliefs typically depict the Philistines and other Sea Peoples carrying long, tapering, two-edged swords with midrib (see Figs. 5.4, 5.6, 5.7). A sample of this type of sword (Fig. 5.8) from the 12th–11th century was discovered near Joppa in Philistia.[36] This sword first appears in Egyptian reliefs[37] with the arrival of the Sea Peoples in the 13th century, and it became the dominant type of cut-and-thrust sword in the eastern Mediterranean.

Fig. 5.8—Long (3' 5") tapering sword from Philistia, 12th–11th centuries

Spear

In addition to swords, the Egyptian reliefs also show Philistine infantry, chariotry, and naval troops carrying one or two spears, each approximately five feet long (Figs. 5.2, 5.6, 5.9[38]). The Bible highlights two Philistine spears for their spearheads of enormous size (Goliath's iron spearhead, weighing 600 shekels (ca. sixteen pounds—1 Sam. 17:7) and Ishbi-benob's bronze spearhead, weighing 300 shekels (ca. eight pounds—2 Sam. 21:16)). Though

Fig. 5.9—Spearhead (4.7" long), hammered from bronze sheet metal

perhaps not represented in the reliefs, daggers, the final type of short-range weapon, have surfaced in excavations at Ashdod; one was made entirely of bronze, the other with a bronze handle and an iron blade.[39]

Medium-Range Weapons

Javelin

The one example of a medium-range Philistine weapon comes from the description of Goliath in 1 Samuel 17. The text says that along with his spear and sword, Goliath also carried a javelin, presumably for hurling a moderate distance.[40] Thus with his sword, spear, and javelin, Goliath had only short- and medium-range weapons when facing David, who carried only the long-range sling. David could and did effectively attack the Philistine from a greater distance, but he would have suffered a significant disadvantage had the two closed to close range.

Long-Range Weapons

Bow

A limited amount of textual and archaeological evidence indicates that the Philistines used the long-range bow. Excavations have recovered Philistine arrowheads (Fig. 5.10).[41] The Bible's parallel accounts of Saul's death state that Philistine archers critically wounded him before he fell on his sword (1 Sam. 31:3; 1 Chron. 10:3). Finally, as discussed earlier, the Egyptian relief with Philistine chariots shows one chariot with what appears to be a quiver, though bows and arrows are noticeably absent from the relief, perhaps for

Fig. 5.10—Arrowhead (2.75"), bronze, with flat mid-rib

ideological reasons. Thus it appears that the Philistines utilized archers like other contemporary armies, though the lack of conclusive proof that their chariots carried archers casts some doubt on the issue.

Defensive Equipment

Also like other contemporary armies, the Philistines protected their warriors with shields, head coverings, and different types of body armor, often portrayed in the Egyptian reliefs. As discussed and pictured earlier (Figs. 5.4, 5.6, 5.7), the Philistines carried round, convex shields varying in size, with a handle in the center, and occasionally decorated with circles apparently representing metal knobs or bosses fastened to the leather covering.[42] The Philistines' headdresses were apparently made from leather and covered the backs of their necks, fastening with a chinstrap. The encircling band that held the protruding "feathers" was decorated in various patterns (Figs. 5.1, 5.2, 5.4, 5.7), perhaps representing rank or tribe. As noted earlier, they wore ribbed corselets on the chest, apparently made of overlapping bands of leather or metal, on top of a shirt. The bands usually curved upward as they met in the middle, perhaps to imitate human ribs, but occasionally they curved down (Figs. 5.4, 5.7).

As discussed above under "Infantry," the Bible's detailed description of Goliath's defensive equipment (1 Sam. 17:4–7) differs somewhat from the typical Egyptian portrayals. He wore greaves and a bronze helmet instead of a feathered headdress, plus scale armor instead of a ribbed corselet. In addition, a shield-bearer went before him carrying what must have been a large shield, rather than the small round shields that consistently appear in the Egyptian reliefs.

In summary, a few of the elements in the Philistines' military gear stand out from the other militaries of the day. Their distinctive headdress and long, tapering sword set them apart somewhat. All in all, though, the Philistines seem to have used offensive and defensive equipment consistent with other militaries in the region for that time period.

TACTICS

The final section of this chapter will describe the strategy and tactics that the Philistines used to conduct their military campaigns, given the limited information from the Bible and Egyptian reliefs. Although the Israelites and Egyptians both give us some information about the Philistines, they were also both enemies, and their descriptions are limited in scope.

Logistics

The Egyptian relief portraying the land battle the Egyptians fought against the Sea Peoples includes some information about how the Philistines and related peoples transported their people and belongings. The relief portrays several heavy carts made of crossed bars or perhaps woven reeds (Fig. 5.11). These carts roll on two solid wheels, pulled by four oxen. They carry women, children, and undoubtedly belongings as well, apparently as part of a civilian population moving along with or behind the army, intending to settle lands that their military conquered. Although some soldiers armed with sword and shield guard the carts in the reliefs, they become victims of a surprise Egyptian attack and must have suffered heavy casualties.

Fig. 5.11—Oxcarts from relief of land battle. Philistine families shown under attack from Egyptian troops (omitted from drawing).

Fortifications

After falling to the Egyptians in the land and sea battles of 1179 BC, the Philistines settled along the southern coastal plain of Canaan. Excavations at their sites reveal that the Philistines established well-planned and fortified major cities, often ringed with thick walls built of sun-dried mud-brick, sometimes strengthened by stone.[43] The cities' walls, up to sixteen feet thick, connected to city gates as large as 45 x 53 feet (Fig. 5.12). Certain Philistine sites also boasted a fortress inside the city wall and a mud-brick-lined glacis[44]—an artificial, solid, steep slope constructed below a city's walls to help keep attackers away. The Philistine fortifications resembled other strong fortifications of the time, but like most others, they eventually fell to stronger foes.

Battle Tactics

As we have seen to this point, the Philistines boasted an effective military consisting of infantry, chariotry, archery, possibly cavalry, and some vassals or mercenaries. They were armed with effective weaponry for their time and protected their cities with strong fortifications. The numerous scriptural passages about the Israelites fighting the Philistines give some indication of Philistine military strategy.

One can detect what appear to be various overall approaches they used when attacking their Israelite neighbors in the hills to the east. First they engaged in border skirmishes, as reflected in the stories of Samson (Judg. 14–16). Toward the beginning of Samuel's ministry, they won a

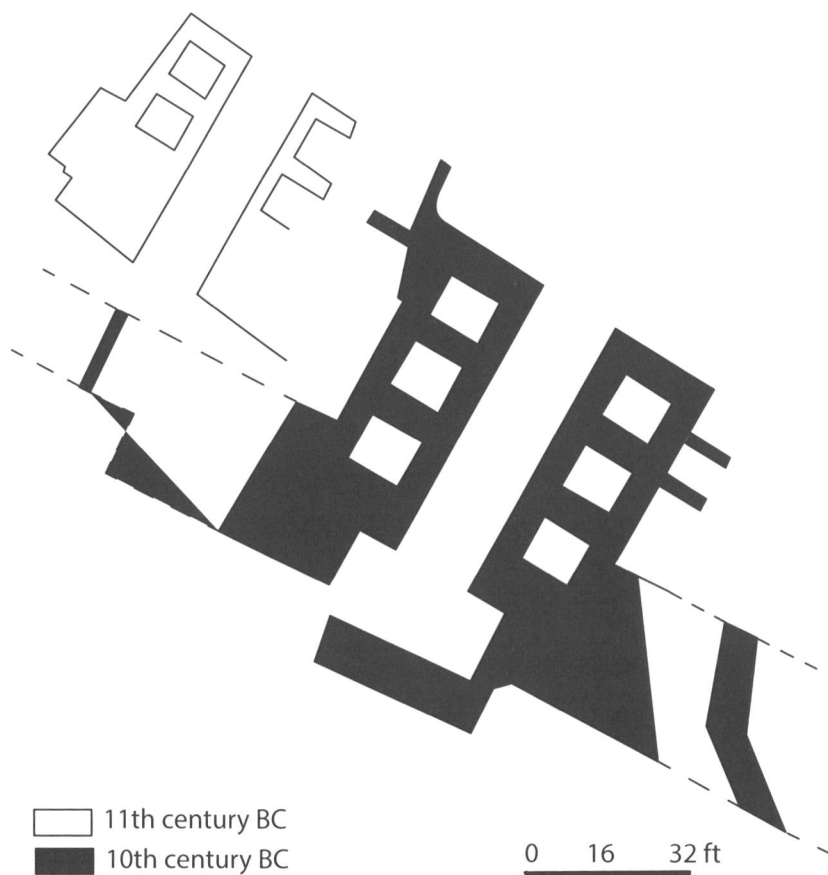

11th century BC
10th century BC

0   16   32 ft

Fig. 5.12—Ground plan of city gates from Philistine Ashdod. King David may have destroyed the smaller gate built in the 11th cent. and King Uzziah may have destroyed the larger, later gate and connected city wall (2 Chron. 26:6–7).

decisive border battle at Aphek (1 Sam. 4), and then tried an unsuccessful attack up into the Israelite hill country (1 Sam. 7). They continued attacking in the Israelite heartland during Saul's early reign (1 Sam. 13–14), but were driven back in what must have proven to be a shocking loss. The Philistines then pulled back to the more familiar coastal regions and tried to take land in the Elah Valley along the Israelite border, but again they suffered a surprising loss (1 Sam. 17). Finally, they boldly moved north to take the Jezreel Valley, successfully drawing King Saul and his army out of the hills and dealing them a crushing blow (1 Sam. 28–29, 31). When David assumed the Israelite throne, they made one move into the hills to erode his increasing strength, but again they fled in defeat back to the safety of their homeland (2 Sam. 5). Sometime after this, David subdued the Philistines, but the Bible does little more than briefly summarize his conquest (2 Sam. 8:1).

Despite recording these battles, the Bible offers little help in understanding particular battle tactics. Most often the Bible describes the Philistine attacks with general terms like "deployed their forces to meet Israel" (1 Sam. 4:2), "gathered their forces for war" (1 Sam. 17:1), and "(drew) up their lines" (1 Sam. 17:21), without describing specifically what those expressions meant or how they appeared. When arrayed for battle, the Philistines apparently relied primarily on their line of infantry assembled in close formation, with support from chariotry and archers (1 Sam. 31:3; 2 Sam. 1:6).

One can better discern Philistine strategy regarding occupation and exploitation of conquered Israelite territory. Once they captured new land, the Philistines established garrisons or outposts at strategic locations (1 Sam. 10:5; 13:3, 23; 14:11; 2 Sam. 23:14). They sent out raiding parties from these garrisons (1 Sam. 13:17–18—in three companies), perhaps to take plunder, suppress rebellion, force payment of taxes, and/or enforce the prohibition against Israelite metalworking (1 Sam. 13:19–22).

The famous confrontation between David and Goliath (1 Sam. 17) offers an excellent example of the relatively uncommon practice of representative warfare. In representative warfare, two armies agreed to decide a battle by having single champions from each army meet to fight. In this way, the two sides thus avoided engaging their entire armies, sparing both sides the greater bloodshed of full-scale battle.[45] In the biblical story, the Philistine champion issued his challenge twice daily to the enemy army arrayed for battle, which sent out its champion only after considerable delay. The surprising victory by the lightly armed and unarmored Israelite sent the Philistines fleeing, pursued by an Israelite army energized by the surprising victory. The Philistines fled rather than honor the promise of servitude as stated in the terms of the conflict (v. 9), apparently not an uncommon response for the side that lost battles of this type.[46] If the defeated army typically did not honor the terms of engagement, this may explain why one does not see representative warfare used more often.

For information and illustrations of the sea and land battles between the Philistines and other Sea Peoples against the Egyptians in 1179 BC, see chapter 2.

Conclusion

Overall, the available textual and archaeological sources paint a less complete picture for Philistine military practices than they did for the Egyptians. Nonetheless, one can still gain a general understanding of Philistine organization, weaponry, and tactics. The Philistines stand out because of their Aegean origin and particular customs—such as their distinct headdress and tapering swords—but otherwise their military practices seem to fit with other contemporary armies in the region. For Israel, this uncircumcised enemy nation to the west gave them particular trouble as they sought to establish themselves in their highland home, but effective leadership coupled with divine blessing ultimately overcame the Philistines' natural advantages.

NOTES

1   Excavations at the Philistine city of Ashdod recovered pottery inscribed with the name *d-g-r-t,* perhaps *Dagarat.* The find dates to the 8th century BC, approximately three centuries later than our story, but it apparently represents an authentic Philistine name. See Trude and Moshe Dothan, *People of the Sea,* 186–87.

2   Excavations for the Philistine occupational levels at Ashkelon and Ekron recovered bones suggesting that the Philistines ate more pork than did the Canaanites, and sometimes dog as well. Twenty percent of the bones recovered were pork, an increase from five percent in the earlier Canaanite levels. The excavations also found dog bones that had marks from butchering, suggesting slaughter for food ("Love That Pork," *BAR,* May/June 2006: 14).

3   Our fictitious warrior has served as a soldier since age twenty, a common age to begin serving as a soldier in the ancient Near East (cf. Num. 1, 26). Our

text calls him old at thirty-five because the available evidence suggests that the life expectancy for common people during this time may have been less than forty. See Philip J. King and Lawrence E. Stager, *Life in Biblical Israel* (Library of Ancient Israel, Douglas A. Knight, gen. ed. Louisville: Westminster John Knox, 2001), 37.

4   According to U.S. Marine Sgt. Joshua A. Draveling, the ability to fall asleep quickly "is a revered ability amongst Marines. Often with an evening of 4–6 hours, every minute is precious—particularly after marching 18–24 miles with 80–120 pounds of gear."

5   The Philistines honored their chief god, Dagon, in part by keeping the following in his temples as trophies of war: Samson (Judg. 16:21–30, apparently in Gaza), the Ark of the Covenant (1 Sam. 5:1–5, in Ashdod), and Saul's head (1 Chron. 10:10, no location given). The Philistines also revered the Canaanite goddess Ashtoreth (also known as Ishtar/Astarte), the goddess of love and war; they took Saul's armor to Ashtoreth's temple after his death (1 Sam. 31:10). Finally, the Philistines worshipped Baal-zebub at Ekron (2 Kings 1:2–16), probably the same as Baal-zebul in the Greek of Matt. 10:25.

6   The Sea Peoples seem to have originated in the area of Aegean Sea in what is today Greece and western Turkey, perhaps on the island of Crete.

7   The number in David's army apparently grew to 600 by the time of 1 Sam. 27:2.

8   Note in the cited passage that David was actually protecting the Judeans and then lying to his Philistine overlord about his actions.

9   After reading this section of the story, Sgt. Draveling commented, "Dagarat's internal dialogue reminds me of many of my own (thoughts) concerning our allies and their leadership in Iraq."

10 See 1 Sam. 28:5–25 for the account of Saul's fear upon seeing the Philistine army, prompting his desperate, ill-advised visit to a witch. Saul apparently understood from the size of the Philistine force and from Samuel's message that fighting the Philistines meant death. He also seemed to think he had no choice, as he fought them anyway and perished with his sons.

11 Note Ahithophel's advice (later rejected) for Absalom to likewise target David (2 Sam. 17:1–4), as well as the Arameans' similar strategy against Ahab (1 Kings 22:31). The Assyrians also targeted enemy leaders, using lightning attacks by the Assyrian king and his elite troops to kill, capture, or put to flight the enemy commander. See Grayson, "Assyrian Civilization," 220.

12 See 1 Sam. 31 for the brief biblical account of the battle and its aftermath.

13 For more complete overviews of Philistine history and culture, see H. J. Katzenstein, "Philistines: History" and Trude Dothan, "Philistines: Archaeology," *ABD* 5:326–33; and Bustenay Oded, "Israel's Neighbours: The Philistines," in *The Biblical World* (ed. John Barton; 2 vols.; London-New York: Routledge, 2002), 1:492–99.

14 For example, Abraham pursued Lot's captors as far as "Dan" in northern Canaan (Gen. 14:14). The place was called Dan only after the tribe of Dan moved there during the period of the judges (Judg. 18), hundreds of years after Abraham.

15 James B. Pritchard, "The War Against the Peoples of the Sea." *ANET*, 262–63.

16 E.g. G. A. Wainwright, "Some Sea-Peoples," *JEA* 47 (1961): 77–79.

17 As per the discussion in chapter 3, the biblical Exodus apparently took place in the 15th or 13th century. If the earlier date is correct, the Israelites preceded the Philistines to the region but struggled for nearly two centuries during the chaotic period of the judges and still were not well established when the Philistines came. If the Israelites left Egypt in the 13th century, they would have arrived about the same time as the Philistines.

18 The present author wishes to acknowledge Steven P. Lancaster and James M. Monson for their insights into this and other geographical and political realities. See esp. *Regional Study Guide: Introductory Map Studies in the Land of the Bible* (Version 3.1; Rockford, IL: Biblical Backgrounds, 2009), 85–89.

19 The parallel passages in 2 Sam. 8:1 and 1 Chron. 18:1 appear to name different places, but the point remains the same—David was now taking territory from Philistia.

20 For discussion a of the term סֶרֶן, see Kenneth A. Kitchen, "The Philistines," in *Peoples of Old Testament Times.* (ed. D. J. Wiseman; Oxford: Clarendon Press, 1973), 67.; and N. K. Sandars, *Sea Peoples,* 166. A number of biblical texts, including 1 Sam. 21:10–12, refer to Achish, the סֶרֶן of Gath, as "king" (מֶלֶךְ), perhaps a synonym.

21 In the Bible one finds that these "lords" pressed Delilah and then captured Samson (Judg. 16), took action when the captive Israelite Ark brought trouble to Philistia (1 Sam. 5–6), led battles against Israel (1 Sam. 7 and 29), and overruled Achish regarding David's participation in Saul's final battle (1 Sam 29:4–11).

22 G. A. Wainwright ("Some Sea-Peoples," 74–75) and Trude Dothan (*The Philistines and Their Material Culture,* 5) both note that the Egyptians also portrayed the related Tjekker and Denyen with the same distinctive headdress.

23 Some authors interpret the reliefs as accurate and assume that the Philistines did not use bows with their chariots. How might one use a chariot

that carries spear-wielding infantry instead of archers? Perhaps the chariots charged to try to intimidate enemy forces, and then allowed the warriors to dismount quickly for hand-to-hand fighting (So argues T. Dothan in *The Philistines and Their Material Culture,* 7). Such an understanding would mean that the quiver on the Philistine chariot probably appears in error. The present author, by contrast, thinks it more likely that the Philistines did fight with bows from their chariots, and that the artists omitted them for ideological reasons.

24 The 30,000 chariots, as per the Hebrew text of the Old Testament, would mean that the relatively small Philistine nation in the 11th century mustered roughly ten times more chariots than did the Hittites and possibly the Egyptians at their peak of power at the battle of Kadesh in 1275 BC. Did the number in 1 Sam. 13 get changed over time? Two versions of the Old Testament text (the Lucianic recension of the LXX (Greek Old Testament) and the Syriac transla-tion of the OT) followed by the NIV support such an idea. These read only 3,000 chariots—still a large number, but one that would much better fit the numbers of chariots known from the armies of the time period.

25 See the discussion in chapter 2 under "Size of Army" for the possibility that the Hebrew word for "thousand" (אֶלֶף—*'eleph*) might also refer to a military unit of unknown size. Were this understanding correct, it would suggest that the small but emerging power of Philistia mustered thirty (or three) units of chariots plus six units of horse(men) plus infantry.

26 See, for example, *HALOT,* פָּרָשׁ, which lists the three possibilities described here but opts for teams of horses pulling a chariot.

27 *HALOT,* פָּרָשׁ, lists this as the only example for a category of meaning de-scribed as "Misc."

28 Trude and Moshe Dothan, *People of the Sea,* 250–51, pl. 28.

29 Note N. K. Sandars' reasonable argument that the ships must have had oars. *Sea Peoples,* 130.

30 Avner Raban and Robert R. Stieglitz, "The Sea Peoples and Their Contribu-tions to Civilization," *BAR* 17, no. 6 (1991): 36–39.

31 Trude Dothan, *The Philistines and Their Material Culture,* 234–49.

32 The Philistines worshipped Dagon (1 Chron. 10:10) as their chief god (Judg. 16:23). They had temples to Dagon at Gaza, Ashdod, and perhaps Beth Shean. A statue of Dagon stood in the temple in Ashdod (1 Sam. 5:2–4). They also had temples to Baal-zebub (Baal-zebul) in Ekron (2 Kings 1:2), and to Ashtoreth (apparently) in Beth Shean (1 Sam. 31:10).

33 See n. 5 above.

34 Bronze had been the most commonly used metal until ca. 1200 BC.

Metalworkers had long relied on trade to procure the locally unavailable tin, which they mixed with the more common copper to make bronze. When the Late Bronze trade routes collapsed ca. 1200, the metalworkers had to use the more accessible iron. Iron, especially from meteors, had long been known and used as a precious metal.

From the 12th to the 10th centuries, iron overtook bronze as the most commonly used metal in the region. 98% of the metal artifacts found in Palestine and the surrounding regions from the 12th century were bronze, with only 2% iron. In the 11th century, the percentage of iron grew to 14%, and in the 10th century, it comprised the majority with 54%. See Jane C. Waldbaum, *From Bronze to Iron: The Transition from the Bronze Age to the Iron Age in the Eastern Mediterranean* (vol. 54 of Studies in Mediterranean Archaeology series. Göteborg, Sweden: Paul Aströms, 1978), 68–73.

35 In *From Bronze to Iron,* 27, J. Waldbaum states that "much, but not all, of the iron from the 12th and 11th centuries comes from sites occupied by the Philistines." Iron agricultural implements have been found in both Philistia and Israel in the 11th century, but all the iron weapons come from Philistine sites. See James D. Muhly, "How Iron Technology Changed the Ancient World and Gave the Philistines a Military Edge," *BAR* 8, no. 6 (1982): 52.

36 See also Yadin, *Art of Warfare,* 344–45; as well as Dothan, *The Philistines and Their Material Culture,* 12, for caution that this sword might not be Philistine.

37 For an analysis of the imagery in the in Egyptian reliefs, see Rodriquez, *Arsenal,* 43–46.

38 The Philistine spearhead and arrowhead shown in Figs. 5.9 and 5.10 came from Tell Qasile in northern Philistia. For illustrations and descriptions, see Amihai Mazar, *Excavations at Tell Qasile, Part 2, The Philistine Sanctuary: Various Finds, the Pottery, Conclusions, Appendixes* (Qedem 20: Jerusalem: Hebrew University, 1985), 4–5, Fig. 1.

39 Trude Dothan, *The Philistines and Their Material Culture,* pl. 2.2.

40 For a thorough discussion of the translation of the words used for "javelin" and "spear" and the interpretation of Goliath's spear shaft as a "weaver's beam," see Boyd Seevers, "Practice of Ancient Near Eastern Warfare," pp. 269–71, esp. n. 737.

41 The excavations at Tell Qasile unearthed four arrowheads. See A. Mazar, *Excavations at Tell Qasile, Part 2,* 4–5.

42 Trude Dothan, *The Philistines and Their Material Culture,* 11–12.

43 Amihai Mazar, *Archaeology of the Land of the Bible 10,000–586 B.C.E.* (Anchor Bible Reference Library; New York: Doubleday, 1990), 317.

44   Among the strongest-known Philistine fortifications were those of Ashdod. See Moshe Dothan, "Ashdod," *NEAEHL* 1: 96–100.

45   Representative warfare was better known as a Hellenistic or Arabic concept. See Roland de Vaux, "Single Combat in the Old Testament," in *The Bible and the Ancient Near East,* trans. Damian McHugh (London: Darton, Longman & Todd, 1966), 128–29. Yigal Yadin (*AWBL,* 267) notes an example from Egypt's 12th Dynasty and suggests that the practice may have died out in the ancient Near East, then returned as an Aegean practice via the Philistines.

46   For a parallel event involving the Hittite military, see Harry A. Hoffner, Jr., "A Hittite Analogue to the David and Goliath Contest of Champions?" (*CBQ* 30 (1968) 220–25). Hoffner points out that a contest of champions must not only involve single combatants, the encounter must take the place of a general engagement by two larger forces. This distinguishes it from a simple duel between individuals. In the Hittite example, Hattusilis, a general who later became king, engaged the "one who marches in front" (cf. Hebrew הַבֵּנַיִם אִישׁ *'îš habbēnayim* —"man between two (armies)"—1 Sam. 17:4), representing the enemy force. Then, when Hattusilis killed their champion, "the rest of the enemy fled," as did the Philistines in 1 Samuel 17:51. One finds a final parallel after the battle when Hattusilis took the weapon he used and devoted it to the goddess Ishtar in her sanctuary, as David dedicated the sword he used to kill Goliath in the sanctuary of Yahweh (1 Sam. 21:8–9).

ASSYRIA:
BRUTAL MASTERS OF THE ANCIENT NEAR EAST—PART 1

6

FORCED TO FIT IN: ASSYRIA CONQUERS LACHISH

Nabu-belu-ukin[1] felt a gnawing sense of conflict over what his duties had called him to do, and he found it a rare and troubling sensation. Usually he just decided what to do, or received orders from his superior officers, and acted without meaningful reflection. That's just how he lived—do what you need to do and don't worry about it. From time to time, people like his Assyrian wife had commented on how his way of thinking led to actions that seemed inconsistent, but until now that hadn't bothered Nabu-belu-ukin. When he forced himself to stop and think about his life, this chariot commander could see how his life had taken a number of twists and turns, but he didn't waste time or energy pondering their ramifications. *Why worry about things? Do what you want, but when ordered, why not just fit in?* Such was the relatively simple but apparently successful philosophy of this tough and determined exile from Israel. It enabled him to fit into and flourish remarkably well in the Assyrian-controlled world of the 8th century BC.

Nabu-belu-ukin had always fit in well, beginning with his birth into a prominent Jewish family in the Israelite capital of Samaria in 740 BC. His parents had named him Jehoiachin,[2] which meant "Yahweh has established (him)," even though they weren't overly religious. A strong, tough boy and the youngest of six children, Jehoiachin had little trouble establishing his own identity. When his oldest brother had gone off to military service, somehow Jehoiachin managed to take over his brother's living space in one of the best parts of their comfortable but somewhat crowded home. But when that brother returned from the army a year later, he pushed Jehoiachin and his belongings back to a much lesser spot. Jehoiachin couldn't win that battle, at least not yet, so he went along with it. He thought it worked best to win by force whenever possible and adapt as needed when winning proved impossible.

Soon Jehoiachin began to make his place in Israelite society as well, thanks to his strong personality and his father's position as an official in the court of Israel's king Pekah. Just before Jehoiachin's birth, his father had helped Pekah overthrow the reigning Israelite king in a bold coup in the royal citadel in Samaria (2 Kings 15:25).[3] For many years thereafter, Jehoiachin's father and family had enjoyed the fruits of that victory.

When Jehoiachin was still a boy, an unwelcome reality began to reimpose itself on Israel. The nation had formerly paid heavy tribute to the powerful but distant nation of Assyria, but it had reversed course at the time of Pekah's overthrow and began withholding the annual payments. Now, some eight years later, the day of reckoning had come. The Assyrian army, led by king Tiglath-pileser III, invaded from the north, intent on demonstrating what happened to those who resisted Assyrian will. In successive campaigns over three years, the Assyrians conquered all of northern Israel as well as its lands in the Transjordan and along the coast (Map 6.1). The Assyrians threatened to return and conquer the rest of the much-reduced nation as well.

Jehoiachin observed that many of Israel's leaders, including his father, seemed terribly distressed by this turn of events, and young Jehoiachin didn't fully understand why. True, many Israelites had died fighting the Assyrians, including two of Jehoiachin's brothers. Losing family members and large parts of one's country was difficult, but Jehoiachin wondered why Israel didn't adapt and submit to Assyria rather than fight. When he suggested this to his father, his father tried to explain that Israel needed to be free and ally with other like-minded nations in the region to avoid paying Assyria's overwhelming tribute. Jehoiachin merely shrugged. Since Assyria clearly had the stronger army, why not just fit into their world? Wouldn't his brothers still be alive if Israel's leaders had done that?

Jehoiachin also noticed that some of the people who had the greatest difficulty with the Assyrian threat were the most religious people, including a few of his friends. They seemed confident that Yahweh, Israel's national God, would save them. Jehoiachin scoffed. He knew that most of those same people worshipped other gods as well, including many of the priests. Even if Yahweh *could* protect Israel from Assyria, *would* he? Why should he be faithful to a nation that wasn't faithful to him?

Meanwhile, though, Jehoiachin's nation was attempting to resist Assyria, and he concluded the best thing to do was to fit in. His

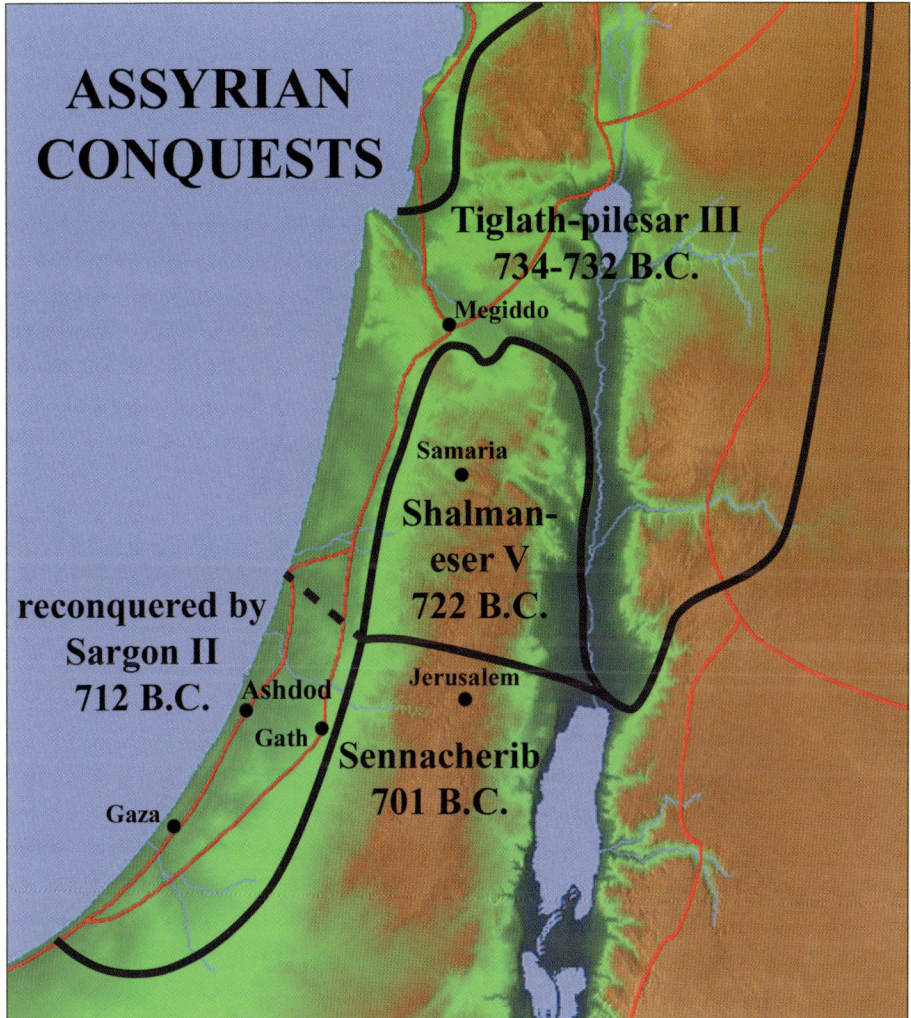

Map 6.1—Expanding Assyrian control in southern Levant

toughness, determination, and willingness to take orders made him eminently suited for a successful military career. He decided early on to become a charioteer. Israel had earned a reputation for its excellent chariotry,[4] and a career as a chariot-warrior or, better yet, a chariot officer, offered excellent possibilities for those who excelled. The official age to begin military service had been twenty, but with the current Assyrian threat, the Israelite army was taking any willing and capable male. A young, strong, focused person like Jehoiachin proved an especially worthy recruit, even at age fifteen.

Soon Jehoiachin left the hilly region of Samaria and went off to a military training camp near the coast to train as a chariot-warrior. Thus he was not in the city of Samaria when the Assyrians, now under Shalmaneser V, invaded and laid siege to the city. The earlier Israelite kings Omri, Ahab (1 Kings 16:23–29), and their successors had built the city well, and it withstood the Assyrians for three years (2 Kings 17:5; 18:9–12). The Israelite troops like Jehoiachin who were outside the city did what they could to harass the Assyrians and relieve the pressure on their capital, but to no avail. In 722 BC, the Assyrians captured the city, deported many of the inhabitants, and made the region into an Assyrian province (Map 6.1). Israel had refused to fit in to Assyrian power and was destroyed as a result. Jehoiachin and many others took note of this, as the Assyrians intended.

Now the remaining Israelites such as Jehoiachin had to decide what to do about the new reality of Assyrian dominance—resist openly, cooperate grudgingly, or embrace the new situation. Jehoiachin had no trouble deciding; he would fit in. In fact, he determined to accept this new reality completely, regardless of the costs. The Assyrians were obviously going to dominate for a long time, so why not abandon the mare and ride the stallion?[5]

Other Israelite charioteers felt the same way. Israelite soldiers had served as mercenaries in the past (e.g. 2 Chron. 25:6), so they understood working under a foreign power. At this point they couldn't hire themselves out to the Assyrians as mercenaries, but they could offer their military skills and join the Assyrian army permanently. They knew that such a move would probably mean leaving Israel forever and moving to Assyria. They also knew that they would have to fight for a nation and for gods that seemed strange and even distasteful, but the alternatives were worse. If they tried to stay where they were, they might be deported to work as forced laborers constructing buildings for Assyria (Fig. 6.1), or be exiled and settled as farmers in some frontier region of the empire to help raise food for the Assyrian army. Even if they were permitted to remain in their now-devastated land, it would mean struggling to survive with those who were left, with much of their food and the goods they produced going as tribute to the conquerors. Who wanted that? Wasn't it preferable to join the conquerors and enjoy the benefits of their might? Jehoiachin had no doubts.

He jumped feet-first into his new world, presenting himself to the new Assyrian governor to offer his services as a charioteer. Jehoiachin even introduced himself using a Babylonian name, Nabu-belu-ukin— "Nabu has established the ruler." The meaning largely paralleled his former Jewish name, except now it acknowledged Nabu, the Babylonian god of wisdom, instead of Yahweh as the one who set up the ruler. In addition, the ruler to whom he now submitted wore an Assyrian crown rather than an Israelite one. Nabu-belu-ukin was turning his back on his king, his people, his homeland, and his God. Since he couldn't win, he would assimilate and do his best to profit from the change. His family and most of his friends didn't approve, but many of his colleagues made the same move. They too cast their lots with their conquerors, but only a few took Assyrian names like Nabu-belu-ukin. Trading a name that honored Yahweh for one that honored an Assyrian god was just too pagan for most of these hardened military men.

Fig. 6.1—Captives doing forced labor for Assyria. Captives pull heavy ropes, dragging enormous stone bull colossus to Sennacherib's palace under construction in Nineveh. Similar dress and appearance with deportees from Lachish (see Fig. 6.7) suggests these are Judeans.

As per Assyrian custom, the new governor at Samaria also served as a high-ranking military official, and he was delighted to accept this group of Israelite charioteers. Assyria had made it a regular practice to incorporate the best of their conquered soldiers into the Assyrian army. All received additional training and had to pass several tests of loyalty. Some then stayed and served in their home regions under the command of the provincial governor, but those whose skills were most needed would be transferred to Assyria to take an assignment in the royal army. The new governor of Samaria began processing these new troops, confident that the king would be glad to get a large group of proven charioteers from this region. Levantine charioteers were renowned for their skill, and getting so many made the governor look good—very good. If a few more joined, he might even be able to send an entire unit of fifty.

The governor did get his fifty, and they passed their training and tests of loyalty. In due time, they were transferred to the Assyrian homeland and were even kept together as a unit. Many foreign soldiers served in the Assyrian army, but this group of Samarian charioteers gained the special distinction of keeping their identity as "the Samarians." No other unit bore the name of a city or nation, especially from a conquered region. The unit was unique,[6] and the man who became their commander, Nabu-belu-ukin, was exceptional.

Nabu-belu-ukin and his unit served their Assyrian masters well, and did their part to help enlarge and control the Assyrian empire during the long and fruitful reign of Sargon II. The Assyrian army relished the new and expanded military compound that Sargon built in his new capital of Dur-Sharrukin (discussed below under "Historical Backgrounds"). At one point their military activity even took the Samarians back near their homeland when Sargon used the army to conquer Philistine cities such as Ashdod and Gath that were located along the southern coast of Canaan (Map 6.1). The men had no qualms about operating as military tools for their conquerors near their home region. In fact, they reveled in their power to help conquer important cities belonging to the Philistines, an ancient enemy of their ancestral people.

The men also became more and more integrated into Assyrian culture, with most of them taking Assyrian wives. These wives bore Assyrian children who grew up speaking Akkadian or Aramaic, like most other Assyrians of the late 8th century BC, and had little appreciation for their fathers' language or background from a distant, conquered land. Indeed, the children had little reason to concern themselves with their paternal

Fig. 6.2—Early Assyrian light chariot with mail-clad warrior and driver, plus infantryman and archer

Fig. 6.3—High-ranking Assyrian officer like Nabu-belu-ukin before Sennacherib at Lachish, standing on a slope. Note conical helmet with earflaps, coat of mail, a short, fringed garment with edge hanging down, leggings, and boots. One hand holds typical officer's mace, other hand rests on sheathed sword.

ancestry, as it caused no concern in their culture. Much of Assyria was comprised of mingled national groups for whom ethnic identity and differences played little or no part.[7] Their fathers had made great sacrifices to fit into the Assyrian world, but just one generation later it came naturally.

When Sargon II died in 705 BC, his death launched a series of events that were rather typical for an ancient Near Eastern empire. Sargon's son Sennacherib, an experienced administrator and military officer, took the throne. Despite the likelihood that Sennacherib would prove to be a capable ruler, many of Assyria's vassals seized the opportunity to cease paying the heavy annual tribute imposed by Assyria. Babylon asserted its independence in the south, as did an alliance of nations in the west that included King Hezekiah of Judah and the rulers of a number of Phoenician and Philistine cities along the coast, with the encouragement of Egypt. In response, Sennacherib suppressed the rebellion in Babylon with the ferocity that one might expect from a new overlord who wished to be feared. Then, in 701 BC, Sennacherib turned his attention to the west.

Sennacherib naturally took the best of his military with him on this campaign, including what remained of his charioteers from Samaria.[8] By now the Samarian unit had been broken up and the charioteers reassigned, and only a handful of the original members remained. Some twenty years had passed, and many had been killed in

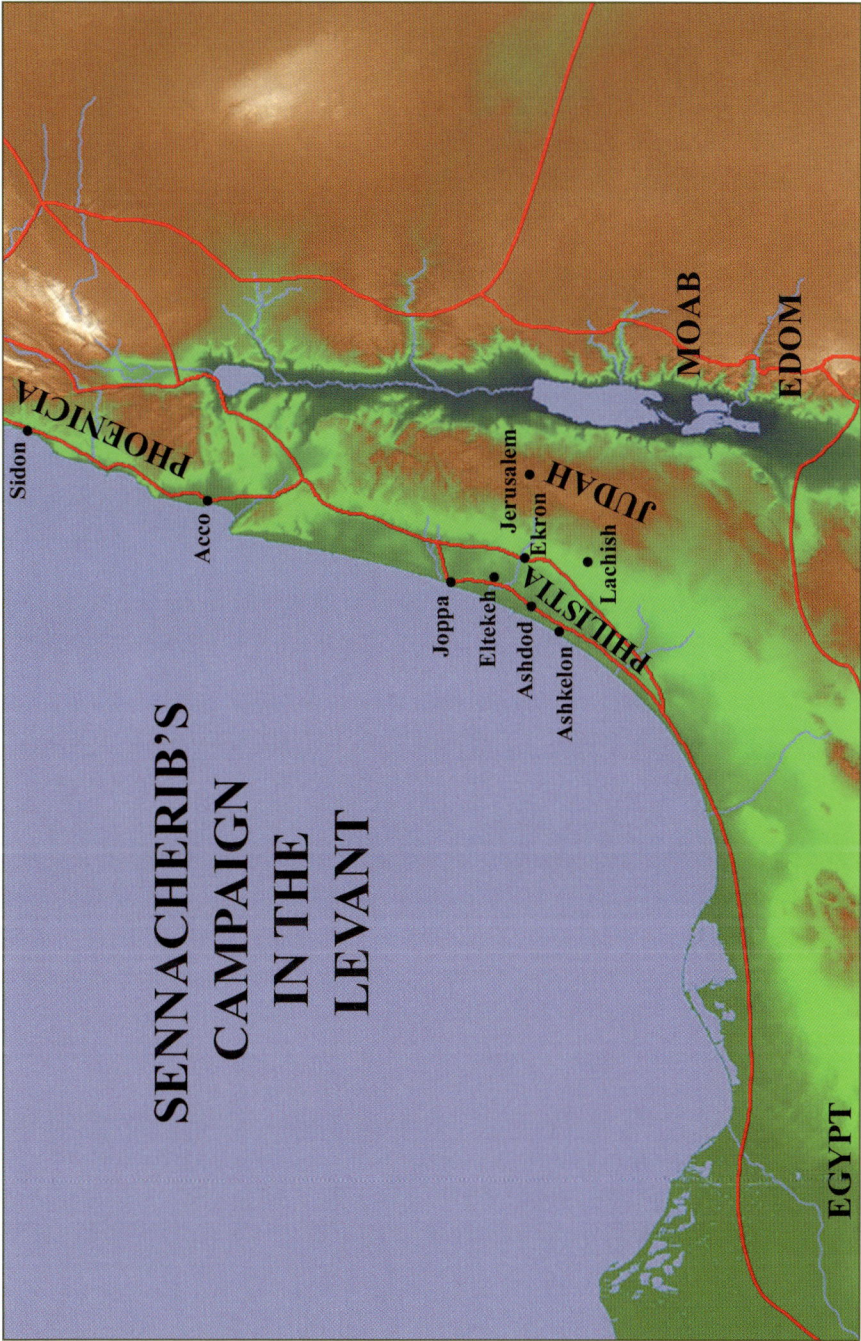

SENNACHERIB'S CAMPAIGN IN THE LEVANT

PHOENICIA

Sidon

Acco

Joppa

Eltekeh

Ashdod

Ashkelon

PHILISTIA

Jerusalem

Ekron

Lachish

JUDAH

MOAB

EDOM

EGYPT

Map 6.2—Sennacherib's campaign in Phoenicia, Philistia, and Judah

battle or retired. The few that remained were now seasoned veterans in the twilight of their careers, with the majority commanding their own units.

Their original commander, Nabu-belu-ukin, had indeed fit nicely into the Assyrian military machine. He was still the same confident, decisive person who had taken command two decades before, only now he also had the experience and wisdom accumulated from numerous campaigns and scores of battles. What he may have lost in quickness over the years, he more than made up for in skill and confidence. Several years earlier he had won promotion to the head of the entire Assyrian chariot force. He also held the title of vizier, or counselor to the king, and had earned a place in the king's trusted inner circle.[9]

Nabu-belu-ukin and his chariots comprised a key part of Sennacherib's army that marched west to attack the disloyal vassal states in Phoenicia, Philistia, and Judah (Map 6.2). By the time the Assyrians arrived at the Phoenician coast, nearly all of the formerly rebellious vassals in the region surrendered and presented their tribute. Only the king of Sidon, perhaps the leader of the rebellion, dared not face Sennacherib. He "fled overseas far-off and disappeared forever,"[10] and Sennacherib replaced him with a man of proven loyalty.

Then the Assyrian army marched south to the southern coastal plain of Philistia (Map 6.2). Sennacherib wrote that numerous kings in the region, including those from Ashdod and the Transjordanian kingdoms of Moab and Edom, "brought me sumptuous presents as their abundant audience-gift, fourfold, and kissed my feet."[11] Next he had to deal with Ashkelon and Ekron, whose former kings had wished to remain loyal to Assyria but had been ousted by residents who wanted to rebel instead. Sennacherib deported the new king of Ashkelon along with his entire extended family in punishment, and he killed the rebels in Ekron, hanging their corpses on the towers of the city's wall. He then reinstated the former kings, imposed heavy tribute on the rebellious cities, and conquered several more cities in the region including, Joppa.

During this part of the campaign, a force of chariots, cavalry, and archers came north from Egypt and Ethiopia to attack the Assyrian army in support of their allies in southern Canaan (2 Kings 19:9; Isa. 37:9). Despite being caught so far from home with no hope of getting meaningful reinforcements, Sennacherib and his Assyrian troops met and defeated the Egyptian force on the plain near Eltekeh (Map 6.2), and then resumed their attacks on Judah.

The Assyrians correctly anticipated little serious resistance from the well-prepared but relatively weak Judeans,[12] so they divided their forces to attack multiple targets concurrently. Sennacherib described for posterity (see quote below in "Historical Background . . .") the successful campaign in which he claims the Assyrians conquered more than forty walled cities and hundreds of unwalled villages, and took over 200,000 captives, plus countless animals, as plunder.

Nabu-belu-ukin and his charioteers fulfilled their usual roles as the Assyrians decimated Judah. Most often they helped intimidate Judean cities into surrendering and paying tribute rather than actually going to battle. Though the charioteers preferred open battle, even they understood that the best victory came without bloodshed, thus saving time, energy, weapons, and lives for the major battles. But when they did fight, the Assyrians, chariot troops played their part with skill and ferocity. Only when they met the Egyptians in pitched battle at the plain of Eltekeh could the chariots take full advantage of their ability to harass, intimidate, and attack the enemy forces, chasing down and killing the enemy troops once their discipline and their battle lines broke. After Eltekeh, they returned to their typical roles of guarding, raiding, showing power and demanding surrender, and hunting down those who attempted to flee.

Even though Nabu-belu-ukin had fought against countless enemies of Assyria in the past, somehow doing it in Judah proved different. Perhaps he was getting too old. He had noticed the smallest twinge of reservation when Sennacherib had announced that they would be attacking Judah, but the chariot commander brushed aside the concern, as he had so many times before. If the Judeans wouldn't adapt, they deserved what they got, didn't they? When the army got to Judah, Nabu-belu-ukin found himself facing many realities that reminded him of his long-forgotten past. Much of the terrain resembled his old home region farther north around Samaria. The style of homes and the dress of the people brought back memories buried decades before. And the language! He hadn't spoken Hebrew for many, many years, even with his fellow Samarians, because speaking the language of a conquered foe was not the best career move for rising Assyrian officers. Now, in this campaign, he kept hearing Hebrew spoken by the locals as he taunted, chased, imprisoned, and killed them. One man he killed was even named Ahijah, the same as his closest friend from among the original Samarian charioteers.[13] Nabu-belu-ukin could disguise his original identity from these Judeans, but he couldn't suppress his growing internal discomfort. He had chosen to blend into the Assyrian world, and now that reality was clashing with the world he thought he had left far behind. He found it a rare and troubling sensation.

One Judean woman bothered him in particular, because she reminded him of the mother he hadn't seen for more than twenty years. This Judean woman was fairly well-to-do, like his mother, and about the same age his mother had been when he had turned his back on her and her world. Unfortunately, this woman's husband had helped lead the resistance in their city, making himself and his family liable for especially severe punishment. When she begged Nabu-belu-ukin to spare the lives of her children using a language she assumed he couldn't comprehend, she didn't realize that he understood every word and caught every nuance. She could not know that something about her reminded him of his own mother years before when she had pleaded with him to spare his family the shame of knowing that this son of whom they had been so proud was about to become a traitor. At the time Jehoiachin had brushed his mother's words aside, telling himself that they meant little. Now Nabu-belu-ukin found that this woman's pleas reopened old wounds long since scarred over. Despite these new and unwelcome feelings, orders were orders. He killed the woman and her family with efficient, practiced strokes of his sword, and ordered her husband's body to be hung on the walls of the city as a sign of what happens to those who show disloyalty to Assyria. *If you don't fit in with those who are stronger, you get what you deserve.*

The sound of the dual pleas from this woman and that of his mother so long ago seemed to echo in his mind as Nabu-belu-ukin and the lead Assyrian troops now approached Lachish (Map 6.2), the second largest city in Judah. Only two cities remained in this campaign—Lachish, the administrative capital for the lower hills southwest of Jerusalem, and the capital city itself. Although much of Judah had seemed familiar to Nabu-belu-ukin, little of its defenses had impressed him to this point. Now his well-practiced eyes scanned and analyzed the city's fortifications as the troops approached (Fig. 6.4), and he knew that the city would give them some trouble. It would undoubtedly fall, but it presented some meaningful challenges and would probably take time.

Nabu-belu-ukin analyzed the city's layout and within minutes knew how the Assyrians would most likely attack. The city of Lachish lay on top of a large mound[14] rising from the low, rolling terrain of the region. The governor's fortified palace sat on a large stone platform dominating the center of the city. Lachish had a double line of walls, as did most well-fortified cities of the time. The outer, lower revetment wall held in place the city's glacis—a hard, manmade, steep slope that supported the upper wall and make it difficult for attackers to approach the upper, main defensive wall. The main wall had towers at regular intervals from which defenders could fire at attackers who might approach the face of the wall.

Nabu-belu-ukin also noted that the hill had good natural protection almost all the way around it due to the valleys that nearly encircled the city. Only on the southwest corner (to the right of the drawing in Fig. 6.4) did the terrain offer a better approach, since there a saddle of land connected the hill of the city to an adjacent hill. The city's planners used the saddle when building the road leading up to the city. They ran the road somewhat parallel to the city wall in order to expose attackers to fire from defenders on the wall. The planners further protected the entrance with two pairs of heavy wooden gates incorporated into a large gate complex. Nabu-belu-ukin noted the usual right turn required of all who passed through the gate compound (since most attackers were right-handed, a right turn left them more exposed). As he surveyed the strong gate complex, he surmised that the Assyrian attack would not focus on the gate. The Assyrians had become proficient at breaking through city walls, and they would almost certainly build a siege ramp directly across the saddle and attack at the more vulnerable corner of the city across from the adjacent hill. Attacking at a corner offered less room for the defenders and more room for the attackers to

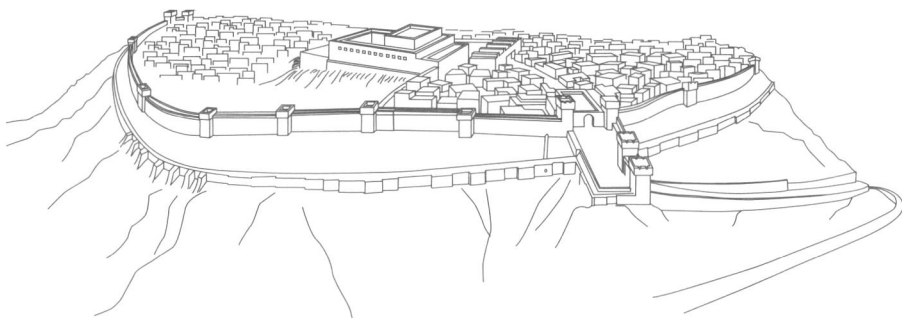

Fig. 6.4—City of Lachish at time of Sennacherib's attack

concentrate their forces to fire on the area of battle. The hill across from the southwest corner would also make an excellent location for the main Assyrian camp, where the officers could stay out of range of the defenders but enjoy a good view of most of the city. From this vantage point, they could easily direct the battle as needed.[15]

Nabu-belu-ukin saw and analyzed all of this quickly, and planned to advise accordingly during the war council that would convene in the next day or so. His advice carried much weight, but here the final decision lay with Sennacherib, as the king would be arriving shortly and would personally direct this battle (e.g. 2 Kings 18:14–17). Nabu-belu-ukin had mixed feelings about fighting with the king present. Sennacherib was a tolerably good strategist and often took advice from his council, but wars and battles were best left to the professionals. Even professionals reported to the king, though, and the king made the final decisions. Nabu-belu-ukin would offer his advice and then follow orders; it's what he always did. He knew how to fit in.

Along with seeing how the Assyrian troops would array in light of the terrain, Nabu-belu-ukin could also picture the entire battle playing out in his mind. He had watched the sequence unfold more times than he could remember. The Assyrians would set their main camp on the hill he had already noted, and establish other camps at various other points around the city. They would ring the city with troops and keep watch day and night to prevent any Judeans from escaping. They would also post chariots and cavalry on the roads and other natural approaches to prevent supplies and reinforcements from reaching the city. The king would order one or more of the highest officers to offer the city's leaders terms of peace, which the Assyrians kept simple. Surrender now and be deported to save the city, or hold out until Assyria destroyed the city, killed all who resisted (Fig. 6.5),[16] and then deported the rest. The inhabitants of Lachish would have to bend to the Assyrian will, either with or without the destruction of the city and the death of many inhabitants.

Unfortunately for both sides, if the defenders had not surrendered by the time the Assyrian army arrived, they probably wouldn't accept the terms of peace either. That meant that the attackers would conquer the city, either by direct assault or by laying siege and letting time, hunger, thirst, and disease do their work.

A direct assault on a relatively weak city could end quickly, with archers and slingers providing cover fire while infantry used ladders to scale the wall and penetrate the city. However, given the strength of Lachish's fortifications and the number of troops that would almost certainly be guarding such a royal administrative center, at least one siege ramp and multiple battering rams would be needed to breach the walls. The Assyrians would bring a large number of the prisoners taken captive earlier in the campaign and force them to move the thousands of tons of stone and rubble needed to construct the siege ramps.[17] The Assyrians would have to feed and supervise these thousands of workers, but the city's defenders were much less likely to fire on their own countrymen as they built the bulk of the ramps. The ramps would rise until they reached the lower city wall, where the city's defenders probably would make an initial stand.[18] Eventually, the ramps would reach the main wall. Assyrian engineers and troops would have to finish the ramps with a thick layer (about three feet) of hard mortar and make a type of road for each battering ram with split logs (Fig. 6.6)[19] to keep the siege engines from sinking into the stones and earth of the ramps.

When the ramps were finished, the attackers would bring the battering rams into position in front of the main wall, with heavy covering fire from archers and slingers to help suppress the fire from the defenders on the walls. The defenders would also be shooting arrows and slinging stones, as well as throwing

Fig. 6.5—Captives stripped naked and impaled on poles at Lachish apparently as a warning against resistance. Earlier king Tiglath-pileser III described a similar act by boasting, "I impaled alive (the enemy king's) chief ministers, and I made his country behold them."

down torches to try to burn up the battering rams before they could penetrate the wall (Fig 6.6). To guard against the defenders' efforts to burn the siege engines and rams, the Assyrians had a soldier in each siege engine to pour water on the beam of the ram and on the engine. The engines' destructive work could take days, but eventually the rams would complete their breaches, and assault troops would storm the city.

If for some reason the attackers could not storm the city either by using ladders or by breaching the wall with rams, they might have to simply seal off the city and lay siege. The defenders had a finite supply of food, medical supplies, military equipment, and possibly even water, although some cities had access to a spring or wells from within the walls.

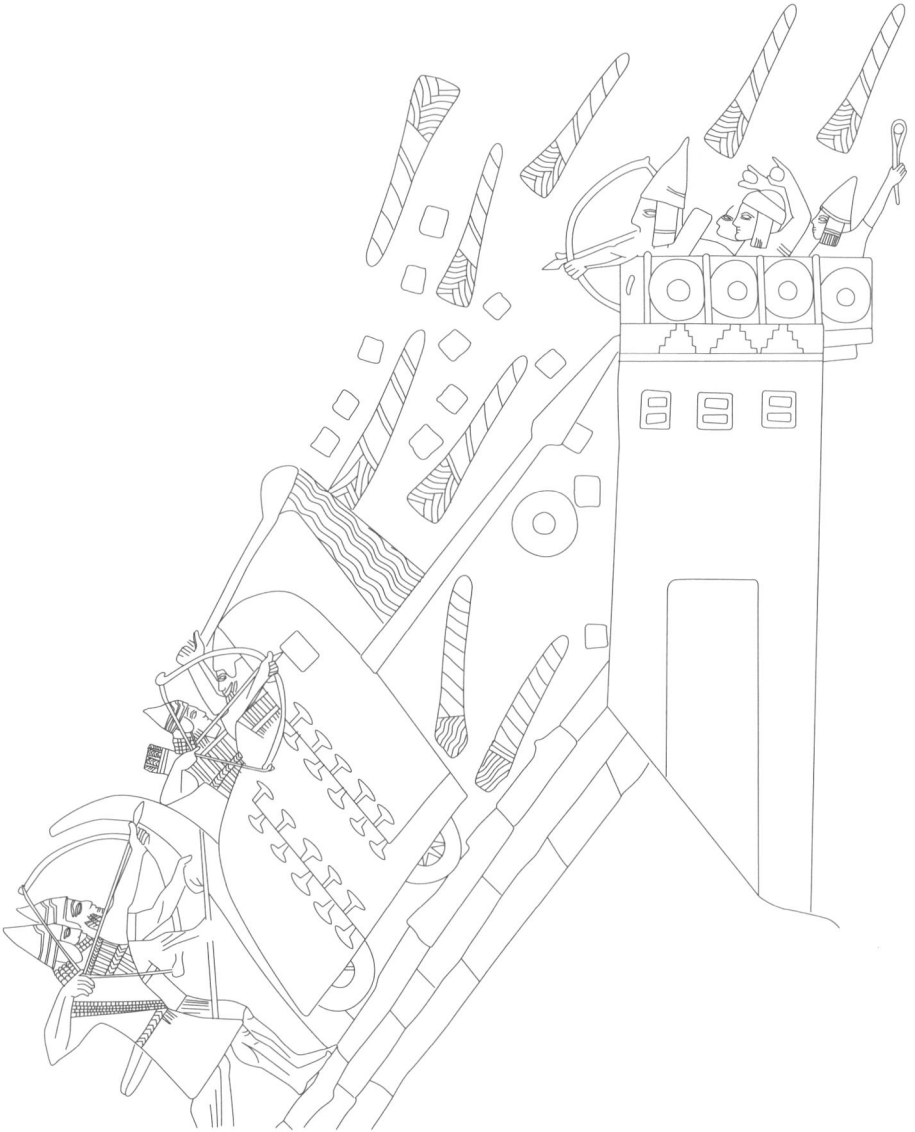

Fig. 6.6—Siege engine attacking Lachish. Note archer and shield-bearer providing cover fire for battering ram on road of logs on siege ramp. Soldiers on top level of ram fire at defenders and pour water to extinguish torches thrown by defenders. Defenders shoot, sling, and hurl stones. Top of defensive tower protected and decorated with shields (cf. Ezek 27:11b*—"They hung their shields around your walls; they brought your beauty to perfection.").

Even if the inhabitants weren't in danger of running out of water, the population of a walled city would swell to many times its normal size as an army approached, since those living in the surrounding villages and countryside would seek the greater safety offered by the city's fortifications. This increased population would drain the supplies within the city more rapidly and, within a limited time, would help foster terrible conditions that typically included starvation and disease. Some cities could hold out for more than a year, but most collapsed within months.

Nabu-belu-ukin didn't foresee the need for such a long siege at Lachish, since he estimated that a ramp and subsequent breach could be completed within several weeks. The Assyrians didn't have more time than that, anyway. The time to return to Assyria at the close of this campaign was fast approaching, and they needed to finish Lachish and conquer Jerusalem fairly quickly. To help hurry the process, Sennacherib would probably send officers ahead to call for Jerusalem's surrender well before Lachish fell (2 Kings 18:13–37). Nabu-belu-ukin remembered from his boyhood the long climb up into the hills to reach Jerusalem, and he didn't relish the idea of going up there with the entire Assyrian army. Hopefully, the Judean king would realize what was best for himself and his nation and save the Assyrians the trouble.

As it turned out, the fall of Lachish played out almost exactly as Nabu-belu-ukin had anticipated. The Assyrians arrayed themselves and demanded surrender. The inhabitants of the city refused, so the attackers brought captives to build two siege ramps, the main one at the southwest corner of the city and a smaller one near the gate. The process took a little more than a month, during which time the top Assyrian officers also rode up to Jerusalem and demanded surrender of the capital using clever and effective psychological warfare (see discussion in chap. 7 under "Psychological Warfare and Cruelty"). King Hezekiah refused, and the officers returned to Lachish. When the ramps at Lachish were complete, the Assyrians brought up seven siege engines with their battering rams to the main city walls, five on the southwest corner and two by the gate. They pounded the walls for several days until they breached the wall at the corner. The attack by the city gate (the ram in Fig. 6.6 attacks the gate) served less as a serious attempt to gain entry than as a way to force the defenders to move many of their troops away from the main point of attack.[20]

The only surprise came when the wall at the southwest corner collapsed, and the Assyrians discovered that the city's inhabitants had built a counter-ramp within the city opposite the Assyrian ramp.[21] Although Nabu-belu-ukin admired the tenacity of these Judeans, the immense amount of work represented by the ramp did little more than buy an extra day or two of battering before the walls collapsed, and present the assault troops with a slightly higher hill to climb to enter the city.

The defenders fought fiercely to keep out the attackers,[22] but the Assyrian military might overwhelmed them. Once the walls were breached, it was only a matter of hours before the Assyrians had penetrated and subdued the city. The fortified governor's palace held out for a few more days, but then it fell as well.[23] By then the Assyrians had looted the main part of the city and cleared out the inhabitants. Once the palace fell and yielded the city's final plunder, the Assyrians burned the entire city.[24]

After the battle, the Assyrians meted out punishment as they thought appropriate. Some of the leaders of the revolt were stretched out on the ground and flayed alive (Fig. 7.13). Others were killed less brutally, and all the survivors were deported.[25] *If you don't fit in, you get what you deserve,* thought Nabu-belu-ukin as he watched the lines of deportees plod off to exile (Fig. 6.7), from which they would never return. But he felt less conviction about his beliefs than in the past. Though he still didn't regret his decision to fit in after the Assyrians had conquered his own city years before, he did admire these Judeans from Lachish for their courage to hold on to their convictions. They had remained true to their God and their world, and it

Fig. 6.7—Deportees from Lachish leaving for exile.

brought them destruction and exile; he had rejected his world and gained success and comfort, but now a growing inner turmoil as well.

HISTORICAL BACKGROUND AND BIBLICAL CONNECTIONS

The latter part of the preceding story takes place as the Assyrians were establishing their control over the kingdom of Judah in 701 BC. They had conquered Samaria, the capital of the northern kingdom of Israel, some twenty years earlier, and had devastated Israel's holdings in the north, east, and west a decade before that. Although Israel and Judah were home to the biblical authors and their people, these two nations were relatively small conquests in the Assyrian strategy to dominate the entire Fertile Crescent (Map 6.3). Who were these Assyrians? From where did they come? What led up to the conquests of Israel and Judah described in the Old Testament, including the fall of Lachish?[26]

The Assyrian nation and empire grew over a long period of time, based out of its homeland on the upper Tigris River in northeastern Mesopotamia (see vicinity of Nineveh on Maps 6.3, 6.4). Nestled up against the mountains to the north and east, it opened toward southern Mesopotamia, from which it adopted the Sumerian culture. The Assyrian homeland also opened up to the west, and a major trade route linked it to the northern Levant. From the west, traders brought much-needed raw materials not found in northeastern Mesopotamia. Immigrating Amorite settlers also came from the west and helped establish strong and aggressive city-states that governed much of early Mesopotamia.

The region's natural fertility produced foods that supported a growing population. Adequate rain in the north, coupled with irrigation from rivers in the drier south, produced good crops of grains, fruit, and vegetables. Agricultural villages dotted the land, some of which grew into larger, walled cities. The region's first great city was Ashur, located approximately sixty miles south of Nineveh along the Tigris River (Map 6.4). Founded in the 3rd millennium BC, the city served as the first capital of the nation and remained the religious center until the end of the Neo-Assyrian Empire. Named for its chief god, Ashur also shared its name with the nation and the people (Ashur–Assyria).

In the early second millennium, the city-state of Ashur built a fighting force to defend itself from warring neighbors as well as from

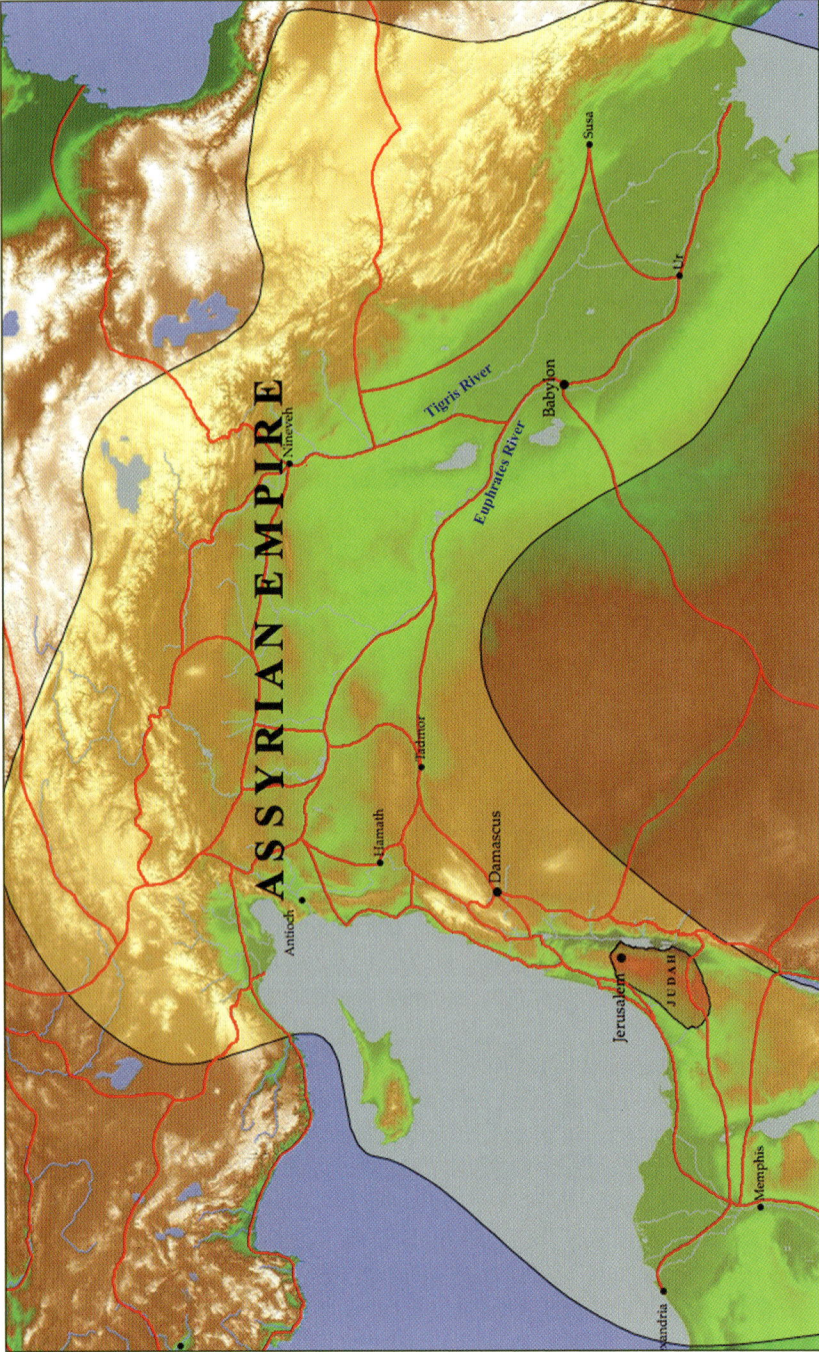

Map 6.3—Neo-Assyrian Empire at peak. Note Nineveh on upper Tigris River, and the barely independent Judah on path from Assyrian homeland toward Egypt. Orange lines denote major roads.

hostile tribes that descended from the mountains. Assyria lacked natural defenses, so it defended itself through quick military raids against established or potential enemies. These defensive actions soon turned offensive, as successful raids gained valued plunder. Assyria's location naturally fostered trade (note Nah. 3:16—"You have increased the number of your merchants till they are more numerous than the stars in the sky"), but soon the military surpassed trade in importance. The nation expanded until about the mid-second millennium in what historians call the Old Assyrian period, during which time Assyria controlled most of northern Mesopotamia. A period of weakness followed, and other powers took much of Assyria's conquered territory.

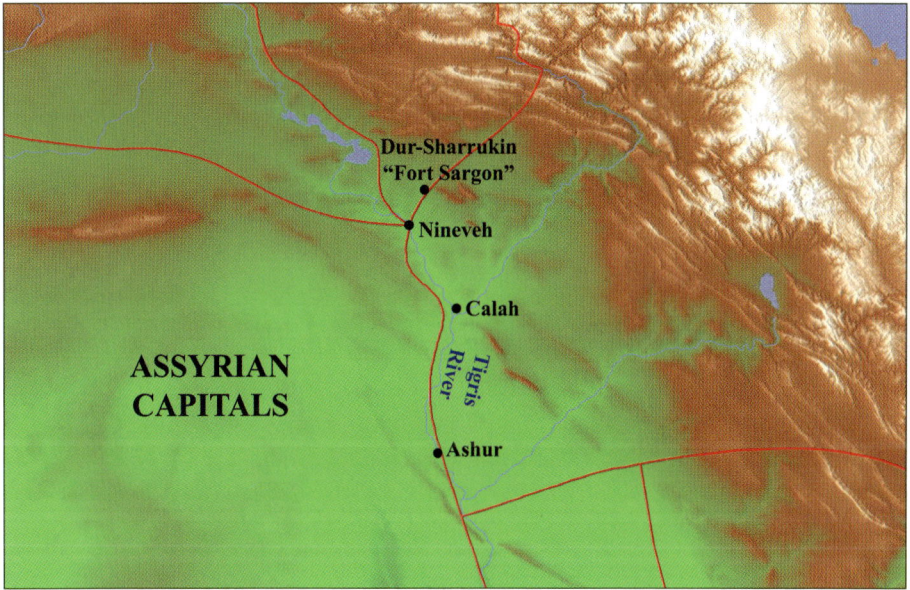

Map 6.4—Four capitals of Assyria through history, all along upper Tigris River. Ashur lies at the southern end of the Assyrian heartland.

A resurgence in the 14th century led to renewed expansion in what became known as the Middle Assyrian Empire. By 1100, Assyrian armies had pushed as far west as the "Great Sea"[27] (the Mediterranean) and south to the Persian Gulf, exerting direct control over an area even greater than during the Old Assyrian period (Map 6.5). The city of Calah (modern Nimrud) was founded about twenty-five miles south of Nineveh during the 13th century, and would later become Assyria's second capital (Maps

6.4, 6.5). The Middle Assyrian Empire ended in the 11th century when rising Aramean power in the west temporarily weakened the Assyrian dominance both in the western and central regions.

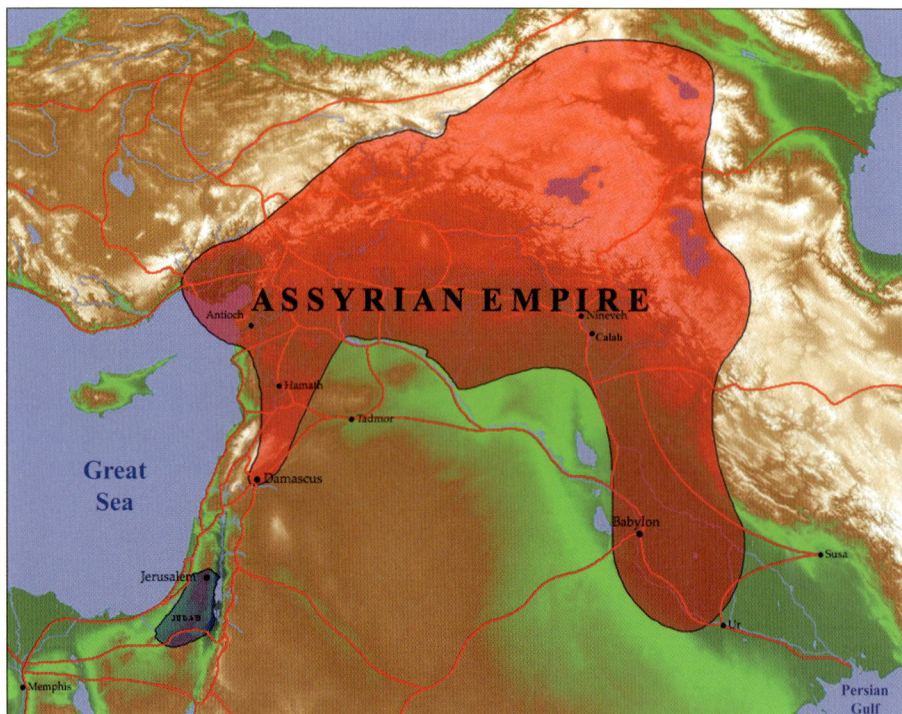

Map 6.5—Extent of Assyrian Empire during Middle-Assyrian period.

By the 10th century, Assyrian rulers had reestablished internal stability and once again began expanding. New vassal states contributed iron, grain, timber, precious metals, horses and other animals, helping set the stage for further conquest. King Ashurnasirpal II rebuilt Calah in the first half of the 9th century and moved the capital farther north for a better staging point for conquests to the north and west. By the mid-9th century, the Assyrian king Shalmaneser III (858–824) pushed to take Damascus. During this period, Assyrian and biblical characters apparently met for the first time. In 853 BC, Shalmaneser faced a coalition of armies from the west in a battle near Qarqar on the Orontes River. Twelve major kings allied against the Assyrians, including Ahab of Israel, who contributed 2,000 chariots and 10,000 infantry to the cause.[28] Curiously, this major battle does not appear in Scripture, apparently because discussing it did not serve the theological purposes of the biblical authors. Shalmaneser claimed victory at Qarqar, but Assyrian records do not mention campaigns for the next three years, suggesting that their forces suffered meaningful losses as well. By 841 BC, Shalmaneser once more campaigned west and received tribute from several kings, including Jehu of Israel[29] (Fig. 6.8). Once again, the event involves a known biblical king but does not appear in Scripture.

Fig. 6.8—Jehu of Israel prostrate before Shalmaneser III, 853 BC.
Caption reads: "I received the tribute of Jehu of the house of Omri: silver, gold . . ."

For the next two and a half centuries, major events in Israel and Judah were linked to those in Assyria. When Assyria focused its attentions and forces on the west, the Israelite kingdoms had to pay tribute. When Assyria had to divert its military elsewhere, the Levantine kingdoms, including Israel and Judah, experienced resurgent power and wealth. The final such respite from Assyrian dominance lasted through the first half of the 8th century. It ended with the aggressive campaigns of Tiglath-pileser III that began in the mid-8th century.

Tiglath-pileser III began a series of attacks that would eventually conquer all of Israel and very nearly all of Judah as well. The Bible prophetically describes this wave of attacks and the futility of resistance as follows:

"[T]he Lord is about to bring against them (Israel)
  the mighty floodwaters of the Euphrates—
  the king of Assyria with all his pomp.
It will overflow all its channels,
  run over all its banks
  and sweep on into Judah, swirling over it,
  passing through it and reaching up to the neck.
  Its outspread wings will cover the breadth of your land.
Raise the war cry, you nations, and be shattered!
  Listen, all you distant lands.
  Prepare for battle, and be shattered!
  Prepare for battle, and be shattered!
Devise your strategy, but it will be thwarted;
  propose your plan, but it will not stand,
  for God is with us" (Isa. 8:7–10).

This floodwater began when Tiglath-pileser III consolidated his power at home and in Babylon and then turned to the west. By 732 BC, he had decimated all of northern Israel and made Galilee into an Assyrian province.[30] His son Shalmaneser V succeeded him on the Assyrian throne and conquered the Israelite capital of Samaria in a three-year siege that ended in 722 BC. Shalmaneser's son, Sargon II, built Dur-Sharrukin ("Fort Sargon," modern Khorsabad) as his new capital about twelve miles northeast of Nineveh (Map 6.4), perhaps as an attempt to undercut the power that officials had built up in Calah over the preceding century and a half.[31] Sargon conquered parts of southern Asia Minor along with Cyprus and expanded Assyria's direct control in cities such as Ashdod and Gath along the southern coast of Canaan.

After his death, Sargon's son Sennacherib moved the capital to the ancient city of Nineveh, Assyria's fourth and final capital, which he expanded and renovated on a grand scale.[32] Sennacherib also continued Assyria's expansion by conquering most of Judah, including Lachish in 701 BC. He very nearly conquered Jerusalem as well, but he returned to Assyria after exacting tribute from Hezekiah of Judah (2 Kings 18–19; 2 Chron. 29–32; Isa. 36–37).

Sennacherib described the reduction of Judah as follows:

As for Hezekiah the Judean, I besieged forty-six of his fortified walled cities and surrounding smaller towns, which were without number. Using packed-down ramps and applying battering rams, infantry attacks by mines, breeches, and siege machines, I conquered (them). I took out 200,150 people, young and old, male and female, horses, mules, donkeys, camels, cattle, and sheep, without number, and counted them as spoil. He (Hezekiah) himself, I locked up within Jerusalem, his royal city, like a bird in a cage. I surrounded him with earthworks, and made it unthinkable for him to exit by the city gate. His cities which I had despoiled I cut off from his land and gave them to (nearby kings who had remained loyal), and thus I diminished his land. I imposed dues and gifts for my lordship upon him, in addition to the former tribute, their yearly payment.

He, Hezekiah, was overwhelmed by the awesome splendor of my lordship, and he sent me after my departure to Nineveh, my royal city . . . 30 talents of gold, 800 talents of silver (and numerous other luxury items).[33]

Sennacherib, of course, does not mention the loss of a large part of his army, as described in the Bible (2 Kings 19:35; 2 Chron. 32:21; Isa 37:36) as well as in later Greek histories; he mentions only that he returned victorious and wealthy. Upon his return Sennacherib built himself a sumptuous new palace in Nineveh that he proudly described as the "Palace without a Rival." Captives, apparently including some from Judah, supplied much of the forced labor to build the grand structure (Fig. 6.1). Sennacherib had one reception hall lined with carved alabaster reliefs depicting the victory at Lachish, his greatest triumph in the campaign (since Jerusalem did not fall). Much of the information about the attack at Lachish and Assyria's weaponry and tactics comes from careful analysis of those reliefs.[34]

Although Hezekiah and his capital survived Sennacherib's attack, his now-much-reduced nation had suffered terribly. God had spared the faithful king and his capital, but he did not spare the nation from great devastation. Hezekiah and his little nation remained free, but now lacked the ability and likely the will to consider resisting the Assyrians again. Judah remained Assyria's vassal for the better part of another century, during which time Assyria even conquered Egypt (in 671 BC). After controlling Egypt for just a few years, however, multiple revolts and internal weakness pushed Assyria into disorder, and its power quickly eroded. The long, brutal Assyrian nightmare finally ended for Judah and the rest of the ancient Near East in 612 BC when Nineveh fell to the Babylonians and Medes. The prophet Nahum described the reaction to Nineveh's fall as follows: "Nothing can heal you; your wound is fatal. All who hear the news about you clap their hands at your fall, for who has not felt your endless cruelty?" (Nah. 3:19).

Although the demise of Assyria was good news for its many victims, Assyria had ruled much of the ancient Near East for more than two centuries. It conquered and ruled an enormous empire through its fearfully effective war machine. The next chapter will describe the organization, weaponry, and tactics of the Assyrian military, the most effective the world had seen up to that time. Assyria had a long history, as noted above, but the following chapter will describe the Assyrian military beginning with the Neo-Assyrian resurgence that began in the 10th century, since this period witnessed the threat and conquest of the Israelite kingdoms as recorded in the Old Testament.

NOTES

1   Nabu-belu-ukin was the name of the actual commander of a unit of Samarian charioteers that served in the Assyrian army under Sargon II and perhaps Tiglath-pileser III. These conquered Israelites were incorporated into the Assyrian military like many others, but they were unique in that their unit retained the name of a foreign place—in their case, the capital of their conquered nation. Sargon wrote of them, "I took as booty 27,290 people who lived (in Samaria). I formed *a unit of 50 chariotry* from them…" See Stephanie Dalley, "Foreign Chariotry and Cavalry in the Armies of Tiglath-pileser III and Sargon II," *Iraq* 47 (1985): 34–35. Nabu-belu-ukin's name and position are historical, but the events of his life that follow come from this author's imagination, supported by research into the world of Israel, the Assyrian military, and the conquest of Lachish in 701 BC.

2   For the biblical account of the later Judean king with the same name, see 2 Kings 24–25. This author suggested the correspondence of the names Nabu-belu-ukin and Jehoiachin to Anson Rainey in personal conversation during March 2010, and Dr. Rainey concurred. Anson Rainey (1930–2011) was one of the world's leading Semitic linguists, historical geographers, and scholars of the ancient Near East.

3   For a discussion of the date of this event as well as the likelihood that Pekah had previously ruled part of Israel from Gilead, see Edwin R. Thiele, *The Mysterious Numbers of the Hebrew Kings* (rev. ed.; Grand Rapids, MI: Zondervan, 1983), 120, 129.

4   Dalley writes, "The Samaritans were among the best in the world at chariotry" ("Foreign Chariotry," 42), a complement that might have applied to other nations along the eastern Mediterranean as well. Sargon incorporated chariots from Samaria, Carchemish, Hamath, and other nearby nations into Assyria's royal army in the 8th century. Of the twelve Levantine kingdoms that Shalmaneser V had battled at Qarqar in 853 BC, three could muster at least 700 chariots, with the force of Ahab of Israel the largest at 2,000.

5   Jehoiachin was about to join the Assyrians, for whom pride demanded riding a stallion rather than a mare. An illustration of the Assyrian attitude toward mares and stallions comes from the annals of Sargon II. When Sargon II routed the forces of an Urartian king, that king fled on a mare, much to the derision of the Assyrian troops. See H. W. F. Saggs, *The Might That Was Assyria* (London: Sidgwick & Jackson, 1984), 259.

6   See also n. 1 above. For an analysis of the Assyrian information pertaining to this unit of Samarian charioteers, see Dalley, "Foreign Chariotry," 31–48.

7   For further discussion on this aspect of Assyrian society, see Saggs, *Might*, 124–30.

8   The Assyrian texts that mention the Samarian charioteers date no later than 710–08 BC. This places them toward the end of the reign of Sargon II, Sennacherib's father and predecessor. Thus, we cannot be certain if the Samarians were still fighting for the Assyrians four years into Sennacherib's reign, approximately twenty-one years after Samaria's fall. However, assuming the historicity of the biblical accounts of Sennacherib's attack on Jerusalem (esp. 2 Kings 18:26–28), the Assyrian army had officers in 701 BC who spoke Hebrew. These Hebrew speakers apparently were recruited from Israel or Judah, but when that would have occurred is unclear—perhaps in 722, perhaps later. Regardless, our current story assumes that Samarians are helping to attack Judah and Lachish in order to add tension to the story.

9   According to Dalley, the real Nabu-belu-ukin bore the title of vizier to the king, and had become "around the seventh most important man in the kingdom" ("Foreign Chariotry," 32).

10 This and subsequent quotes from this campaign are taken from *COS*, 2.119B.

11 Middle Easterners, both ancient and modern, typically take gifts when they visit someone, especially when visiting someone important (note 1 Sam. 9:7–8, for example). Thus, presenting "sumptuous presents" when visiting an offended, powerful overlord would have proven especially important.

12 Since more than thirty years had passed since Tiglath-pileser III had first invaded northern Israel, the Judeans had had plenty of time to prepare for this likely eventuality. Multiple biblical passages (e.g. 2 Chron. 32:1–8; Isa. 22:1–11) describe King Hezekiah's preparations, including blocking up water sources outside of Jerusalem, channeling the water from the Gihon Spring into Jerusalem through a tunnel, repairing the city wall and reinforcing it with towers, adding a second city wall (perhaps to include the part of the city that had expanded onto Jerusalem's western hill), manufacturing and stockpiling weapons, expanding the military, leading religious reform, and making political and military alliances with other like-minded nations. Multiple archaeological finds reflect this preparatory activity, including the above-mentioned tunnel, now called Hezekiah's Tunnel in the modern City of David (2 Kings 20:20), the twenty-five-foot wide (!) Broad Wall (Isa. 22:10) in the modern Jewish Quarter of Jerusalem, built to protect the western part of the city, and the *l'melek* ("belonging to the king") seals found on hundreds of storage jars that apparently reflect Hezekiah's efforts to store enough provisions for the army.

Unfortunately, the Bible also notes that the Assyrians conquered all of Judah with apparent ease (2 Kings 18:13) except for the capital of Jerusalem, reportedly saved only by divine intervention (2 Kings 19:32–36).

13   Ahijah ("Yahweh is my brother"; *ahi*(PAP)-*i-ú* in Akkadian) was one of two personal names of the Samaritan charioteers that included part (-jah/yah) of the divine name Yahweh. See Dalley, "Foreign Chariotry," 32. The name Ahijah appears more than twenty times in the Old Testament to designate some eight different individuals.

14   As with most major ancient Near Eastern cities, Lachish was located on top of a hill in order to better protect it from attackers. The hill on which Lachish sat covered thirty acres at its base and eighteen acres on top. Cities needed a water source such as a river or spring, typically located down low in a valley, but they needed to be up high for defense. So the inhabitants built up high and brought up water each day, or used wells, or stored enough rainwater in cisterns for their needs. As time passed and cities were destroyed by human or natural events and subsequently rebuilt on their hills, multiple levels would accumulate and the mound would rise, creating a better defensive position.

15   For drawings and discussion of the Assyrian camp, see Ussishkin, *CLS,* p. 118, figs. 65, 73. The broad, flat hill on which the Assyrians apparently made their main camp now serves as the site of Moshav Lachish, built by Israeli settlers in the 1950s.

16   The three impaled individuals are shown at the base of the city in front of the main siege ramp with the battle raging on one side and the deportees leaving the city on the other. Thus, it is not clear if they were set up before the battle as a warning not to resist, during the battle as a warning not to continue resisting, or after the battle in order to sear one final gruesome image into the minds of the deportees as they left for exile.

17   Ussishkin, the excavator at Lachish, estimates the dimensions of the main ramp as 150–180 feet long bottom to top and 210–225 feet wide at the base, rising at a grade of thirty degrees ("Defensive Judean Counter-Ramp," 71; *Conquest of Lachish,* 50–54). Eph'al (*City Besieged,* 84–85, esp. n. 156) notes that a ramp this size would have required approximately 19,000 tons of stone, earth, and rubble, and could have been completed in as little as 35 days. It would have required a work force with porters working in shifts of 500 around the clock. Each porter could carry basketfuls of material with a load of thirty-five pounds a distance of one-fifth of a mile at a rate of three rounds per hour. The porters would also need the support of other laborers to do jobs like gathering stones and filling the baskets.

In a somewhat similar situation, Alexander the Great used "many tens of thousands of men" to carry the rubble from Old Tyre on the mainland of Phoenicia to construct a kilometer-long causeway out to the island of Tyre, enabling him to conquer that city in 332 BC (*Diodorus of Sicily* 17:40.5 (trans. C. Bradford Welles; Loeb Classical Library; Cambridge: Harvard University Press, 1963)).

18   Excavators digging at the revetment wall on the southwest corner of the city uncovered evidence of a battle at that location. They recovered twenty-seven arrowheads, one of which was still embedded in the wall, as well as two sling stones of rounded flint about the size of tennis balls. See Ussishkin, "Defensive Judean Counter-Ramp," 73.

19   For a description and pictures of the siege ramp, see Ussishkin, *Conquest of Lachish,* 50–54; and Ussishkin, "Defensive Judean Counter-Ramp," 66–73. For a thorough treatment of the whole process of laying siege to a city, including ramps and siege engines, see Eph'al, *City Besieged.*

20   For discussion of the two-pronged attack, see Ussishkin, *Conquest of Lachish,* 99–102, as well as figs. 68 and 78.

21   For discussion and pictures, see Ussishkin, "Defensive Judean Counter-Ramp," 66–73.

22   Hundreds of arrowheads and sling stones recovered from the area of attack, as well as clear signs of burning, bear witness to the ferocity of the fighting. See Shanks, "Destruction of Judean Fortress," 48–65. Note in upper-left corner of Segment IV of the Assyrian reliefs (Ussishkin, *Conquest of Lachish,* fig. 69), the defenders appear to be throwing even burning chariots or carts down on the siege engines in a desperate attempt to burn them up before they could complete their deadly work.

23   Archaeologists recovered hundreds of arrowheads from the three major areas of battle—around the wall on the southwest corner of the city, at the gate, and at the governor's palace (Ussishkin, *Conquest of Lachish,* 54).

24   Excavations uncovered a thick burn layer (up to two meters) in the city, but no valuables or skeletons. Evidently the Assyrians looted the city thoroughly and cleared the inhabitants before putting it to the torch. Though no skeletons were recovered in the city, four caves on the northwest corner of the hill were found to contain approximately 1,500 bodies dumped there in a mass burial, many with disarticulated skulls. These may represent those killed either during the battle or possibly afterward, or perhaps both. See Ussishkin, *Conquest of Lachish,* 54–58. Also note figs. 69 and 83 for representations of plunder, apparently taken from the governor's palace.

25   For the graphic portrayal of these events as carved by Assyrian artists on

Sennacherib's palace in Nineveh, see Ussishkin, *Conquest of Lachish,* figs. 69–71, 84–88.

26 For more complete overviews of Assyrian history, see A. Kirk Grayson, "Mesopotamia, History of (Assyria)," *ABD* 4:732–55; and especially William C. Gwaltney Jr., "Assyrians," in *Peoples of the Old Testament World* (Alfred J. Hoerth, Gerald L. Mattingly and Edwin M. Yamauchi, eds; Grand Rapids: Baker, 1994), 77–106, from which much of the following information was drawn.

27 When the later Assyrian king Ashurnasirpal II likewise reached the Mediterranean Sea in the early 9th century, he boasted, "I made my way to the slopes of Mount Lebanon and went up to the Great Sea of the land Amurru. I cleansed my weapons in the Great Sea and made sacrifices to the gods. I received tribute from the kings of the sea coast, from the lands of the people of Tyre, Sidon, Byblos. . . . They submitted to me" (lit. "they seized my feet" (in surrender). (*RIMA* 2, pp. 218–19 (1:iii 84b-92a)).

28 *COS,* 2.113A.

29 *COS,* 2.113C, D, E, F. 2:113F gives the text from Shalmaneser's "Black Obelisk" uncovered at Calah which depicts Jehu and lists Jehu's tribute as "silver, gold, a golden bowl, a golden goblet, golden cups, golden buckets, tin, a staff of the king's hand, and javelins(?)."

30 Tiglath-pileser III described his activity in Israel in 732 BC as follows: "I carried off to Assyria the land of Bit-Humria (Omri) Israel, its auxiliary army, all of its people. . . . They killed Pekah, their king, and I installed Hoshea as king over them. I received from them ten talents of gold, x talents of silver, with their possessions and I carried them to Assyria" (*COS,* 2.117C; also note variant text in 2.117G). For the complementary biblical description, see 2 Kings 15:29–30. In 729 BC, Tiglath-pileser III notes receiving tribute from "Jehoahaz (Ahaz) the Judahite," the king who sent gold and silver to petition Assyria's aid against Pekah of Israel and Rezin of Damascus (2 Kings 16:5–8).

31 Saggs, *Might,* 97–98.

32 The walls of Sennacherib's Nineveh stretched nearly eight miles and expanded the city from 180 to 1,000 acres. The walls had fifteen major gates, and based on the reported courses of bricks laid and the known size of the bricks, the walls stood more than forty feet thick and forty-five feet high. Inside the city, Sennacherib laid out new streets and squares, and built a magnificent new palace with a great park and extra protection against floods. He added extensive gardens, for which he drew the water of the Khosr River, augmented by streams and canals from up to thirty miles away (Saggs, *Might,* 99, 190–93).

33 *COS,* 2.119B.

34 The British excavator of Sennacherib's palace, Austen Henry Layard, described his discoveries at the palace as follows: "In this magnificent edifice I had opened no less than seventy-one halls, chambers, and passages, whose walls, almost without an exception, had been paneled with slabs of sculptured alabaster recording the wars, the triumphs, and the great deeds of the Assyrian king. By a rough calculation, about 9880 feet, or nearly two miles, of bas-reliefs, with twenty-seven portals, formed by colossal winged bulls and lion-sphinxes, were uncovered." Unfortunately, many of these reliefs had been badly damaged by fire, probably when the palace was destroyed at the fall of Nineveh in 612 BC. The heat turned much of the alabaster to lime, causing the reliefs to crumble as soon as they were excavated (*CLS,* pp. 66–67).

The room displaying the conquest of Lachish apparently served as a reception room at the end of a triple entrance, each flanked by a pair of huge, bearded man-bulls. The first pair stood eighteen feet tall, with each pair successively smaller, giving the one who passed the impression of a much longer and more impressive entry. At the end of this entrance sat the "Lachish Room," the reliefs arranged so the one entering would be struck first with the scene of the storming of the city (*CLS,* fig. 60). Any foreign dignitary entering this reception room could not help but be impressed by the power and might of Assyria, and the tremendous risk involved in not paying Assyria's required tribute.

ASSYRIA:
BRUTAL MASTERS OF THE ANCIENT NEAR EAST—PART 2

7

MILITARY ORGANIZATION

Although the Assyrians developed the greatest military the ancient Near East had yet seen and used it to dominate their part of the world for centuries, in most ways their military organization resembled that of other major armies the time. They relied primarily on infantry and chariotry, and developed extensive cavalry as well. These branches served under a hierarchy of officers who reported to the king. The Assyrian military differed in that it came from a culture more militaristic than most others, so many aspects of the culture from the kingship on down focused on military success.

The Assyrians left a wealth of texts and pictures pertaining to their military activities, especially during the period from the early 9th century to the end of the empire. Many of the most striking pictures come from bas reliefs (scenes in low relief carved into the surface of the material, usually slabs of alabaster or stone, to present imagery more vivid than if flat). Many of these reliefs decorated the royal palaces at Calah, Dur-Sharrukin, and Nineveh. The Assyrian kings also used wall paintings and repoussé (raised imagery on sheets of metal, usually bronze, made by hammering from the reverse side), the best of which come from a temple at Balawat, a royal residence in the country twelve miles northeast of Calah. Many of these Assyrian images serve to glorify the king and demonstrate his military prowess by portraying the Assyrian military in action. The Assyrians also left many texts that also contain much military information, but the texts require careful interpretation. In the words of one Assyrian scholar, "The Assyrian royal scribes were prone to hyperbole, hypocrisy, and even falsehood. The modern historian must tread warily through this dangerous forest."[1] Even allowing for exaggerations, the Assyrian sources offer fascinating views into the military machine that mastered the Middle East of its time.

Recruitment and Training

Since the Assyrians developed such a highly militaristic culture, likely every healthy adult male from the king on down served in the military when called. Originally the crown would call up troops for limited periods of service during the year, after which the men would return home and resume their normal lives. As the kingdom expanded and the need for troops increased, three types of soldiers emerged: the career soldiers, who served full time, the men who contracted to use land in exchange for periodic service, both civil (road building, canal maintenance, etc.) and military; and those mustered for a specific campaign. Civil and military organization overlapped, and many officials both ruled over a certain number of villages and had to levy and lead troops from those villages.[2] Such levied troops serving under regional governors comprised the majority of the army, but Assyria also had a growing "royal army," a standing army under the command of the king.

Eventually the needs of the military grew greater than the supply of native Assyrians. By the time of Tiglath-pileser III in the mid-8th century, the army began conscripting troops from conquered regions. The Assyrian reliefs often depict foreigners serving together in units wearing native dress and using the same weapons (bows, slings, and swords of different types). By the end of the empire, the majority of troops apparently came from outside of Assyria, despite the fact that foreigners were more likely to desert or turn and fight against their Assyrian overlords (cf. 1 Sam. 14:21).[3] In later periods, native Assyrians tended to function in the more important branches of chariotry and cavalry, with foreigners serving more often as infantry. One also finds numerous exceptions to this rule, like with the unit of fifty charioteers from Samaria discussed in the last chapter, or another fifty charioteers and 200 cavalry that Sargon says he enlisted from Carchemish.[4]

The royal or standing army, with its native and foreign troops, comprised the core of the military. It supplied the king's bodyguard and elite troops who fought under his direct command in battle. The standing army also gave the king a strike force ready to move at a moment's notice. The royal army had its headquarters and main training facility in the nation's capital, which moved from place to place over time, as discussed above. The headquarters housed large numbers of troops and animals and great quantities of supplies, along with royal apartments for the king and his retinue. The king carried out a major inspection of the military each new year. Other troops, both in the royal and provincial forces, were stationed and trained at garrisons and barracks throughout the empire.[5]

Military Branches

As mentioned earlier, the Assyrian military used infantry and chariotry, and developed a significant cavalry during the Neo-Assyrian period. With its landlocked heartland far from any large bodies of water, Assyria had no significant navy, but it built or acquired ships when needed. Each of these branches will be discussed below.

Infantry

The sources typically describe the army using general terms that give little indication of the army's size or organization, such as "I mustered my chariotry and extensive troops."[6] A company of fifty under the command of a captain apparently comprised the basic unit, and was made up of files of ten.[7]

As with most armies, the Assyrians relied heavily on their infantry, supported by chariotry, cavalry, and engineers. Major cities such as Ashur and Arrapkha (modern Kirkuk) supplied entire regiments of infantry, and rural regions also contributed foot soldiers through levies raised and commanded by local officials/military officers. As already noted, many foreign lands, such as Aram in the west or Chaldea in the south, contributed meaningful numbers as well.

Regional officials/officers formed the base of the command structure. The next-higher level was made up of provincial governors, and above them, at the third-highest level, were palace officials such as the palace steward, the palace herald, and the chief cupbearer (listed in 2 Kings 18:17 and Isa. 36:2; transliterated "Rabshakeh" in certain translations). Like at the lower levels, many of these highest officials also served military roles. Thus, not only did the chief cupbearer serve at the palace, but one also finds him serving with the army at Lachish and delivering Sennacherib's demand for surrender at Jerusalem (2 Kings 18–19). The second-highest level of command consisted of three more officers: the field marshal ("Tartan" in 2 Kings 18:17), who carried out the king's commands and led campaigns when the king did not accompany the army;

the vice-chancellor, who advised on affairs of state; and the chief steward or major-domo, who controlled access to the king.[8] At the top of the hierarchy, of course, stood the king, who often but not always led the army on campaign. Senior officers including the king seem to have carried maces as symbols of authority (Fig. 6.3).

Many officers commanded infantry made up of different types of troops, including elite Guards who always accompanied the king (but note their failure to protect him in 2 Kings 19:37). Many served as spearmen, attacking with spears perhaps five feet long and protecting themselves with helmets and round shields (Fig. 7.1—left). These often served as the shock troops both in open battles and when attacking fortified cities.

The infantry also included different types of archers and slingers. Sometimes these wear different types of clothing in the reliefs, apparently reflecting varying ethnic groups (Fig. 7.1—center). Other times, the differences seem connected to their function. Light auxiliary archers and slingers wore cloth garments and often head coverings and went about barefoot, while heavily armed troops had conical helmets with earflaps, partial or complete coats of mail, and boots (Fig. 7.1—right). Archers and slingers who fired from the rear of the battlefield had no shields, while those who supplied close covering fire for siege engines were typically protected by a fellow soldier carrying a shield with one of many different shapes, sizes, and materials. Note in Figure 6.6 the shield-bearer protecting an archer with a tall, full-body shield curving back at the top. Archers also had a quiver

Fig. 7.1—Spearman, light auxiliary archer, heavily armed slinger.

strapped over one shoulder and often carried a sword (see archer and slinger in Fig. 7.1) as well as their bow, in case they needed to fight hand-to-hand.

The infantry also included support troops such as engineers and personnel in charge of the supply train carrying food, tools, supplies, and siege equipment like rams and disassembled siege engines. The engineers would have gone ahead of the army to make necessary preparations so that the army could advance. They often cut new roads or enlarged existing ones, especially in the mountains, using picks and axes made of copper or iron. When a river was too deep for the army to ford, the engineers built rafts to ferry troops and equipment or built bridges of rafts lashed together with planks laid on top to serve as roads.[9] When the army laid siege to a city like Lachish, the engineers oversaw the construction of the ramps and the siege engines. Apparently they brought the engines in wagons, then assembled and operated them on site. The engineers may also have included the sappers, who tunneled under city walls to make them collapse. One might also include with the support personnel others like diviners, interpreters, intelligence officers, and the scribes who kept records like quantities of plunder and drew imagery to be depicted later on scenes back home.[10]

Chariotry

As with the infantry, the Assyrian chariotry required greater resources than the Assyrians naturally could provide—in this case, equestrian skill and an adequate supply of horses. Horses had become highly important for the military by the early 1st millennium, so the Assyrians conquered horse-producing regions to the north and northeast. They brought in horses by the thousands as tribute, as well as men skilled in horse training. One also finds frequent mention of horses and chariots in the lists of plunder, like "2,702 horses in teams and chariots, more than ever before . . . for the forces of my land."[11]

Unfortunately, the vague descriptions in the texts give little indication of the organization or numbers of the chariots. Units of fifty and titles for chariot officers are known, but how many there were and how they fit into the overall structure is not so clear. As with the Egyptians, the Assyrian texts provide incomplete but better information about numbers of enemy chariots than of their own. Shalmaneser III claims to have faced nearly 4,000 chariots from five kings at Qarqar in the 9th century, and Sargon II took a total of 700 chariots from five Levantine kingdoms he conquered in the late 8th century.[12]

In contrast to the vagueness of the texts, the reliefs portray a number of dramatic changes in the construction of Assyrian chariots over time, and offer some help as to their function. The frequent changes probably reflect attempts to improve this vital part of the military. Because of the reliefs, we know that chariots in the Neo-Assyrian Empire began as light vehicles with six-spoked wheels carrying an archer and driver (Fig. 6.2), much like in New Kingdom Egypt. By the early 9th century, reliefs show chariots with three horses, perhaps including a spare who didn't help pull the chariot but made for a quick replacement should one of the others get injured or killed.[13] As cavalry increasingly assumed the function of supplying light, mobile firing platforms, the Assyrians chariots grew in size. By the end of the empire, one finds chariots with four horses pulling larger, heavier vehicles that carried three or even four occupants (Fig. 7.2) using one or two shields. The chariot-warriors still typically fought with a composite bow, but sometimes used spears as well. These larger chariots required larger horses, which the Assyrians brought from Nubia and Egypt either in trade or as tribute.[14]

Cavalry   Though horses had been known in Mesopotamia from the 3rd millennium, only when advances in bridles in the early 1st millennium enabled soldiers to let go of their reigns and use their weapon, could soldiers use horses as cavalry. The Assyrians took advantage of this advancement to develop an extensive cavalry, though the changes took some time to develop. When Assyria first started using mounted troops, they fought in pairs with one rider holding a shield as well as the reigns for both so his partner could use his weapon, typically a composite bow. Eventually the riders learned to operate independently.[15] Cavalry troops had natural advantages over chariots—cavalry didn't require the big, expensive, and somewhat fragile wheeled box to carry their soldiers, plus horses alone could navigate terrain too difficult for chariots.

In contrast to the heavy horses that pulled the later, heavier Assyrian chariots, the cavalry required smaller horses that the Assyrians continued to bring from regions to the north. The Assyrian cavalrymen used a simple blanket rather than a saddle, apparently without stirrups or spurs. The dismounted cavalryman pictured at Lachish (Fig. 7.3) wore a conical helmet, a corselet made of scale armor, a tasseled garment over leggings, and boots. An elliptical bow case is strapped to his back, and he carries a spear and wears a short, sheathed sword. His well-decorated stallion sports a nicely groomed mane, a tail tied in a knot, and its decorated bridle sports a plume on top, making the horse appear taller.

Its advantages over chariotry notwithstanding, maintaining the cavalry still would have represented formidable logistical challenges for the army. This chapter has already mentioned the problems with obtaining and training the horses. The army would also need to supply large quantities of grain and straw for the horses during their training and for the entire time

Fig. 7.2—Heavy Assyrian chariot, late Neo-Assyrian Empire. Note four horses pulling vehicle with large, eight-spoked wheels, ridden by driver, archer, and two shield-bearers.

and distance of each campaign, as well as back home between campaigns. The army needed a good supply of replacement horses as well, and both cavalry and chariotry troops risked getting stranded in battle if an enemy soldier shot or speared one of the large equestrian targets that they were riding or driving. When shown with protection, the horses appear to wear coverings of leather (Figs. 6.2, 7.2).

Assyrian cavalry fought with either bow or spear, thus either from long or short range. Cavalry operated particularly well in open battle or in hilly or wooded regions, but not against fortified cities. In open battle, like at Eltekeh (mentioned earlier), the mounted archers (cavalry and chariotry) may have closed enough to fire the first shots. Then they may have moved to the wings to continue firing when the armies drew near enough for the archers in the infantry to begin their attack.

Fig. 7.3—**Dismounted cavalryman at Lachish**

As the battle lines closed further, the mounted spearmen could have begun the charge, followed by spearmen on foot.[16]

Navy

As noted at the beginning of this section, the Assyrians had little need for a proper navy most of the time. The army usually operated far from large bodies of water, but often along the major Mesopotamian rivers. The three main Assyrian capitals (Ashur, Calah, and Nineveh) were all located along the Tigris River, and the Assyrians used the river extensively for transportation.[17]

The army made use of different types of river vessels. One of the most common was the *kelek,* a large raft made from numerous inflated sheep- or goatskins attached to the bottom of a wooden frame. The *kelek* transported goods by floating downstream to the desired destination, where it was dismantled. The Assyrians also used coracles—large, round, flat-bottomed sturdy reed baskets sealed with bitumen that worked well for ferrying goods short distances. When these simple river craft wouldn't suffice, the Assyrians hired craftsmen from Phoenicia to build conventional boats with prow and stern, powered by oars. Sennacherib used such ships, manned by Phoenician sailors, to sail down the Tigris to the location of Baghdad, then cross to the Euphrates in a canal before sailing the rest of the way down to the Persian Gulf. From there he launched an attack on Elam in the eastern Gulf coast in what is today southwestern Iran.[18]

General Information
Unfortunately, the Assyrian sources describing the branches of the military just discussed supply only fragmentary information about the size of the Assyrian army. They describe much more clearly the roles of the Assyrian kings and gods, discussed next.

Size of Army

As was the case with Egypt, the Assyrian texts and reliefs present an incomplete and often questionable picture regarding the numbers of their own troops and those of their enemies. The earlier Assyrian royal annals seldom give numbers of troops or casualties, but when they do, they list rather believable numbers in the hundreds and low thousands. The numbers seem to grow logically as the empire grew in size and wealth. Shalmaneser III (late 9c) claimed to have 44,000 troops; Tiglath-pileser III (mid-late 8c) 72,950; Sargon II (late 8c) 90,580; Sennacherib (early 7c) 208,000.[19] One provincial governor reportedly commanded 1,500 cavalry and 20,000 archers, suggesting that the entire army from more than a score of provinces could potentially number in the hundreds of thousands, though a king rarely summoned all available troops at one time.[20]

On the other hand, the Assyrian records often appear suspect as well. Annals from the later Neo-Assyrian Empire list rather large numbers that are more difficult to accept. Sennacherib claimed that the Elamites lost an incredible 150,000 men in a battle against him in 691 BC. One can also see that successive reports by the same king about the same campaign give increasingly larger numbers for plunder and captives, though these number could conceivably be including later tribute and additional deportations.[21] All in all, the Assyrian army clearly grew quite large, though just how large remains unclear.

The same would be true for the branches within the army. The numbers of infantry, chariots, and cavalry are given only piecemeal, and a comprehensive picture remains beyond the scope of what our present information can provide. Our information can give some indication of the relative proportion of infantry to chariots and chariots to cavalry for some of Assyria's enemies, though the numbers come from Assyria and thus may be suspect. For example, Shalmaneser III claims to have defeated a coalition of twelve kings and their armies at Qarqar in 853 BC. Five of these contributed chariots in numbers ranging from thirty to 2,000[22] (from Ahab of Israel), and only Damascus and Hamath brought cavalry (1,200 and 700, respectively). The three largest purportedly brought chariotry and infantry in ratios of 1:17, 1:14, and 1:5 (lower because of Ahab's large chariot force). The two who brought cavalry brought equal numbers of cavalry and chariots. By contrast, in the late 8th century Sargon II gave chariotry and cavalry to his Babylonian governor at a ratio of ten cavalry for every chariot, apparently illustrating the dominance of cavalry by that time.[23]

Role of the King   In general, ancient Near Eastern kingdoms expected their monarchs to lead them effectively in battle (cf. the justification for Israel asking God for a king in 1 Sam. 8:19–20). For the militaristic kingdom of Assyria, this function was paramount. "The chief occupation of the Assyrian king and state was warfare. All other interests were subordinate to this central concern and over the centuries Assyria developed military expertise far surpassing that of any other contemporary nation."[24]

Usually the kings led by marching with their armies to make command decisions on the spot. Often, but not always, they personally fought in battle. Sargon II personally led one successful cavalry charge that penetrated the enemy camp and neutralized their chariotry by shooting the horses.[25] Sargon apparently was killed later in battle, and Esarhaddon died en route to Egypt while on campaign. If the king didn't accompany the army, he maintained good communication and passed on orders to his field commanders through the Assyrian system of communication, discussed below under "Intelligence."

The Assyrian kings often led the military well, and they gave credit to their gods for that success. Ascribing credit to their gods didn't keep the kings from pride, however. Adad-narari II in the early 8th century wrote, "I am king, I am lord, I am powerful, I am important, I am praiseworthy, I am magnificent, I am strong, I am mighty, I am fierce, I am enormously radiant, I am a hero, I am a warrior, I am a virile lion, I am foremost, I am exalted, I am raging."[26] Such pride earned the condemnation of Israel's God, who said through the prophet Isaiah, "I will punish the king of Assyria for the willful pride of his heart and the haughty look in his eyes. For he says: 'By the strength of my hand

I have done this, and by my wisdom, because I have understanding. I removed the boundaries of nations, I plundered their treasures; like a mighty one I subdued their kings'" (Isa. 10:12–13).

The Assyrian kings credited their gods with their military successes, and justified the entirety of their expansionistic policy on theological grounds, much like in Egypt and other ancient Near Eastern empires. Esarhaddon wrote in the 7th century, "Ashur, father of the gods, empowered me to depopulate and repopulate (deport conquered populations), to make broad the boundary of the land of Assyria."[27] When rebellious vassals refused to pay tribute, the Assyrians wrote that the vassals had acted sinfully, so defeating them in war simply brought about justice. For example, Sargon explained punishing the disloyal vassal king of Carchemish by saying, "In my 5th regnal year, Pisiri, the Carchemishite sinned against the treaty of the great gods (by making a forbidden alliance). . . . I lifted my hands to Ashur, my Lord." Sargon exiled the king and his family and plundered the palace and exported the residents who had joined in the rebellion and settled Assyrians in Carchemish in their place.[28]

Role of the Gods

The Assyrians believed that their gods accompanied the king and the army, and they portrayed this using standards, much like the Egyptians did. The texts sometimes mention one of the gods or Ishtar, goddess of battle, accompanying the king into battle, probably represented by some kind of standard. Other texts note a pair of standards on the king's right and left, though which gods the standards represent is not consistent. Sometimes people on foot, perhaps priests, carried these standards. Other times the reliefs show them mounted on chariots (Fig. 7.4). The standards typically appear as circles mounted on poles with some sort of sacred emblem inside the circle. Often a spear protrudes from the top, and tassels dangle beneath. The standards were carried or set in chariots during the march, and were set on the ground or left fastened to ceremonial chariots for certain religious functions.[29]

The Assyrian kings knew what their gods wanted them to do through one or more types of divination. The Assyrian priests often received direction from the god(s) by slaughtering an animal and examining its organs. Before killing the animal, the priests would write on a clay tablet a question like "Will the troops of either (of various enemies), or any enemy whatever, strive and plot against me?" The priests would set the tablet before the god, slaughter the animal, and interpret the shapes, sizes, colors, or various abnormalities of the organs to determine the god's answer. (Compare David's four questions to Yahweh about one military action in 1 Sam. 23:1–12.)

Fig. 7.4—Divine standards and ceremonial chariot. First standard depicts god Ashur with drawn bow, on bull. Second shows spearhead between two streams, flanked by bulls.

The Assyrians thought the gods also communicated with them through prophetic utterances or through astrology. Prophecies came when a priest went into an ecstatic state and gave a message purportedly from the god, typically approving the king's action and offering encouragement.[30] Then, toward the end of the Neo-Assyrian Empire, astrology took over as the primary way to hear from the gods. Priests observed celestial events (e.g. eclipses, thunder, positions of planets) and applied the message appropriately (cf. the thunder that launched the Israelite victory over the Philistines in 1 Sam. 7:10). Messages might be something like the following: "When at the observation of the moon it is high, the enemy will take the land by force" or "When a halo surrounds the moon and Jupiter stands inside it, the king of Akkad will be shut in by force."[31]

WEAPONS

A military establishment as great as Assyria's relied on its gods, and on effective weaponry. The Assyrians used short-, medium-, and long-range weapons typical of the era as well as defensive implements and equipment like chariots and siege engines. Their chariots and siege engines show a meaningful amount of change over the course of the Neo-Assyrian Empire. Assyrian pictorial records preserve in great detail the appearance of many weapons, far more than their texts describe how those weapons were used.

The Neo-Assyrian Empire stretched over the time period (9th–8th centuries) that witnessed the transition from bronze to iron as the primary metal for producing weapons. Both had to be imported into Assyria in large quantities, as the home region lacked the necessary supplies of these metal ores. Assyria had traded in metals since the beginning of the 2nd millennium, but their craftsmen remained technologically and artistically inferior to those in kingdoms like Urartu in the mountains to the north. Thus, the Assyrians brought in refined metals and finished objects whenever possible, either through trade, tribute, or plunder. In one case Sargon II listed 305,000 bronze daggers as part of the plunder from a successful campaign in Urartu. Excavators at Khorsabad, Sargon's ancient military compound of Dur-Sharrukin, unearthed 160 tons of iron and iron implements that Sargon collected from his campaigns.[32]

Short-Range Weapons

The Assyrians used these metals to make a number of different weapons for hand-to-hand fighting, including swords and spears and sometimes maces, daggers, and axes.

The role of maces and daggers is unclear, even though one sees many different maces in reliefs and finds frequent mention of daggers in the texts. Reliefs often show high-ranking officers, up to and including the king himself, carrying maces of many different designs.[33] However, they may have served as a symbol of office and as a ceremonial weapon rather than as an actual weapon of war. Likewise, the Assyrians had many daggers, as suggested by the large number taken from Urartu, but the daggers also appear to have functioned frequently for ceremony and ritual. How much they were used in battle is uncertain.[34] The Assyrians also used axes, but apparently they were used most often as tools.[35]

Mace, Dagger

Swords, by contrast, served as a common and important military weapon[36], though some had highly decorated hilts and sheaths with lions or bulls (Fig. 7.5—bottom), and must have functioned more ceremonially. Most Assyrian swords were straight with double-edged blades; a few had blades that were curved or slightly leaf-shaped (Fig. 7.5—top). The royal annals reflect the weapon's importance with common statements like "I felled with the sword (some large number) of their fighting men."[37]

Sword

Soldiers typically wore their swords over the left thigh attached to a belt. Often the belts connected to one or more shoulder straps to relieve some of the weight from the belt.

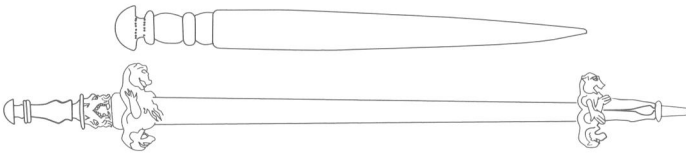

Fig. 7.5—Assyrian swords. Top—common, leaf-shaped sword from mid-late 8th century. Bottom—ornate sword decorated with lions from early 9th century.

Spear   Finally, the Assyrians also used spears frequently, both in the infantry for hand-to-hand fighting on foot (Fig. 7.1—left) and in the cavalry (Fig. 7.3).[38] Earlier spears are shown as relatively short, with a length of perhaps five feet. Beginning in the time of Sargon II in the late 8th century, the spears (now perhaps better called lances) of the cavalry reach approximately nine feet in length. The shafts appear to be made of wood, inserted into a socketed spearhead. The spearheads were typically leaf-shaped (Fig. 7.6 top) or rhombic with a thick midrib for strength (Fig. 7.6 bottom). The butt ends are sometimes shown set into ferrules, probably for decoration and/or for planting in the ground when not in use. The ferrules occasionally appear with tassels or streamers (Fig. 7.6).[39]

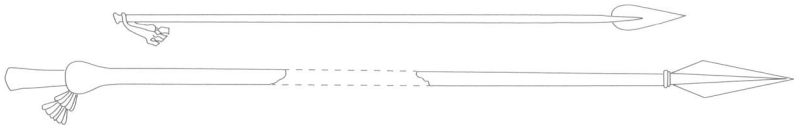

Fig. 7.6—Assyrian spears. Top—shorter spear with leaf-shaped spearhead. Bottom—longer spear with socketed rhomboid spearhead with large midrib. Both have added decorations at butt end.

Medium-Range Weapons

Javelin   Like most other contemporary militaries, the Assyrians used javelins, a smaller version of the spear meant for throwing a moderate distance.

Assyrian reliefs sometimes show their chariots carrying javelins, apparently for throwing at enemy troops or horses. In one battle, Sargon led an attack of cavalry against an enemy's chariotry, and he and his cavalry disabled the chariots by shooting the horses with arrows and javelins.

Long-Range Weapons

The bow seems to have served as the Assyrians' main long-range weapon, perhaps even the army's primary weapon. One author described the bow as "the national weapon carried by everyone."[40] The

Bow

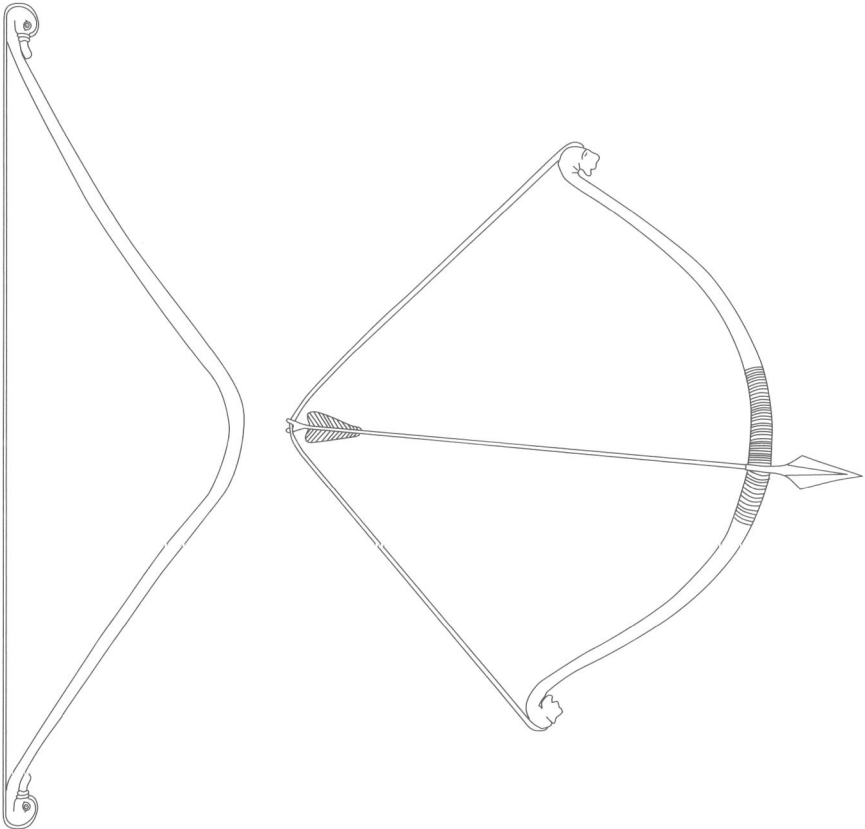

Fig. 7.7—Assyrian composite angular bows. Note heads of ducks on left, lions on right.

large numbers of arrowheads found at sites of battles attest to its importance. The Assyrian king declared war and began sieges by shooting an arrow in the direction of the enemy (Fig. 7.11 where the king is portrayed shooting at the besieged city, though obviously well after the siege commenced). Sennacherib's reliefs portray the king, immediately after the victory at Lachish, sitting on his throne, holding a bow in one hand and two arrows pointed upward in the other, apparently to symbolize victory.[41] Assyria had large numbers of archers in its infantry, both lightly and heavily armed, with different types of dress reflecting the different regions from which they came (Fig. 7.1—center). Charioteers also used the bow as their primary weapon, though their bows, as well as those used by cavalry and troops in siege engines, appear smaller than the bows of archers in the infantry (note the size difference of the bows in Fig. 6.6).

The Assyrian reliefs occasionally show their archers using simple bows made from a single piece of wood, but most often they used more powerful composite bows made of multiple layers of wood glued together. Assyrians often used angular composite bows, where the relatively straight arms met at the handle in an angle that disappeared when the bow was drawn. Often the ends where the string attached were shaped like heads of ducks or occasionally lions (Fig. 7.7) to make it easier to attach the string as well as for decoration.[42]

Assyrian arrows varied somewhat in size and design. The shaft would have been made of some light, tough wood, and the arrowheads of bronze or iron. Some arrowheads ended in a tang that was inserted into the shaft, though the superior design had a socket into which the shaft was inserted and fastened. Most arrowheads ranged in length from approximately two to four inches, often with a reinforcing rib that tapered at the front. The tail typically had two feathers and ended in a crescent or V-shaped notch (Fig. 7.8). Archers carried their arrows in quivers and

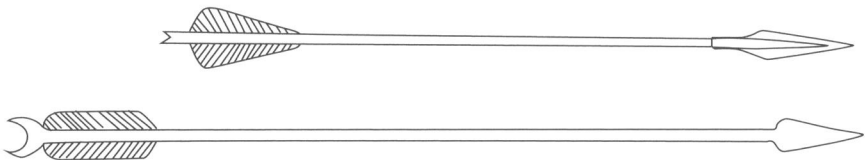

Fig. 7.8—Assyrian arrows.

their bows in bow cases of widely different sizes and designs, often decorated with geometric or floral designs. The quivers sometimes had a rod on one side to stiffen it and make it easier to attach to a shoulder strap.[43]

Assyrian reliefs picture slingers beginning in the late 8th century,[44] operating in pairs with piles of sling stones at their feet. Some are heavily and some are lightly armored (Fig. 7.1—right). They used slings with long straps apparently made of leather, and at Lachish at least, slung flint stones approximately 2.5 inches in diameter, well rounded to fly straighter. In contrast to the Egyptian slinger in Fig. 3.10, who is apparently whirling his sling horizontally overhead, the Assyrian slingers appear to whirl their slings vertically at their sides. The distinction may reflect different methods actually practiced, or may simply appear different due to artistic representation.

Sling

Defensive Equipment

In addition to their offensive weaponry, the Assyrian soldiers also used defensive equipment such as helmets, scale armor, and shields of various kinds.

The reliefs show literally scores of different types of helmets, apparently reflecting changing needs, styles, and possibly what they had taken from others as tribute or plunder. Helmets were made of hammered sheet metal with pieces attached by rivets. Many of the typical styles were conical, quite common in the ancient Near East during the 1st millennium, apparently to deflect downward blows by one's enemy. Sometimes conical helmets had earflaps and/or reinforcing ribs at the rim (Fig. 7.9—left). Another common style looked more like a squat, inverted funnel, again at times with earflaps and ribbing, as well as neckguard (Fig. 7.9—center). A third and final common style sported a crest sometimes curving forward (Fig. 7.9—right) made of metal and adorned with some type of bristles or feathers, perhaps somewhat like the earlier distinctive Philistine headdress (Fig. 5.1, etc.).[45]

Helmet

In addition to helmets, the Assyrians also protected many of their troops with scale armor. Some of the light auxiliary archers and slingers wore only cloth or leather garments, but the higher-tiered troops enjoyed the protection of expensive and heavy scale armor, made of either bronze or iron. Assyrian metal scales recovered at Lachish each had a rib running down the center, perhaps for strength as well as to keep the overlying scales hanging straight. The scales also had holes for sewing them to an undergarment. Most often, armored troops wore scale armor just on their corselet to protect their upper torso. Those who needed more

Armor

protection, like some heavy archers, also had a skirt-like covering ex-tending to their ankles, and some had scale-armor neck protectors ap-parently attached to their helmets.

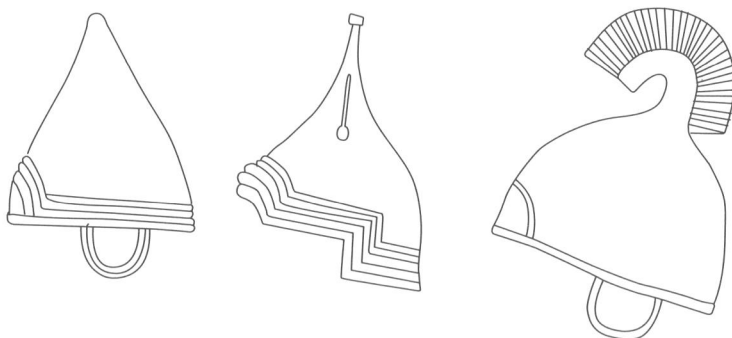

Fig. 7.9—Basic types of Assyrian helmets.

Shield
Most troops also carried shields of various sizes, shapes, and mate-rials.[46] The variations likely represent different approaches to balancing the conflicting needs of protecting oneself with the need for mobility. The simplest shields were round and flat (Fig. 7.1—left), apparently made from a single piece of metal, approximately 2.5 feet in diameter. The sol-dier held on to a handle fastened to the center of the shield with rivets. Other round shields bore concentric circles, apparently reinforcing ridges (Fig. 7.10—left), with the spaces between the ridges sometimes decorated with geometric and floral designs.

Other shields of various shapes show patterns suggesting wick-erwork in various patterns, often resembling brick-work (Figs. 7.10—center, 7.12). The wickerwork would have been lighter than metal, but obviously still strong enough to stop an arrow. Some round shields were larger (about four feet in diameter), conical, and made of metal, appar-ently to better protect the soldiers' sides and to deflect arrows (Fig. 7.10—right). Some shields were rectangular and either flat or curved (Figs. 6.2, 7.12). The very largest shields had curved tops, flat bottoms resting on the ground (Fig. 6.6), apparently made from wicker, and were held by a shield-bearer to protect himself and an archer during a siege.

Chariots
The chariot was apparently developed around the 17th century BC by

the Mitannian peoples in Syria and northern Mesopotamia and became a major military implement throughout the ancient Near East. The Assyrians developed close contact with the Mitanni and likely adopted the chariot within the next three to four centuries. By the beginning of the Neo-Assyrian Empire, the Assyrians were using light chariots with two riders pulled by two horses, very much like Egyptian chariots of the 18th Dynasty, apart from a few relatively small differences. The Assyrian chariots used an elliptically shaped shaft connecting the car to the horses' yoke and carried a slanting lance or standard mounted to the back of the car (Fig. 6.2).

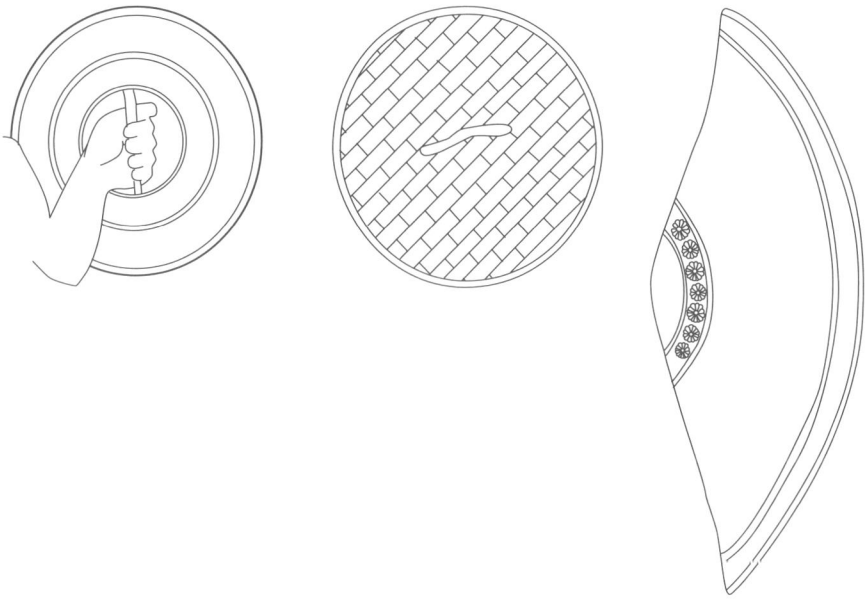

Fig. 7.10—Basic types of Assyrian shields. Reinforced metal (left), wickerwork (center), conical metal (right).

Assyrian chariots carried various weapons in addition to the chariot-warrior's bow. Their early chariots usually had two quivers attached at crossed diagonals along the side of the car next to the warrior (Fig. 6.2). Later the design shifted to one or two quivers mounted vertically on the front (Fig. 7.2), with perhaps one or two set diagonally on the side as well. Sometimes the chariots also carried a javelin plus one or two axes in the quivers along with the arrows in case the charioteers had to fight hand-to-hand.

Earlier, this chapter noted the progression to larger, heavier chariots during the course of the Neo-Assyrian Empire. The chariot wheels show a dramatic increase in size, sometimes even higher than a man. The number of spokes in the wheels increases from six to eight, and the wheels are occasionally studded with nails (Fig. 7.2). Decorations for the horses on these later chariots grow more ornate, with tassels, disks, crests of bristles or feathers, and perhaps streamers. The horses often wear protective leather coverings, sometimes with elaborate decorations (Figs. 6.2, 7.2).[47]

Siege Engines

As was the case with the chariot, the Assyrians used siege engines throughout the Neo-Assyrian Empire, and the design changed repeatedly over that time. Essentially the engines consisted of a battering ram mounted on a frame and covered by protective materials, all of which could be rolled up to the wall of a city under attack. Usually the engine also carried archers who provided covering fire so the men manning the ram could create a breach in the wall.

Assyrian reliefs portray some six different styles of engines.[48] Each had a rather rectangular box apparently made of wood and covered with wickerwork or perhaps leather, which was sometimes decorated. The box rolled on four or six wheels and housed one or two rams. The engine usually had one tower (though one style possibly had two) on the front, usually to protect archers who provided covering fire from within or on top of the tower. The heads on the rams took various shapes including pointed like a large spearhead (Fig. 6.6), and blunt (Fig. 7.11). The earliest designs date from the early 9th century, and appear much larger than those used later. The later designs, such as the one used at Lachish, are more compact, perhaps to make it easier to transport the engines to the desired target.

TACTICS

After discussing the organization and weaponry of the Assyrian military, this chapter now turns to military tactics and related matters of strategy. What motivated the Assyrians' extensive military practice? When did they fight? How did they organize their marches and supplies? Why were they

Fig. 7.11—Siege engines from early 9th century. Six-wheeled tower with rounded top, perhaps three stories high, with blunt-nosed ram. Also higher, second tower behind the first, apparently to provide additional covering fire.

so brutal? What were their strategies for pitched battle, and laying siege? And finally, what do we know about matters after the battle such as treaties, plunder, and prisoners of war?

Motivation

As noted earlier, Assyria's military activity began out of necessity, but this gave way to greed with an overlay of religious justification. Assyria's exposed position in the northern Mesopotamian river plain left it vulnerable to attack from nearby peoples. The Assyrians defended themselves by taking the offensive, but the plunder from successful campaigns soon shifted their primary motivation from protection to greed and pride. Their military enabled them to acquire materials that they lacked, such as timber, stone, metal, and horses, and the threat of repeated military action resulted in annual tribute from those they conquered. Continued success brought a greater area of control, plus honor to the nation and to the king who led them. The Assyrians justified their actions theologically, expanding the status of their chief god Ashur from that of a regional deity to one who claimed sovereignty over the entire ancient Near East. The Assyrians found this mixture of greed, glory, and religious fervor an intoxicating one, and they imbibed as much as they could.

Strategy

Over Assyria's long history, with its periods of expansion and contraction, one can see its overall strategy for building, maintaining, and benefiting from its empire. From the records of the Assyrians' frequent campaigns, one can also see elements of strategy in matters such as logistics, psychological warfare, and cruelty, which enabled them to carry out their overall plans.

Season for War

Like most armies in the region, the Assyrians preferred to begin their campaigns some time around late April until early June, after the winter rains and following the completion of the wheat harvest, when the farmers became available. The Assyrians' frequent campaigns into the mountains often took place during the summer so the king and his troops could escape the summer heat, which could reach up to 120 degrees Fahrenheit on the Assyrian plain. The farmers always hoped to finish the summer campaigning before the heavy agricultural activity in October and November, but as the military needs grew, men could find themselves under arms at any time during the year.[49] If the campaign continued through the winter, the army chose a suitable spot to wait it out.

Fig. 7.12—Soldier crossing river using inflated goatskin as flotation device.

The March

Typically, the army launched its campaigns after assembling at a general staging site called the Review Palace, the great military compound at the capital. Once preparations were complete, the king inspected the troops, the religious personnel performed their rites, and the army set off. Imperial standards led the way (cf. Fig. 7.4), accompanied by priests and diviners. Next came the king with his bodyguard and elite troops, followed in turn by the chariotry, cavalry, levied infantry, and finally, the support train. For major campaigns the army would add contingents of levied troops at predetermined meeting points on the way to the field of battle. When the situation called for great haste, the king sometimes departed with just the chariotry or the standing army without waiting for the levied troops to assemble. For example, Sennacherib says that when he left for Babylon, "I did not wait for my forces, nor did I hold back for the rear guard."[50]

The army marched perhaps fifteen to thirty miles per day, depending on the need, the terrain, and the conditions. Numerous campaigns in the nearby mountains forced Assyrian engineers to widen roads or cut new ones. Kings boasted of passing through rugged terrain "where even birds cannot fly." At other times rivers blocked the path, and the army relied on boats, floating bridges (see earlier discussion under "Navy"), or required soldiers to paddle across using inflated animal skins as flotation devices (Fig. 7.12).[51] Kings boasted how many times they (along with the army) crossed the Euphrates "in its flood." At other times water was scarce and the need for it grew critical. One Assyrian ruler acknowledged losing forty troops due to the lack of water.[52]

Food and Logistics   The army on the march could bring only part of the food it needed, typically using mules as pack animals and carts pulled by mules or oxen. The supply train carried a quantity of barley for the men, plus barley and straw for the horses. Provisions were issued daily. When the army captured enemy stores, the king sometimes allowed the soldiers to eat "without measure." Part of the organization of the empire included selecting sites for garrisons and having local governors or allied rulers stock them with food and supplies from which the army could draw as it passed through. When in enemy territory, the army ate off the land a great deal and looted as needed.

Intelligence   In addition to supplies, the Neo-Assyrian Empire required an effective system of intelligence gathering and communication. Governors and officials in border areas collected and passed on information, as did paid spies and captured and interrogated enemy troops. Second Kings 18:19–35 may reflect an example of Assyrian intelligence. In this instance, an Assyrian officer comes to Jerusalem urging the people to surrender. He knows about Hezekiah's religious reform and the theological basis for resisting, and he uses them to motivate the people to surrender the city. Apparently the Assyrians obtained that information from an informer of some kind.

However they gathered the information, the Assyrians passed it back to the capital over a system of roads kept in good repair for royal messengers. They carried information written in cuneiform on small tablets or on scrolls written in Aramaic. The messengers used a system of horses kept at relay stations, enabling them to deliver information from the Levant to the capital in just a few days.[53] People such as officers, officials, captives, and informers followed the information at a more normal speed to follow up on it as needed.

Battle Tactics

The Assyrians used the intelligence they gathered to help them achieve their military objectives. When they wished to subdue or to reconquer a region, they had various ways to achieve their goal. They preferred victory through psychological warfare if at all possible, and they were masters at it. Their acts of cruelty and subsequent proclamation of those acts helped them win many battles without firing an arrow. When they did have to fight, they had options—engaging in pitched battle, storming a city, and laying siege to a city, all of which are discussed below. One also finds in the annals tactics like night marches, ambushes, deception and infiltration, and guerilla warfare.

Even though their military was unmatched for its time, the Assyrians preferred not to use it. They preferred to threaten to use it and have the enemy surrender without engaging.[54] Battles consumed time, energy, and manpower, even for the victors, so the Assyrians preferred to secure an enemy's surrender and tribute without fighting, whenever possible. Not destroying the enemy left open the possibility that they could rebel in the future, but not destroying them also left them better able to pay more tribute.

When conquering a region, Assyria often practiced a form of psychological warfare by using a limited amount of actual force but threatening much more. Once they targeted a region, they used diplomacy and threats to try to motivate surrender. If these didn't work, they sent in the army, selected the easiest target from among several small cities, and conquered it. Then they subjected the place to extreme acts of cruelty, including looting, burning, murdering, raping, flaying, mutilating, and enslaving the population. They then broadcast news of these acts to nearby cities to convince them to surrender without further attack.[55]

Psychological Warfare and Cruelty

This practice may explain the Assyrians' actions as portrayed in the aftermath of their conquest of Lachish. They impaled some captives on poles (Fig. 6.5), killed or dismembered others, apparently flayed still others (Fig. 7.13), and deported the surviving inhabitants before looting and burning the city. Perhaps they treated Lachish so brutally to help motivate Jerusalem's surrender and thus avoid having to take the army up into the Judean hills to attack that well-fortified city. Clearly, Sennacherib used the victory and subsequent acts of brutality at Lachish for further propaganda, decorating his reception room in his new palace in Nineveh with a long row of scenes depicting the conquest of Lachish and its aftermath. Officials visiting Sennacherib in his palace would meet the king in this room, with its striking visual representations of what would happen to those who didn't submit to the Assyrian will.

Such acts have earned the Assyrians the reputation of acting with particular cruelty. In addition to committing the brutal acts mentioned above, they also blinded; decapitated; removed noses, ears, and extremities; and created piles of bodies or body parts in front of targeted cities. Their rulers and kings boasted about these acts. Tiglath-pileser III wrote that he "impaled alive (the enemy king's) chief ministers; and I made his country behold them" (cf. Fig. 6.5). Ashurnasirpal II boasted, "I fixed up a pile of corpses in front of the city's gate. I flayed the nobles, as many as rebelled, and spread their skins out on the piles. . . . I flayed many within my land and spread their skins out on the walls." Another ruler "removed the hands and lower lips of eighty of their troops. I let them go free to spread the news of my glory."[56] "The news of my glory" undoubtedly included news of the atrocities and would hopefully discourage others from resisting demands for surrender (compare Nahash's treatment of the inhabitants of Jabesh Gilead in 1 Samuel 11:2).

In their defense, the Assyrians seem to have reserved the cruelest acts for the most rebellious subjects. Disloyal subjects became the objects of

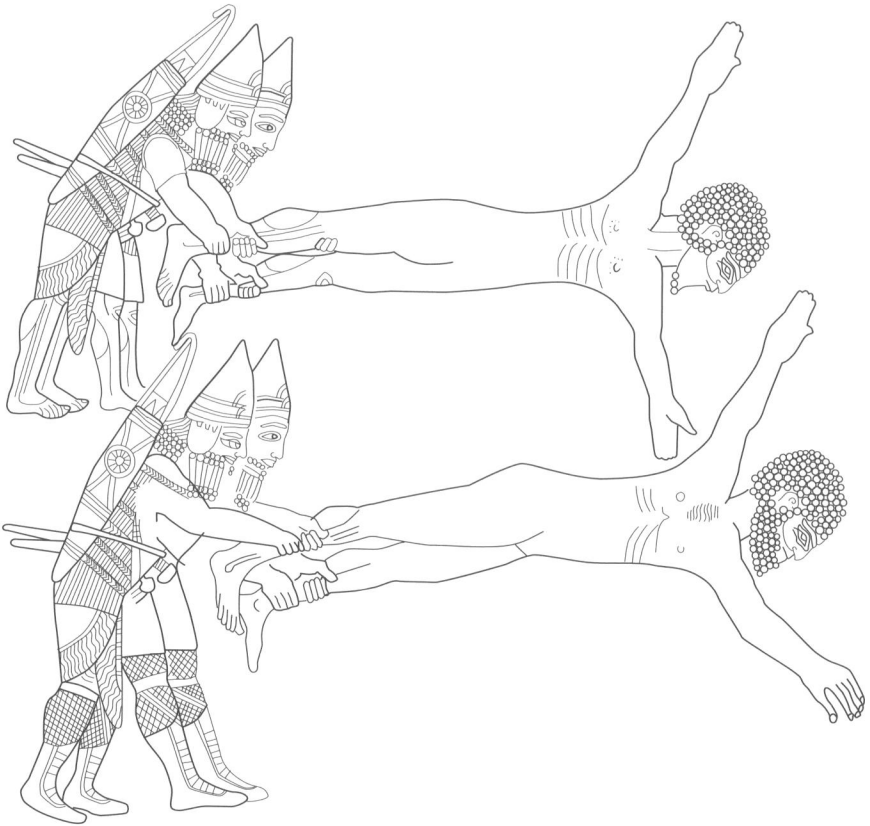

Fig. 7.13—Archers stretch out naked captives from Lachish, possibly for flaying

punitive campaigns, and if repeated punitive campaigns didn't prevent further rebellion, Assyria deported the population. Tiglath-pileser III appears to have attempted to get Israel to cooperate as a vassal (2 Kings 15:19–20, 29), but when it wouldn't, Shalmaneser V finished conquering the nation, made it an Assyrian province, and deported a large number of Israelites.

Apparently the threat of destruction and cruelty often worked. The Assyrian annals frequently tell of the army marching to a region and collecting tribute without further military action. Shalmaneser III collected tribute from Jehu of Israel and other regional rulers in 841 BC (see Fig. 6.8 and accompanying text). Approximately one century later, Tiglath-pileser III did likewise with Menahem of Israel (see 2 Kings 15:19–20, where Tiglath-pileser III is called Pul). In some cases, a king like Ahaz of Judah voluntarily paid tribute and became Assyria's vassal in exchange for military aid (2 Kings 16:7–9).

When cities or nations didn't give in easily, the Assyrians often used additional psychological tactics to encourage surrender before attacking, with 2 Kings 18:17–37 providing an excellent example. During the attack at Lachish, Sennacherib sent three high-ranking officers to Jerusalem to call for the city's surrender. They used several arguments to emphasize the futility of resisting Assyria. Knowing that Judah was expecting Egypt to protect them, the officers pointed out how unreliable Egypt was. They also knew the Judeans were trusting Yahweh to deliver them, and noted that Hezekiah had removed a number of places of worship in his recent religious reform, implying that Yahweh might now be less inclined to help. Next, the Assyrians taunted Judah for its limited military ability, especially compared to Assyria.

The Judean officials could offer little response. They asked the Assyrians to speak in Aramaic rather than Hebrew so the common Judeans couldn't understand these taunts, but the Assyrians continued in Hebrew to make sure the commoners knew what was at stake.[57] They pointed out how all Judeans would suffer or benefit based on their leaders' decisions. If they continued resisting and the city went under siege, the inhabitants would have to "eat their own excrement and drink their own urine." By contrast, if the leaders surrendered, the people would be deported in peace to a pleasant land full of "grain and new wine, a land of bread and vineyards, a land of olive trees and honey," where each could enjoy a good life and "eat fruit from your own vine and fig tree and drink water from your own cistern" (2 Kings 18:27–32). The Assyrians concluded their appeal with a final warning not to obey the king and trust in Yahweh. Though their arguments

Pitched
Battle
in Open

were strong, the Assyrian officers had to leave without securing Jerusalem's surrender.

When psychological warfare and cruelty did not produce the desired surrender and payment of tribute, the Assyrians also had a number of options on how to fight. For their initial military action in frontier regions, they often used small strike forces. These units harassed the local troops and civilians and conducted raids, perhaps to lower the morale of their enemies (compare similar Philistines raids in Israelite territory—1 Sam. 13:16–23).

The Assyrians also met opposing armies in pitched battles in the open. In such fighting the armies engaged in continuous warfare until one side achieved victory, probably within a matter of hours. Chariots were best suited to this type of fighting.[58] Unfortunately, the annals often report on such battles using terms too vague to describe the tactics used.

In one of the few accounts that clearly describe the tactics used, Sargon led an attack of cavalry that focused on the enemy chariotry. The Assyrian troops had suffered greatly on this campaign up into the mountains and moral was low, especially in the infantry. Sargon in his chariot personally led the charge with just his cavalry. The Assyrian horsemen targeted the enemy chariotry and immobilized the horses with arrows and javelins. The Assyrian cavalry then attacked the opposing commander's headquarters, cut up the infantry guarding it, and forced the enemy cavalry to surrender since they had insufficient room to maneuver in the mountain pass.[59]

The royal annals seem to indicate that Assyria fought more pitched battles during the time of expansion before they had established their superiority, such as under Shalmaneser III in the mid-9th century. From the time Tiglath-pileser III solidified Assyria's dominance in the mid- to late 8th century, they seem to have fought fewer battles out in the open. By then, Assyria's enemies knew that they had little chance of matching strength against strength, so they opted for other tactics such as seeking protection behind city walls. For example, during Sennacherib's campaign to the west in 701 BC as described earlier, his army seems to have fought only one pitched battle—against the Egyptians on the plain near Eltekeh. Apparently no other army dared take them on head to head. Most simply capitulated, and those who didn't hoped their fortifications would keep out the Assyrians. On this campaign, only Jerusalem succeeded.

During his campaign against Judah, Sennacherib reportedly

conquered forty-six walled cities and an unspecified number of smaller towns, rather typical claims for this type of campaign. In his earlier campaign against Babylon, Sennacherib had reported conquering a total of eighty-eight fortified cities and 820 villages.[60] Reports of other campaigns claimed the conquest of as many as 100, 150, or 250 cities—all large, round numbers. Regardless of the accuracy of these numbers, the campaigns apparently decimated regions that had withheld tribute and served as warning to others in the area to choose more wisely.

The campaigns of Sennacherib also seem to mark a general shift in Assyrian tactics. Sennacherib seems to have used more archers, both on foot and mounted, and slingers than had his predecessors. By the late 8th century, the siege engines were smaller and more easily transported. The Assyrians still used spearmen, but overall the tactics seem to favor more long-distance rather than hand-to-hand fighting,[61] perhaps to reduce casualties. This safer, more transportable style may reflect the need to sustain a viable fighting force over long periods covering long distances as the empire continued to expand and the army had to campaign over more territory.

Many Assyrian campaigns, like those of Sennacherib, seem primarily aimed at punishing vassals who decided to withhold tribute and hopefully hold out inside their fortified cities. Why would vassal states like Judah and cities along the Philistine and Phoenician coasts decide to withhold tribute and risk facing the Assyrian might? Even when they had years to prepare, as Hezekiah did,[62] what chance did they stand against the Assyrian military machine? They were taking a very high-stakes gamble, and to some degree, had time on their side.

Attacks on Cities

Vassals under a power like Assyria had to pay enormous amounts of tribute annually or else risk military retribution. Most or all wished to avoid paying the tribute, but had to weigh the chances of having the Assyrian army come to exact revenge. With such a large empire, Assyria had too many priorities to address them all adequately, and the vassals knew that. If Assyria sent its army in one direction for a year or multiple years of campaigning, vassals in other parts might well contemplate rebelling. Then, even when Assyria did send its army to a region, it only could allocate so much time to that particular campaign. The army had to return within a limited amount of time, and then perhaps switch to other priorities that had arisen. If a vassal or group of vassals could hold out longer than Assyria could afford to attack, the Assyrians might have to withdraw and possibly not return, at least for a time. Conversely, Assyria needed to break the rebels' morale and resistance quickly, and it often divided its forces to attack multiple targets simultaneously.[63] The risks were great—large amounts of money and numbers of lives hung in the balance in this international game of cat and mouse.

Though not stated in the biblical text or Sennacherib's annals (and not to discount the impact of losing a large number of troops, as described in 2 Kings 19:35–36), Jerusalem may have survived in part because Sennacherib ran out of time and decided to return to his capital without conquering this final city in Judah. He had already received tribute from Hezekiah (2 Kings 18:14–15) and inflicted severe damage by destroying many of his cities and giving large parts of his kingdom to nearby nations. Hezekiah would likely have little ability and motivation to resist further, even if the campaign ended with Jerusalem's walls intact.

When a rebellious vassal lost the gamble that the Assyrians couldn't or wouldn't attack and didn't surrender when the army showed up, the Assyrians needed to conquer the city. As described earlier, this could mean scaling the walls or otherwise penetrating the city's defenses in a relatively short period of time, breaching the walls to take the city in somewhat longer time frame (as at Lachish), or laying siege for an extended period of time.

Reliance on the walls for defense reduced the intensity of the engagement on both sides, allowing for a longer period of attack.[64] But the extended period also worked against both defender and attacker. The defenders were probably weaker to start with, and the increase in population with the approach of the army used up the city's stores of food and supplies more quickly and increased the likelihood of disease. Likewise, the attackers could only last so long, though they had the advantage of reinforcements if they weren't too far from home. As noted above, attackers often could allocate only a limited amount of time to the campaign, and walled cities sometimes did survive.

Usually, the attacker tried to penetrate the walls using surprise, deception, ladders, tunnels, or very often, breaches. The earlier account of the fall of Lachish describes the process of breaching walls as best as we currently understand it. As with many other aspects of the Assyrian military, the texts are quite vague: "I laid siege to the city _____, I conquered it and destroyed it." Pictures, archaeological remains, and analysis by those familiar with military strategy[65] fill in some of the gaps.

After the Battle

Following the successful conquest of a city or a victory out in the open, the Assyrians collected plunder, dealt with prisoners, (re-)established treaties, and otherwise dealt with the situation to best serve the needs of their empire.

Plunder

As noted already, gaining plunder served as the primary motivation for Assyrian military activity. The Assyrian records justified it theologically, then boasted about what they took. "By the command of Ashur, my lord, I took prisoners. . . . I carried off their booty, possessions, property, herds, and flocks and brought them to my city Ashur."[66] The Assyrians took as plunder items as mundane as barley, bread, beer, and oxen, and as exotic as purple wool, ivory (decorated) furniture, a bronze bathtub, and a tent decorated with gold. They also captured large numbers of animals. Sennacherib claims to have taken from Babylon 7,200 mules and horses, 11,073 asses, 5,230 camels, and 800,100 ewes for the crown, plus noting that the soldiers took more for themselves.[67] Whenever possible, the Assyrians took great quantities of metals both finished and unfinished, with amounts as high as twenty talents of gold, 2,300 talents of silver, 3,000 talents of bronze, and 5,000 talents of iron.[68]

Prisoners

The Assyrians also targeted capturing people, both for punishment and for a supply of labor. Often they would take away the defeated king and his family, apparently as punishment for leading the rebellion. They likewise deported increasingly large numbers of commoners, with numbers as high as 200,150 from Judah and 208,000 from Babylon. Sargon says of the king of Ashdod, "I counted as booty his gods, his wife, his sons, his daughters, the property, the possessions and treasures of this palace, together with the inhabitants of his land."[69]

Treaties

Once the Assyrians had defeated and looted an enemy, they organized the city or region in the manner most helpful to Assyria. When necessary, they incorporated conquered regions as Assyrian provinces. Repeatedly, rebellious vassals were liable to end up in provinces with Assyrian governors appointed to administer them and oversee the annual tax due to Assyria. Whenever possible, Assyria preferred to leave nations and cities as vassals, assuming they would remain loyal (submissive) and pay the assigned annual tribute. It was better to leave the administrative work to others and just collect the income.

For those who maintained their position as vassals, they had to swear an oath of loyalty in the name of some gods, sometimes non-Assyrian gods, sometimes Ashur. The vassals had to promise not to appeal to other nations for help against Assyria, in addition to other stipulations. If they broke the treaty, the gods would punish them. The Assyrians also took foreign princes and nobles as captives to ensure that treaties would be honored as well as to train them as loyal officials[70] (compare Daniel and friends taken captive for training—Dan. 1:3). Sennacherib installed one such official on the throne in Babylon "who was raised in my palace like a young puppy."[71]

Other
Events
after
the Battle

Although the Assyrians went to great lengths to punish regions that rebelled, they sometimes also took steps to rebuild conquered areas, perhaps for no greater reason than to make these subjects capable of producing more tax or tribute in the future. They deported large numbers of people, but repopulated some with deportees from other regions (such as Samaria—2 Kings 17:23–24). They often founded new settlements or rebuilt older ones and settled people, such as retired soldiers, there. In one case they planted orchards, repaired the embankment of the Euphrates, and built a temple and a palace for the new governor to be stationed there. This helped cultivate new lands to produce more food as well as establish centers where the army could resupply when on the march.[72]

A successful campaign ended with a victory parade in the Assyrian capital. The king led the parade in his chariot of state, followed by conquered royalty in chains.[73] The king often had inscriptions done to record his great exploits and honor the gods. Ashur and the other gods had done their part, and the king and the army had done theirs. Assyria had won again and enriched itself with more spoils. Assyria was the brutal master of the Middle East—at least for the time being.

NOTES

1   Grayson, *ARI* 1: XXI-XXII. Elsewhere, Grayson analyzes four battles between Assyria and Babylon in which both sides claimed victory, and he concludes that the Assyrians lost each time. He summarizes by saying, "Assyrian sources are always to be regarded with the greatest skepticism." ("Problematical Battles in Mesopotamian History," in *Studies in Honor of Benno Landsberger on his Seventy-Fifty Birthday April 21, 1965. (Assyriological Studies* 16; Chicago: University of Chicago, 1965, 342). In one example of apparent exaggeration describing the battle at Qarqar, Shalmaneser III claimed a smashing victory over a coalition of twelve kings. He boasts of having killed 14,000 enemy, such that "the field was too small for laying flat their bodies." Yet he had to return three more times over the next eight years to fight the

same coalition, suggesting that the victory wasn't so complete (*COS*, 2.113A, n. 35).

2   Grayson, "Assyrian Civilization," 213, 218.

3   Grayson, ARCT, 960, 966.

4   *COS* 2.118A.

5   Grayson, "Assyrian Civilization," 219.

6   *RIMA* 2, p. 255 (18:1–5).

7   Grayson, "Assyrian Civilization," 217.

8   Grayson, ARCT, 963.

9   This method of constructing a bridge was used in Baghdad as late as AD 1957 (Saggs, *The Might That Was Assyria*, 199).

10 Saggs, *Might,* 243–44.

11 *RIMA* 2, p. 178 (5:128–31).

12 *COS* 2.113A; 2.118A, B, D, E.

13 So, *AWBL,* 297–98, but Madhloom argues that the chariots must have had four horses even if the artist drew only three (*Chronology,* 16–19).

14 Dalley, AMMO, 418. In "Assyrian Civilization" (217), Grayson notes that the additional men in the chariots typically bore shields, and that the bows used by charioteers and cavalry were often smaller than those of the archers in the infantry.

Even after the cavalry eclipsed the chariotry in military importance, Assyrian kings continued to use chariots for prestige and for hunting. For example, Adad-narari II boasted that he killed 360 lions and 240 wild bulls "from my chariot . . . and on my swift feet with the spear" as well as 6 elephants (*RIMA* 2, p. 154 (2:122–27)).

15 Grayson, "Assyrian Civilization," 218.

16 *AWBL,* 297.

17 At Calah, excavators uncovered a quay more than 700 feet long, sunk twenty-one feet deep into the riverbank, rising thirty-three feet above bedrock. Sennacherib built a similar quay at Nineveh, and used it to bring limestone colossi to his capital (Saggs, *Might,* 197).

18 Ibid., 198–99, 255–56.

19 Dalley, AMMO, 417–18.

20 Saggs, *Might,* 253.

21 Dalley, AMMO, 418.

22 Curiously, Shalmaneser III gives nearly an identical number of chariots for his own army, 2,002, for the campaign in his 14th regnal year (ca. 845), along with 5,542 cavalry. Earlier in the same report, he claims to have crossed the Euphrates with 120,000 men (*COS* 2:113B).

23   Dalley, "Foreign Chariotry," 37–38.

24   Grayson, "Assyrian Civilization," 217.

25   Saggs, *Might,* 259.

26   *RIMA* 2, p. 147 (2:13–15).

27   Saggs, *Might,* 247. Though the kings clearly ascribed their position and success to their gods, the number and identity of the gods varies. Tukulti-Ninurta II, for example, was among the most inclusive, listing thirteen "great gods" who had made him king (*RIMA* 2, pp. 164–75 (1:1–25)).

28   *COS* 2:118A.

29   Madhloom, *Chronology,* 13–14; pl. 10, 11.

30   The Bible contains many examples of Yahweh communicating to Hebrew kings through prophetic messages. These Hebrew and Assyrian prophecies have some similarities, but the Hebrew prophets often delivered messages of judgment from a God whose moral requirements the king had violated, a striking difference from Assyrian prophecies.

31   Saggs, *Might,* 245.

32   Ibid., 183–85.

33   Madhloom, *Chronology,* 61–63; esp. pl. 31; Rodriquez, *Arsenal,* 115–25.

34   Note images and analysis in Rodriquez, *Arsenal,* 66–71.

35   Rodriquez, *Arsenal,* 87–93.

36   For more detailed description and analysis, see Rodriquez, *Arsenal,* 50–64.

37   *COS* 2:113.

38   See also Rodriquez, *Arsenal,* 146–60.

39   Madhloom, *Chronology,* 52, pl. 26.

40   Gad Rausing. *The Bow: Some Notes on its Origin and Development* (Bonn A. R., Germany: Rudolf Habelt, 1967), 86.

41   Ussishkin, *CLS,* fig. 89.

42   Yadin, *AWBL,* 296. See also Rodriquez, *Arsenal,*190–205 for discussion and images of various types of Assyrian bows.

43   Yadin, *AWBL,* 296; and Rodriquez, *Arsenal,*223–32.

44   See Rodriquez, *Arsenal,* 241–44 for further imagery and discussion.

45   For descriptions and pictures of these many helmets, see Madhloom, *Chronology,* 37–44, pl. 18–19. Excavators at Lachish recovered a crest perhaps from a helmet of this third type. See Ussishkin, *CLS,* 55, fig. 49.

46   Madhloom, *Chronology,* 54–58, pl. 27–29 describes and illustrates more than thirty-two different styles and designs of shields.

47   Ibid., 8–15.

48   Ibid., 33–35, pl. 16–17; *AWBL,* 313–16.

49   Saggs, *Might,* 251.

50   Quote from *COS* 2:119; general information from Grayson, "Assyrian Civilization," 219.

51   People were still using this same method of transportation along the Tigris River at Mosul as late as the 1970s (Saggs, *Might,* 167).

52   *COS* 2:115B.

53   Grayson, "Assyrian Rule," 966.

54   Compare the American military tactic of "Shock and Awe" used in the 2003 invasion of Iraq.

55   Ibid., 961.

56   Quotes from *COS* 2:117A; Saggs, *Might,* 262; *COS* 2:115B. Clearly, the Assyrians committed these acts and then boasted about them in texts and pictures, but were they more brutal than other nations or just more honest and open about their actions? One author tries to lighten the dark picture painted by Assyrian atrocities by pointing out that "all peoples have in the heat of war been guilty of atrocities." Though this may well be true, the Assyrians, clear policy and the number of times they carried out such cruelty does seem to suggest that they were more brutal than most.

57   The Assyrians did the same thing earlier at Babylon, appealing past the Babylonian officials to the city's populace (Saggs, *Might,* 91).

58   Eph'al, "Warfare and Military Control," 91.

59   Saggs, "Assyrian Warfare," 152–53.

60   *COS* 2.119.

61   Madhloom, *Chronology,* 46.

62   See n. 12 above.

63   Eph'al, "Warfare and Military Control," 97.

64   Ibid., 94.

65   Yadin's *AWBL* is dated but still useful for the perspective of this general and archaeologist. More recently, Eph'al's works, including *The City Besieged,* are likewise helpful for their analysis by that warrior and historian.

66   *RIMA* 2, p. 133 (1:16–22).

67   *COS* 2.119.

68   *COS* 2:114G.

69   *COS* 2:119A, B, E.

70   Dalley, AMMO, 420; Grayson, ARCT, 964.

71   *COS* 2:119A.

72   *COS* 2:115B; Grayson, "Assyrian Civilization," 221.

73   Grayson, "Assyrian Civilization," 219.

BABYLON:
HEIR TO ASSYRIAN DOMINANCE

8

"YAHWEH YOUR GOD DECREED THIS DISASTER": BABYLON DESTROYS JERUSALEM

King Nebuchadnezzar (Fig. 8.1[1]) had required Nebuzaradan to perform a number of interesting and difficult tasks for him over the years, but this was the first time he had asked him to supervise the destruction of a city. Nebuzaradan had served as one of Nebuchadnezzar's bodyguards for nearly all of the nineteen years that Nebuchadnezzar had ruled as king of Babylon, and several years ago the king had promoted Nebuzaradan to captain of the unit.[2] Nebuzaradan thus had become responsible for the king's safety, but more and more Nebuchadnezzar entrusted him with other jobs as well.

Having grown up in his father's palace and then having served as king for nearly twenty years, Nebuchadnezzar was quite aware of the fawning, hypocrisy, self-promotion, and backstabbing prevalent among most royal officials. He had little patience for such behavior, discouraged it whenever possible, and promoted those like Nebuzaradan who demonstrated more skill and sound character than self-promotion.[3] Thus, when Nebuchadnezzar could not personally supervise the events that followed the capture of Jerusalem, he assigned the trusted Nebuzaradan to destroy this particularly rebellious city.

By this point in 586 BC,[4] the Babylonians had brought their army to Jerusalem, the Judean capital, three times. Back in 605 BC,

Nebuchadnezzar had plundered Jerusalem and other cities in the region shortly after his key victory at Carchemish (Map 8.1), which opened up to him control of the Levant (discussed below under "Historical Background and Biblical Connections"). In 597 BC, the Babylonians had once again conquered and plundered Jerusalem, this time for breaking its covenant that promised loyalty and annual tribute to Babylon. Just two years later, the obstinate Judeans had rebelled yet again, and now they would get no more mercy. Nebuchadnezzar usually tried to avoid unnecessary killing and destruction, but these Jews deserved severe punishment for their repeated rebellion.

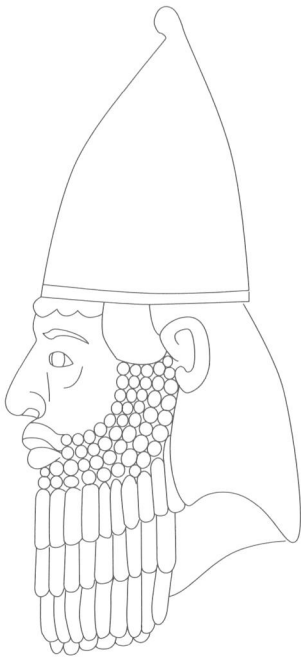

Fig. 8.1—Nebuchadnezzar II, the greatest king of the Neo-Babylonian Empire.

Like his king, Nebuzaradan had grown tired of this rebellious city. On the one hand, Nebuzaradan understood the Jews' reluctance to pay the heavy annual tribute to Babylon. Nebuchadnezzar had to find a way to pay for the spectacular building projects he wanted to carry out in his capital, and he passed most of the financial burden on to his subject nations. Nebuzaradan understood that the required amounts of tribute were often excessive, pushing the subject kings to look for a way out.

A nation as far away as Judah would naturally wish to ally with a power like Egypt (Map 8.1; cf. Ezek. 17:11–21) to escape the Babylonian demands. Unfortunately for Judah, Egypt was no longer strong enough to compete with Babylon. The only real hope for rebels like Judah was that the Babylonian army wouldn't have time or opportunity to return and carry out punishment. Seven years had passed since Judah's last rebellion, but the Babylonian army had finally arrived, and Judah would not survive. Nebuzaradan could appreciate the reasoning behind Judah's course of action, but he would not tolerate it; Babylon had a vast empire to control, and couldn't afford to send its army to such a small, distant nation three times in two decades.

However, Nebuzaradan did appreciate one aspect about these stiff-necked Judeans: Their religion and god intrigued him and, in some ways, appeared admirable. Nebuzaradan was a polytheist and

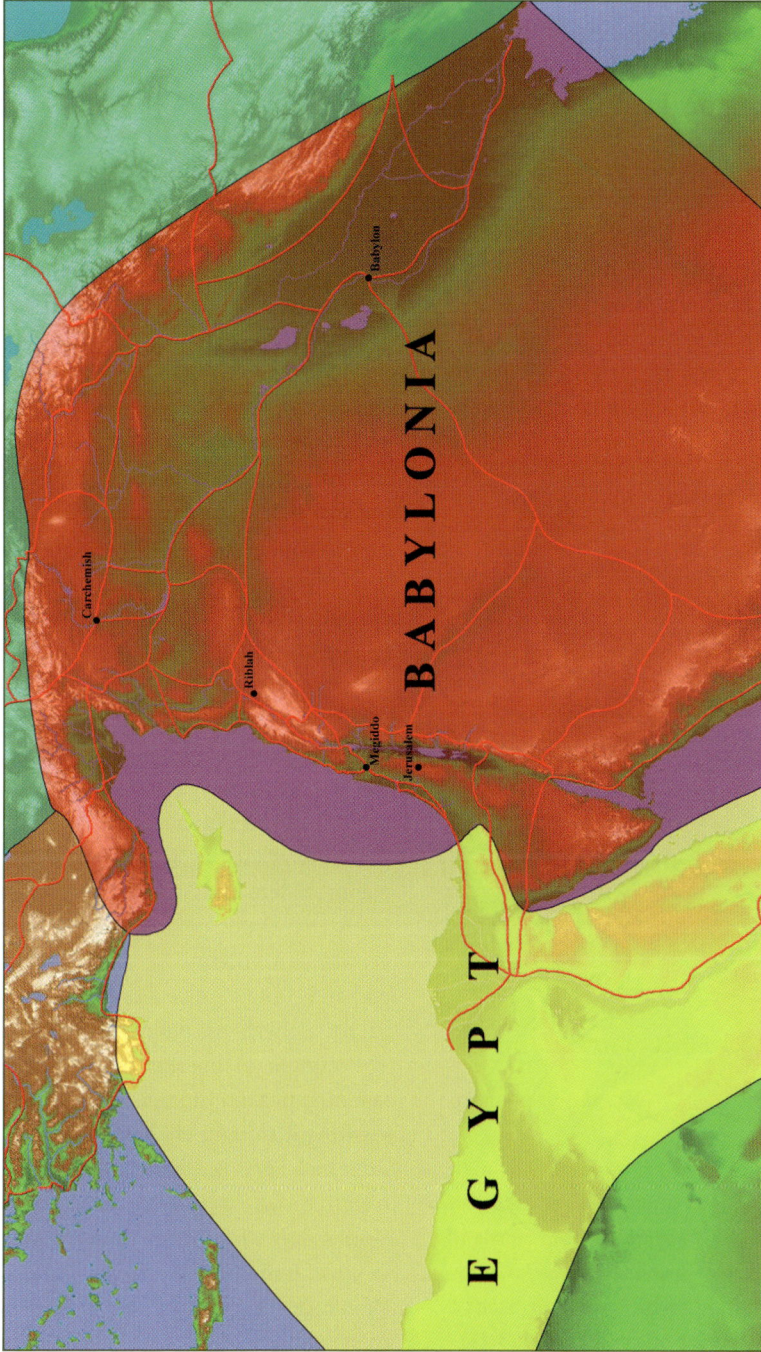

Map 8.1—Empires of Babylonia and Egypt at the time of Nebuchadnezzar.

worshipped the numerous Babylonian gods like the rest of his countrymen, but he couldn't generate much enthusiasm for them. All these gods, with their competing claims and stories, somehow didn't seem authentic. In addition, the gods often didn't seem to fulfill what they supposedly promised.

By contrast, Nebuzaradan found the Israelite god strangely attractive. For one thing, a single god who demanded exclusive worship stood out in the otherwise-polytheistic landscape of the region. Could it be true that Israel's god, Yahweh, was indeed the one great creator and redeemer, as the Israelites believed? Their interesting stories argued for it, but their behavior often suggested otherwise. Nebuzaradan knew that the Israelites were commanded to worship only Yahweh, but any visitor could easily see shrines to other gods in the land, including temples to foreign gods in Jerusalem within sight of the temple of Yahweh itself. Even worse, it had been Solomon, one of Israel's greatest kings, who had built many of these pagan temples.

Despite the clear infidelity of many of Yahweh's supposed followers, the exclusive and highly moral demands of Israel's national god appealed to many devout foreigners like Nebuzaradan. The Babylonian captain knew that even Nebuchadnezzar had genuine admiration for the Israelite god and some of the exiles that served in his court[5]—as did Nebuzaradan. The captain of the guard had heard several intriguing stories of Israel's god showing his might even after his subjects had been taken into exile,[6] and Nebuzaradan wondered why these stories didn't inspire the Judeans still in their homeland to greater fidelity. Wouldn't their god punish them for this?

Fig. 8.2—Babylonian official. Nebuzaradan may have resembled this Babylonian from façade of Darius' tomb. Ezekiel described powerful Babylonians with "flowing turbans on their heads . . . like Babylonian chariot officers" (Ezek. 23:15).

In fact, Nebuzaradan did believe that the Israelite god was punishing them for their faithlessness, and using the Babylonians to do it. Since the Babylonians had the strongest military of the time, many peoples' gods could claim to be using the Babylonians as their instruments of judgment. This seemed especially true for Judah. Nebuzaradan had even learned about a particular Judean prophet named Jeremiah who had been prophesying exactly what Nebuzaradan would have expected. The Judeans were in covenant with their god, they hadn't been loyal to that covenant, and now Yahweh was using Babylon to chastise them. Nebuzaradan figured the events of 605 and 597 BC had been warnings that had gone unheeded, and now Israel's god meant business, just like the Babylonians did. At least, Nebuzaradan hoped that was the case. He found it much more comforting to think that he and his fellow Babylonian soldiers were instruments of divine purposes. Otherwise, the killing and destruction would seem almost pointlessly cruel.

By the time Nebuzaradan had to oversee Jerusalem's destruction, he and the Babylonians had already killed many and destroyed much. The Babylonian army had laid siege to Jerusalem for eighteen months. Had Nebuchadnezzar so chosen, he could have concentrated more of his army's forces and equipment to break through the city wall and capture the city sooner. But Nebuchadnezzar had decided to divert most of his forces to fight elsewhere and leave just enough troops to maintain an effective siege. Starvation and disease could weaken the defenders almost as well as the Babylonian military, and wouldn't cause as many casualties among the Babylonians. And that's exactly how it happened. The attackers had established their camps, built a siege wall to keep the inhabitants in and reinforcements and supplies out, and began constructing a siege ramp for the battering rams. After eighteen months, all the food in the city was gone, the siege ramp was completed, and battering rams breached the walls (2 Kings 25:3–4; cf. Ezek 4:1–2). Most of those who had survived the siege had been so weakened by starvation and disease that they could muster little resistance to the storming Babylonian troops.

The Babylonian officers also found it difficult to control the blood-bath and pillaging; their troops had spent eighteen months laying siege to a strange city far from home and were in no mood for restraint when they finally breached the walls. The author of the following quote described the fall of a different city, but he could easily have been talking about the conquest of Jerusalem: "I have looked upon evils and seen my sons destroyed and my daughters dragged away captive . . . and the innocent children taken and dashed to the ground in the hatefulness of war, and the wives of my sons dragged off by the accursed hands of the (enemy)."[7] Once inside Jerusalem's walls, the conquering Babylonians likely committed similar atrocities and thus helped fulfill Jeremiah's prediction: "Whoever stays in this city will die by the sword, famine or plague" (Jer. 38:2). Apparently the Babylonians' actions also inspired the psalmist to write about them: "Happy is the one who repays you according to what you have done to us. Happy is the one who seizes your infants and dashes them against the rocks" (Psalm 137:8–9).

The killing continued even after the city fell. It took a little over a day to capture the majority of the city and another few days to root out the last pockets of resistance, and many Judeans died in the process. The Babylonians discovered that King Zedekiah, along with a party of men, had somehow managed to escape the city, but the Babylonians quickly dispatched mounted troops to hunt them down. The Judean king and his sons, as well as a portion of his army, had fled nearly fifteen miles to the east before being captured and brought back to the fallen capital.

Several days later, a delegation of Babylonian officers that included Nebuzaradan traveled north to Nebuchadnezzar's headquarters to report on the fall of the city, and they took along the king and his sons as trophies. Nebuchadnezzar was directing his overall campaign in the west from the city of Riblah, an administrative and military center[8] in northern Syria (Map 8.1). When the party arrived from Jerusalem, he had Zedekiah's sons executed on the spot, and immediately afterward, had the king blinded[9] and sent into exile in shackles, with the deaths of his sons the last images Zedekiah would ever know (2 Kings 25:4–7). Nebuzaradan almost felt pity for the Judean king, but he was getting what he deserved. Nebuzaradan understood that Zedekiah "did evil in the eyes of the LORD" (2 Kings 24:19). The king ultimately bore responsibility for the actions of his nation, and he and that nation had betrayed both Yahweh, their god, and Nebuchadnezzar, their human overlord. Both now brutally punished the king and his nation.

Thus the Babylonians had already done much killing and destroying, and now Nebuchadnezzar commanded Nebuzaradan to continue; he sent his captain back to Jerusalem to complete the deportation and destruction. Nebuchadnezzar knew that such complete demolition of a subject nation meant little or no tribute from them for many years. But other subject nations undoubtedly were watching Judah's fate, and many would be deciding whether or not to continue paying tribute. Nebuchadnezzar thought it better to sacrifice the tribute from one nation than risk losing it from many more. It would prove impossible to send his army to punish all the nations that might decide to revolt if they thought they could get away with it. Yes, Judah's punishment had to be severe for many reasons.

Nebuzaradan arrived back at Jerusalem almost a month after the city had fallen, and set about razing the once-proud city. Although he had never been in charge of this process, he knew how to deal with the corpse that Jerusalem had become. First, he would have to remove the heart and vital organs. Though it caused him a few misgivings, he began by ordering his troops to burn the Judeans' formerly magnificent temple to Yahweh. As soon as the flames had consumed most of the temple, he ordered them to continue with the other major buildings. He had no qualms at all about burning the palace of the rebellious Judean king, as well as the other administrative buildings and the homes of the Judean elite. The king and most of the leaders had led the infidelity against their god and promoted revolt against their human overlord. Now they would pay with the destruction of the city's best works of architecture and the fine homes that had belonged to their families for years, in some cases many generations (2 Kings 25:9; Jer. 52:13).

Once the heart and vital organs were gone, he would need to dismember and dispose of the body. Nebuzaradan had his troops break down the city's walls by creating enough breaches so that only a major, well-organized effort would be able to seal up the city and make it defensible again.[10] He processed most of the surviving Judeans to be taken into exile (cf. Fig. 6.7), including the rest of the inhabitants of Jerusalem and the leaders of the outlying regions. Nebuzaradan deported the majority of Judah's population, leaving only the poorest farmers to continue to till the land (2 Kings 25:10–12; Jer. 39:8–10; 52:16). He gave to these formerly landless agricultural workers the ownership of what little usable farmland remained in Judah. They seemed pleased with their jump in personal holdings and status, but Nebuzaradan felt they were more like new owners of a valuable horse—which had just been killed.

Finally, it was necessary to take everything of value associated with the body. The troops had nearly finished gathering the items made from precious metals (gold, silver, or bronze). They collected them at the temple since many of those valuable items were kept there already. As usual, the Babylonians had to scour the city and the temple complex for the valuables the Judeans had tried to hide. The conquerors had to apply special persuasive methods to extract the locations for many of the treasures from those who knew where they were hidden. The Babylonian officers also had to go back through their own soldiers' quarters to dig out the valuables that some of their troops had looted, and then discipline those who tried to keep that loot for themselves. Once these processes were complete, the army's supply units set about breaking up the large bronze items used in worship at the temple (2 Kings 25:13–17; Jer. 52:17–23), and then began listing, packing, and loading everything for transport to Riblah and then Babylon. Though Judah was relatively small, it yielded a meaningful amount of plunder, and Nebuchadnezzar would be pleased.

The disposal of the corpse was nearly complete. Although the king and his sons had been dealt with, the rest of the head remained. Nebuzaradan gathered the nation's other high officials from among those being sent into exile. He took the chief priests, the highest surviving military commander, the king's advisors, and those in charge of the outlying population. He returned with them to Nebuchadnezzar at Riblah and Nebuchadnezzar had these men executed as well (2 Kings 25:18–21; Jer. 52:24–27). This completed the decapitation of the nation and sent a warning to the leaders of Babylon's other subject nations of what could happen to them if they rebelled and withheld tribute.

Thus Nebuzaradan had completed the assignment Nebuchadnezzar had given him—he had dismembered and disposed of the corpse of Jerusalem, enriching and strengthening his king and his nation in the process. Nebuzaradan appreciated Nebuchadnezzar's words of commendation, but also reflected on his part in the process. He had had more than his fill of death and destruction, but he knew that such punishment was necessary if one wished to maintain an empire. Although Babylon had defeated Judah and carried off the symbols of the Israelite god Yahweh, this captain of the guard returned to his hope that his loyal, sometimes brutal service also served whatever gods really existed. He felt sure that Yahweh was real and must have been using the Babylonians to punish his disloyal subjects. Part of Nebuzaradan's confidence came from his personal interaction a few days earlier with the Judean prophet Jeremiah, which he mulled over once again. . . .

Jeremiah had preached in Jerusalem for many years, mostly calling for Judah to repent and obey its covenant with Yahweh or else face exile. His more recent messages about the imminent destruction of the city and the temple had become well known in Judah and even in the Babylonian court. Babylon had its paid informants in Judah's capital city, as it did in other subject nations throughout the empire. Thus, word had been coming back from Jerusalem for some time[11] that this prophet had been delivering a repeated message of submission and surrender to Babylon. At the beginning of the attack on Jerusalem, Nebuchadnezzar had given clear orders to his officers to protect and release this prophet, who by that time had been imprisoned by his own people (Jer. 39:11–13). Nebuzaradan wasn't sure if Nebuchadnezzar's orders came more from respect for Israel's god and prophet or from the desire to reward loyalty to Babylon. Nebuzaradan assumed that the king's motives were mixed, as was often the case with most people. Either way, this captain was under orders to help Jeremiah, a command that he was quite willing to carry out.

Nebuzaradan ultimately released Jeremiah twice. When the Babylonians first captured Jerusalem, he freed Jeremiah from his imprisonment at the Judean military headquarters where unbelieving Judean officials had confined him. Nebuzaradan was especially glad to hear that his actions helped fulfill some of Yahweh's earlier promises to the prophet—that he would not die in the conquest but be released (Jer. 39:15–18). However, when Nebuzaradan returned to Jerusalem from Riblah a month after the city fell, he was dismayed to discover that other Babylonian officers had taken Jeremiah captive once more and had processed him for exile with the other deportees. Thus the captain had to travel a few miles north to the Babylonian military center where the exiles were being held. He found Jeremiah among the anxious Judeans[12] who were eating a poor meal of bread and water while they finished packing a few necessary belongings (Ezek. 12:3–20) for the long, unwelcome trip to Babylon.

Nebuzaradan freed Jeremiah once more. He then rebuked Jeremiah's fellow countrymen with stern words that sounded like they could have come from Jeremiah himself, followed by words of comfort to the prophet:

> "The LORD your God decreed this disaster for this place. And now the LORD has brought it about; he has done just as he said he would. All this happened because you people sinned against the LORD and did not obey him.

> "But today I am freeing you from the chains on your wrists. Come with me to Babylon, if you like, and I will look after you; but if you do not want to, then don't come. Look, the whole country lies before you; go wherever you please." . . . Then the

commander gave him provisions and a present and let him go (Jer. 40:2–5).

Nebuzaradan then looked at the despondent, confused Judeans preparing for their journey into exile, a journey from which most would never return. Nebuzaradan shook his head. He had grown up in a culture that worshiped other gods, but he served Yahweh better than most of these Judeans had done. He understood well that Yahweh expected real loyalty from his people, which they hadn't displayed. Why couldn't they comprehend that? Certainly they had suffered and would continue to suffer at the hands of Nebuzaradan and the other Babylonians, but they had brought it on themselves. Yahweh their had God decreed this disaster for this place. And now Yahweh and the Babylonians had brought it about. Nebuzaradan was simply his instrument, and he was more loyal to Yahweh than most of them.

HISTORICAL BACKGROUND AND BIBLICAL CONNECTIONS

The preceding story took place during the peak of Babylonian power, just a few decades after the fall of Assyria and a few more decades before the rise of Persia. When Assyria's capital of Nineveh fell in the late 7th century BC, the neighboring Babylonians to the south assumed the role of heir to Assyrian dominance. The Babylonians enjoyed a brilliant but brief period as masters of their world before falling in the late 6th century to the next power, Persia, whose homeland lay just to the southeast.

When Babylon finally eclipsed Assyria at the end of the 7th century, it brought an end to the centuries-old rivalry between these neighboring nations. These two peoples shared a similar culture in their homelands, located in northern and south-central Mesopotamia, respectively. Whereas Assyria originated in the northern reaches of the Tigris River, the Babylonian homeland centered around the city of Babylon, located along the south-central Euphrates River (Map 8.2) near where the two great rivers flowed closest together, almost due south of modern Baghdad.

Like the Assyrians, the Babylonians could claim a history that stretched back at least to the 3rd millennium BC,[13] when the city of Babylon apparently began. The inhabitants of Babylon benefited from the fertility and abundant water of the central Mesopotamian river plain, but like Assyria, they lacked the natural geographic barriers to protect them from invaders. The Mesopotamian river valley actually helped funnel the Assyrians and other invaders from the north and west toward Babylon, and the marshlands to the southeast did little to stop armies from that direction. In addition, invaders from the mountains in the east and northeast preyed on the cities of central Babylonia when given the opportunity, much as they did on Assyrian cities in the north.

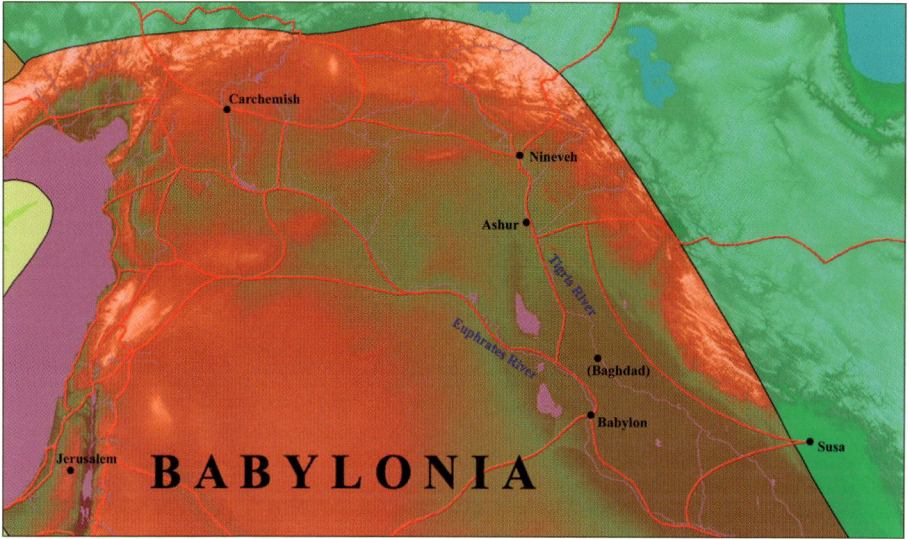

Map 8.2—Heartland of Babylonian Empire at its peak during Neo-Babylonian period.

Despite these disadvantages, the city of Babylon gradually grew to dominate south-central Mesopotamia during the 2nd millennium BC, and from time to time, it extended that dominance to more distant regions as well. The Amorite migrations from the west that had helped strengthen Assyria in the early 2nd millennium (see discussion under "Historical Background and Biblical Connections" in chap. 6) did the same for Babylon, and helped inaugurate the first of three periods of power in Babylon's history, also similar to Assyria. The Old Babylonian period (ca. 2000–1600 BC) included the reign of Hammurabi in the 18th century, when that highly capable king promulgated his now-famous law code and united nearly all of Mesopotamia under one power for the first time. This dominance did not last long, however, as competing powers such as Assyria quickly took back lands the moment Babylonian power began to wane.

Kassite invaders from the Zagros Mountains to the east and south (Map 9.1) conquered Babylon by the beginning of the Middle Babylonian period (ca. 1600–1000 BC) and established a dynasty in Babylon that lasted for more than 300 years. Less militaristic than their predecessors, they relied more on diplomacy to unite southern Mesopotamia, as well as establishing treaties with Assyria, Egypt, and others. This stability encouraged the spread of Babylonian culture, including the Babylonian dialect of the Akkadian language. Babylonian Akkadian became the *lingua franca* for diplomacy throughout the wider region, as illustrated by its use in the el-Amarna archive in Egypt dated to the 14th century. By the 12th century, Babylonian power had waned. Elamites from the southeast sacked Babylon and captured the statue of Marduk. A Babylonian king named Nebuchadnezzar I led a brief resurgence and recaptured the statue, an event that helped elevate Marduk to the position of supreme deity in Babylon. Nevertheless, the 2nd millennium closed with Babylon relatively weak.

The Neo-Babylonian period (ca. 1000–539 BC) began with Assyria dominating in northern and central Mesopotamia. By the early 8th century, a tribal group from far southern Mesopotamia called the Chaldeans had established themselves well enough to compete with Assyria for power in Babylon. Throughout the 8th century, the Assyrians and Chaldeans alternated control of Babylon, with Assyria the more frequent winner.

These struggles in the 8th century connect Mesopotamian and biblical history for the first time. A Chaldean known in the Bible as Merodach-baladan took control in Babylon in 721 BC and held it for more than a decade. His efforts to encourage others to resist Assyria reached as far as Judea, as described in 2 Kings 20 and Isaiah 39. His overture to Judah's king Hezekiah undoubtedly had greater political designs than simply wishing Hezekiah well after his recent illness. The prophet Isaiah warned the Judean king against allying with Babylon, and predicted Judah's captivity in Babylon nearly a century and a half before it occurred.

Meanwhile, turmoil continued in Mesopotamia. In an effort to keep the region stable, the Assyrian king Esarhaddon put two of his sons on the thrones of Assyria and Babylon in the mid-7th century, but the situation degenerated into civil war. Assyria emerged the victor, but the war drained Assyrian resources and exposed its increasing vulnerability. Babylon recovered quickly and helped galvanize resistance to the long-standing Assyrian control.

In 625 BC, a leader of the resistance named Nabopolassar assumed power in Babylon and established what would become known as the Neo-Babylonian dynasty. He ruled until 605 BC and helped bring about the collapse of Assyria. A contemporary king named Cyaxares led the Medes, an ancient Iranian people group, to assume Elamite power in the east and participate in the dismemberment of the Assyrian Empire. In 614 BC, Cyaxares and the Medes conquered the major Assyrian city of Ashur (Map 8.2), and immediately afterward, they formed an alliance with Nabopolassar. Two years later, their armies combined to attack and conquer Nineveh, fulfilling the prophecies of Zephaniah (2:13–15) and Nahum (entire book) that the great Assyrian capital would indeed fall.

Mesopotamia found itself free from Assyrian domination for the first time in centuries, but once again, it was in turmoil. Although the Assyrian capital lay in ruins, enough of its formerly mighty army still remained to form a viable force. Babylon seemed poised to assume Assyrian power, a scenario not to the liking of the distant, but highly interested Egyptian nation. Egypt wished to recapture some of its former holdings in the Levant, but it needed a weakened Mesopotamia to make it happen.

Thus, this formal rival of Assyria now reversed its policy and came to Assyria's aid in a vain attempt to restrain the rapidly increasing Babylonian might. In 609 BC, Pharaoh Neco set out with an Egyptian army toward Carchemish on the Euphrates River to establish a stronger Egyptian presence in northern Mesopotamia. The Egyptians had to pass through Judah, and the Judean king Josiah sought to check the Egyptian advance at the key site of Megiddo (see Map 8.1, and note the similar strategy by the Canaanites in the opening story in chap. 3) apparently in an attempt to aid Babylon. Unfortunately, Josiah, the last godly king of Judah, died in the battle (2 Kings 23:29; 2 Chron. 35:20–24), and the religious reforms he had been leading came to an abrupt end. The Egyptian army resumed its march northward toward Carchemish, and the Judean nation resumed its march toward apostasy and destruction.

At about this same time in Babylon, Nabopolassar turned over command of the Babylonian army to his energetic and highly capable son Nebuchadnezzar II. The crown prince led his army to victory at Carchemish in the spring of 605 BC, decisively defeating the Egyptians and the remnants of the Assyrian army (Jer. 46:2). Babylon's allied Medes decided to concentrate on lands to the north and east, leaving Babylon to inherit most of the lands to the west that were formerly under Assyrian control. Nebuchadnezzar and his army swept south through the Levant to consolidate his new holdings and receive tribute. As part of this sweep, the Babylonians plundered

Jerusalem and took Daniel and his three friends for training in Babylon (Dan. 1:1–6), perhaps to help govern the newly subjected Judah.

The final Judean kings did not remain loyal to their new Babylonian overlord for very long. In 601 BC, Jehoiakim king of Judah switched allegiance to Egypt (2 Kings 24:1–5), contrary to the advice of the prophet Jeremiah (Jer. 27:5–11). Nebuchadnezzar and the Babylonian army responded by attacking and conquering Jerusalem in 597 BC. They looted the palace and the temple, and exiled the new king Jehoiachin and 10,000 leading citizens of Judea (2 Kings 24:10–17), including the prophet Ezekiel. An unsuccessful revolt in Babylon in 595 BC encouraged further rebellion, and Judah once again allied with Egypt. Although it took several years before their army could arrive, the Babylonians again attacked, laying siege to Jerusalem for eighteen months beginning in 587 BC. This time the Babylonians looted and destroyed both the temple and the city, as described in the earlier story of Nebuzaradan (see also the book of Lamentations). This ended Judah's independence, just as Assyria had ended the independence of the northern nation of Israel some 135 years earlier.

Nebuchadnezzar grew wealthy from his conquests of Judah and other ancient Near Eastern kingdoms. His extensive conquests helped finance numerous building projects in his capital, which he gradually transformed into a truly magnificent city (Dan. 4:28–30). Nebuchadnezzar's Babylon even boasted two of the seven wonders[14] of the ancient world—Nebuchadnezzar's famous Hanging Gardens and the large, impressive Ishtar Gate on the northern side of the city.

Despite Babylon's wealth and strong defenses, the city and empire grew weak after Nebuchadnezzar's reign and would eventually fall to the Medes and Persians. Five less capable successors followed Nebuchadnezzar on the Babylonian throne in just over two decades, and Babylon's brilliant but brief domination came to an end. Cyrus II conquered the city for Persia almost without a fight in 539 BC (cf. Dan. 5). The city's inhabitants welcomed their new Persian overlords, apparently eager to be rid of the final Babylonian rulers.[15]

MILITARY ORGANIZATION

Although the Babylonians succeeded the Assyrians in dominating the ancient Near East from their homeland in southern Mesopotamia, we know far less about the Babylonian military than we do about the Assyrians. The

Babylonians left comparatively little military imagery, leaving us to rely on rather limited textual data.[16]

We know relatively little about the Babylonian military despite the greatness of its empire and the clear military prowess of Nebuchadnezzar II, its early champion. The Bible depicts Nebuchadnezzar's army by simply noting its "horses and chariots, and with horsemen and a great army" (Ezek. 26:7). The Babylonian chronicles recount how the later Babylonian king Neriglissar (560–556 BC) led simply "his army" against an enemy's army, when he "reached and inflicted a defeat upon them and conquered the large army. He captured his (enemy's) army and numerous horses."[17] These brief, general accounts tell us precious little about the troops, weapons, or tactics of the Babylonian forces, but they are two of the better contemporary descriptions of the Babylonian military. We do know that the Babylonians followed the Assyrians in their domination of the ancient Near East, and apparently in most of the Assyrian military practices as well. The little available information seems to fit well with the earlier, better-known Assyrian military practices.

Their scanty records tell us that the Babylonians' army included infantry, chariotry, and cavalry,[18] much like the Assyrian army before them. In at least one campaign to Asia Minor, the aforementioned Neriglissar also conducted naval operations. He captured an enemy island and its stronghold of 6,000 troops "by means of boats,"[19] but the account gives no indication what the boats were like or where he obtained them. The Babylonian crown apparently raised its needed troops by general levy or by contractual obligation. For example, temples owned sections of land called "bow-fiefs," which farmers could cultivate in exchange for their commitment to serve in the army as an archer.[20]

The records tell us just a bit more about who led the Babylonian troops. Typically, the king or a prince acted as general commander, with support from "the officers."[21] Nabopolassar, father of Nebuchadnezzar and founder of the Neo-Babylonian Empire, typically led the army personally. Near the end of his reign, crown prince Nebuchadnezzar began to accompany Nabopolassar and gradually took command. Sometimes both king and prince led parts of the army (cf. Saul and Jonathan in 1 Sam. 13:2). On one campaign, Nebuchadnezzar took command while his father went home; later the king returned to lead the capture of a city[22] (cf. David and the capture of Rabbah in 2 Sam. 11–12). Similarly, toward the end of the empire, Belshazzar the prince commanded the army in the absence of his father King Nabonidus.[23]

The Babylonian gods also seem to have played a major role in their military and in the society at large. A diviner always accompanied the army[24] (cf. Samuel's role with Saul's army in 1 Sam. 13). After a victorious campaign, the Babylonians "abducted the gods" (statues) of the vanquished to demonstrate the superiority of their own gods. When King Nabonidus neglected the rites honoring Marduk, Babylon's chief god, the annals make repeated mention of it. Such neglect may have hastened the end of the empire by making the people open to the takeover by Cyrus.

WEAPONS

The near absence of pictorial representations and detail in texts makes any meaningful discussion of Babylonian weaponry most difficult. Two examples will illustrate this. The chronicles note that Nebuchadnezzar "put his (enemy's) large army to the sword,"[25] giving one of the few references to a Babylonian weapon of any kind, but the reference to "sword" could be a figure of speech rather than an actual weapon. Equally vague, the chronicles also note that Nebuchadnezzar and Nabopolassar used siege engines in their campaigns during the early and late Babylonian Empire, but other than describing them as "large siege towers" "brought . . . up to the wall" to capture a city,[26] the texts give little indication of their number, size, design, or use. Such sparse information gives only hints about the weapons the Babylonians used, but these hints fit well within the far clearer information available from the earlier Assyrian military. Babylonian weaponry may have differed little, if at all, from that of their Mesopotamian predecessors.

TACTICS

In contrast to the extremely limited available information about weaponry and organization, the Babylonian sources provide better help in understanding their overall military tactics.

Motivation
The Babylonians seem to have been motivated by the desire for wealth and power, much like other militaries of the time. They went on raids to capture plunder, noting that they took "vast booty" from conquered regions and "plundered them extensively."[27] They also used their power

to depose and impose kings of their choice in conquered lands[28] to better help retain control.

Strategy

Various elements of military strategy also appear in the Babylonian records, all of which fit well with the general military activities of the time. The Babylonians' desire for prominence helped launch their empire in the late 7th century. They gained their independence from the Assyrians, then drove these northern rivals from southern Mesopotamia. Next, they pressed northward along the Euphrates to push back the Assyrians and take more territory for themselves. They allied with the Medes and others when mutually advantageous, and fought against enemy alliances, experiencing both victories and defeats. Though they had followed this same general strategy for much of their long history, by the early 6th century it worked well enough to secure them an empire.

The Babylonians continued using their army to conduct raids into outlying areas to collect booty, as noted above, or to guarantee the collection of tribute from already-subjected cities and peoples. They further used their military to suppress rebellions, and whenever possible, expand their control into regions they felt they could conquer and govern. Nebuchadnezzar's campaigns in and around the Levant, described earlier, fit this pattern well. He defeated the Assyrian and Egyptian forces at Carchemish, and when that victory opened the door for control throughout the Levant and possibly even Egypt, he exploited the opportunity as best he could. Nebuchadnezzar took control of the Levant but apparently couldn't conquer Egypt,[29] though he apparently grew wealthy from the lands he did conquer.

Obviously, the Babylonian army marched a great deal to conquer the lands in its empire and then maintain that control. The limited texts that mention marching note some of the exceptions to what must have been the most common experience—marching great distances along the flat, open Mesopotamian river plain. These texts occasionally note crossing the great Euphrates and Tigris Rivers while on the march, as well as marching in the mountains during campaigns, apparently a challenging experience for Babylonians who were used to the broad river plain. Neriglissar's ambitious campaign in 557 BC took his army to the mountains of Anatolia to capture a king in his mountain stronghold. This required pursuing the enemy "a distance of fifteen double-hours of marching through difficult mountains, where men must walk single file,"[30] as well as conquering an island fortress by naval action,

The March

mentioned earlier. Though they were necessary to control such a vast empire, these experiences obviously seemed unusual for the flatlanders from Babylon.

Battle Tactics

Babylonian military tactics included both battle in the open field and at or within cities, often changing from one to the other quickly. For example, when the Assyrian army marched to attack Babylon, Nabopolassar left the city with his army to engage the attackers out in the open. "He did battle against the army of Assyria and the army of Assyria retreated before him. He inflicted a major defeat upon Assyria and plundered them extensively."[31] The chronicles describe several battles in the open by Nabopolassar, though Nebuchadnezzar and other Babylonian kings must have had similar experiences not preserved in existing records.

Nabopolassar also attacked cities held by the enemy, including one on an island in the middle of the Euphrates.[32] During one campaign, Nabopolassar admitted to an unsuccessful attack against a city, but was quick to add his subsequent victory over the Assyrian army, which used the occasion to attack the Babylonian forces.[33] Such battles against cities seem to have involved direct attacks (probably assault against the gate or scaling the walls with ladders), and could last anywhere from "all day" to ten to fourteen days.[34] These attacks sometimes ended with the victors destroying the captured city by fire.

If direct attack didn't work, the Babylonians could choose to lay siege to an important enemy city. For example, the Babylonians laid "heavy siege" to Nineveh, which fell after three months, and later to Jerusalem, which held out for eighteen months, both described previously.[35] The Babylonians built siege ramps to conquer Jerusalem (Jer. 32:24), apparently to bring battering rams against the walls. In a few cases, the accounts mention siege equipment like large towers, but tell precious little about their number, appearance, or use.

After the Battle

After victories in the field or at a city, the Babylonians followed up with the usual military activities of the time, though, as usual, the available data is sketchy.

As noted already, the Babylonians fought in large part to gain plunder, so plundering appears frequently in their texts. In one typical account, Nabopolassar's troops "carried off the vast booty of the (conquered) city and the temple and turned the city into a ruin heap."[36] Victory over an enemy meant victory over its gods, so the Babylonians also "abducted their gods"[37] by taking the enemy's idols as war trophies. The Babylonians often took exiles as part of the plunder. The biblical accounts of Babylon conquering Judah illustrate these practices, as when Nebuchadnezzar took sacred vessels from temple (Dan. 1:2) and exiles from Jerusalem three times (described in the story of Nebuzaradan). The Babylonian records also occasionally mention other specific plunder, such as horses or fruit from enemy orchards.[38]

NOTES

1   This image was adapted from the medallion of the Babylon International Festival conducted by the Iraqi national government in 1987. Where the Iraqis got the image of Nebuchadnezzar is unknown. The medallion overlaid the images of Saddam Hussein and Nebuchadnezzar II in an attempt to portray Hussein as a modern Nebuchadnezzar. So far, history does not seem to have accepted that comparison as valid.

2   The biblical books of 2 Kings and Jeremiah name Nebuzaradan (Akkadian for "Nabu has given me offspring") no less than sixteen times. His title "chief of the guardsmen/cooks/slaughterers" has been variously understood as chief bodyguard, chief cook, or chief executioner. (Compare Potiphar's nearly identical title in Gen. 37:36.) Nebuzaradan appears as captain of Nebuchadnezzar's guard and as the official fulfilling various roles in the Babylonian dismemberment of Jerusalem and Judah in the early 6th century BC.

3   Note, for example, Nebuchadnezzar's actions toward his court advisors as recorded in Daniel 2. At this point, Babylon's new king seems to have grown so frustrated with his apparently questionable and self-seeking advisors that he decided to raise the stakes dramatically in his interaction with them. After having a dream one night, Nebuchadnezzar demanded that his advisors go beyond their normal responsibility of telling him the interpretation of his dream, and give him the very content of the dream. If the advisors really did receive the interpretations of dreams from the gods, as they claimed, Nebuchadnezzar perhaps wondered why the gods couldn't also tell them the substance of a dream.

But the advisors couldn't meet the demand, and Nebuchadnezzar would have killed them all had an exile from Judah named Daniel not come up with the content and interpretation, and then credited his god rather than himself. Nebuchadnezzar promoted this exile, apparently thinking that such skill and character deserved reward. Although we don't know that the king ever again threatened to kill advisors he thought untrustworthy, neither do we see him in the book of Daniel putting much trust in their interpretations or advice. It seems that when Nebuchadnezzar found capable and trustworthy people like Daniel or Nebuzaradan, he promoted them much more quickly and relied on them much more extensively than his official advisors.

4   The Bible gives the date for the fall of Jerusalem using the relative dating common to the time—the ninth day of the fourth month of the eleventh year of King Zedekiah of Judah (2 Kings 25:2–3). This falls in either 587 or 586 BC, depending on when the Judeans began counting Zedekiah's regnal years. See Mordechai Cogan and Hayim Tadmor, *II Kings: A New Translation with Introduction and Commentary* (Anchor Bible 11; Doubleday, 1988), 317, n. 2 for further discussion.

5   Note, for example, Nebuchadnezzar's confessions of appreciation for Israel's god and the exiled Israelites in Dan. 1:18–20; 2:46–49; 3:28–30; and 4:1–3, 34–37. Though he apparently didn't abandon his polytheism, these stories suggest that Nebuchadnezzar did acknowledge the clear power of Israel's God, at least at those times. Daniel's apparent concern for Nebuchadnezzar (Dan. 4:19, 27) further supports the idea that this Babylonian king had at least some good character, especially compared to Daniel's apparent disdain for the later, corrupt Belshazzar (Dan. 5:17–28).

6   The stories in Daniel 1–5 bear testimony to the power of Israel's God despite the Babylonian conquest of Judah, though not all would have occurred by the time of Jerusalem's fall in 586 BC.

7   *Iliad* 22.58–71. Though this quote by the mythical Priam of Troy may be entirely legendary, it describes well the commonly brutal aftermath of a city's fall.

8   Located some 200 miles north of Jerusalem on the Orontes River, Riblah had earlier served as a fortress and checkpoint for the Assyrians, then the Egyptians (2 Kings 23:31–34), and now as Nebuchadnezzar's headquarters during his campaigns in the west.

9   Blinding unfaithful subject kings may not have been uncommon, as suggested by the appearance of this fate among the curses threatened in the treaty of Ashurnirari V of Assyria and Mati'ilu of Arpad (*ANET*, 533b). A related but lesser punishment of blinding larger numbers of males in just one eye is also known from Mesopotamia (Cogan and Tadmor, *2 Kings*, 318, n. 7) and the Levant (1 Sam. 11:2), apparently designed to humiliate and partially disable the victims.

10   Nehemiah completed this very task some 150 years later under difficult circumstances, and he did so in just fifty-two days (Neh. 3–6). The short time needed testifies to his effective leadership, but he also benefited because the greatly reduced population after the exile meant Nehemiah needed to restore a much smaller city. The eastern city wall along the Kidron Valley would have remained roughly the same, but the western wall would have reverted to the older wall running along the central valley on the west side of the City of David. This western wall would have been an interior wall when the Babylonians destroyed the city, suggesting that they may have done it little damage. If so, Nehemiah's may have needed relatively minor restorative work on approximately forty percent of the city's wall.

11   According to Jeremiah 1:2–3, the prophet's ministry began during the reign of Josiah and lasted until sometime after the fall of Jerusalem, apparently ca. 627–586 BC. This long period of prophetic ministry would have helped produce a wide familiarity with his message. According to Jeremiah 39:11–12, Nebuchadnezzar indeed knew of the prophet and his ministry, and gave orders for the Babylonian troops to protect and aid Jeremiah. How Nebuchadnezzar learned of Jeremiah is unknown, but the common use of spies and informants during this era makes the scenario described in this story at least possible.

12   Jeremiah 52:29 states that 832 Judeans were heading into exile at this time, but that number may be incomplete. The previous verse says that the Babylonians took 3,023 exiles in 597 BC, compared to 2 Kings 24:14, which gives 10,000 for the same event. Perhaps the numbers in Jeremiah 52 count only the heads of households or just the males.

13   Much of the following historical review came from Bill T. Arnold's "Babylonians" in Alfred J. Hoerth, Gerald L. Mattingly, and Edwin M. Yamauchi, eds., *Peoples of the Old Testament World* (Grand Rapids: Baker, 1994), 45–66.

14   Various lists of the so-called seven wonders have existed through history. The earliest lists apparently included Babylon's Ishtar Gate as well as the Hanging Gardens, but later lists replaced the Ishtar Gate with the lighthouse at Alexandria, Egypt.

15   For the Greek accounts of this conquest, see *Her.* 1:190–91; and *Cyr.*7:5.1–34.

16   For example, the Babylonian Chronicle Series in *Assyrian and Babylonian Chronicles* covers both the Babylonian and Persian periods, but offers only brief, highly selective, and fragmentary accounts. Interestingly, this series is also objective and impartial enough to actually acknowledge defeats, a rare trait for ancient Near Eastern annals.

17   *ABC* p. 103; Chronicle 6.

18 Note, for example, the reference to Nebuchadnezzar's "numerous horses and chariotry" that he had to refit after his unsuccessful invasion of Egypt (*ABC* p. 101; 5:8).

19 *ABC* p. 104; 6:20–23.

20 Stephanie Dalley, "Ancient Mesopotamian Military Organization," *CANE* 1:422.

21 *ABC* pp. 107–8; 7:10, 19, 23.

22 *ABC* p. 19, 97–98; 4:5–15.

23 *ABC* pp. 107–8; 7:10, 14, 19.

24 Oates, *Babylon,* 178.

25 *ABC* p. 102; 5:22.

26 *ABC* pp. 93–94; 3:35–36; p. 100; 5:22.

27 *ABC* p. 100; 5:12–1; pp. 19, 97; 4:1–4.

28 *ABC* 102; 5:11–13. Nebuchadnezzar deposed and exiled the Judean king Jehoiachin and placed his uncle Mattaniah on the throne instead, renaming him (also a further indication of authority) Zedekiah (2 Kings 24:10–17). Cf. Egypt's similar action in 2 Kings 23:34.

29 *ABC* 101; 5:6–8.

30 *ABC* 20–21, 103; 6:11–17. "Fifteen double-hours of marching" may suggest a distance of some ninety miles, if one assumes thirty hours at approximately three miles per hour. Cf. Albright's discussion of a similar description for Sargon's Assyrian army in "New Light on Magan and Meluha," *JAOS* 42 (1922): 317. Regardless of the distance, a long march single file through the mountains clearly merited notation in the flatlanders' chronicles.

31 *ABC* 91; 3:4–5. Cf. his earlier account in 88: 2:10–13 and the later experience of Nebuchadnezzar against the Egyptians in 99; 5:4–5.

32 *ABC* 93; 3:33.

33 *ABC* 92; 3:16–22.

34 *ABC* 87; 2:2; 92; 3:21; 109; 7:iii.14.

35 For the Babylonian account of the conquest of Nineveh, see *ABC* 94; 3:38–45. Although Jerusalem held out against the Babylonians much longer than Nineveh had done years before, this probably had more to do with Nebuchadnezzar's apparent decision to apply only limited resources to the attack on Jerusalem, as described in the story of Nebuzaradan above.

36 *ABC* 94; 3:45, 48.

37 *ABC* 91; 3:7–8.

38 *ABC* 103; 6:9–10; 105; 7:11–13.

PERSIA:
FINAL RULERS FROM THE EAST

9

THE MEDES AND PERSIANS CONQUER BABYLON

Chrysantas[1] commanded a division of Median cavalry, a high position in the Medo-Persian army of Cyrus II. Both the Medes and Persians boasted long, proud traditions of raising, riding, and fighting with horses, so both peoples produced exceptional cavalrymen. Chrysantas was no exception. He had grown up with horses; in fact, his father, a nobleman, had him trotting around on small horses almost as soon as Chrysantas had learned to walk. Before he turned ten, Chrysantas could ride well, use a bow and javelin from horseback, and had learned to place a high value on honor (see discussion below under "Recruitment and Training"). He had mastered the skills and toughness needed for the military, and his social position and natural abilities had him serving as a cavalry officer almost as soon as he joined the army at age twenty.

Chrysantas had still been in his late teens when the Persians had won their independence from Median rule (550 BC) and shortly thereafter forged an alliance with their former overlords. The proud Medes found it difficult to accept the increasingly superior position of the Persians in their sometimes uneasy alliance, but they could not deny the skill and success of Cyrus II (Cyrus the Great) of Persia (Fig. 9.2). Although Cyrus ruled as a Persian for the Persians, his mother was a Median noblewoman, giving the Medes some solace in serving under a half-Mede. Nonetheless, all could see the increasing dominance of the Persians in their alliance, so the Medes relied on powerful and talented Median officials and officers like Chrysantas to watch out for Median interests and maintain ethnic pride. Chrysantas filled his role well.

By 539 BC, nearly a dozen years had passed since the Persians had won their independence and almost ten since Chrysantas had joined the military. He had served his requisite four years, then continued as a professional cavalry officer. None could outdo his equestrian skills, and few could match his talent as a commander. He had risen in the ranks until he commanded an entire division of one thousand cavalry—Median cavalry, of course. His unit always performed its duties well in both battle and peacetime, and its commander made sure Median interests and needs received adequate attention and resources. By the time Cyrus led the Medo-Persian army toward the great city of Babylon in 539 BC, Chrysantas had earned a respected place in the army's war council.

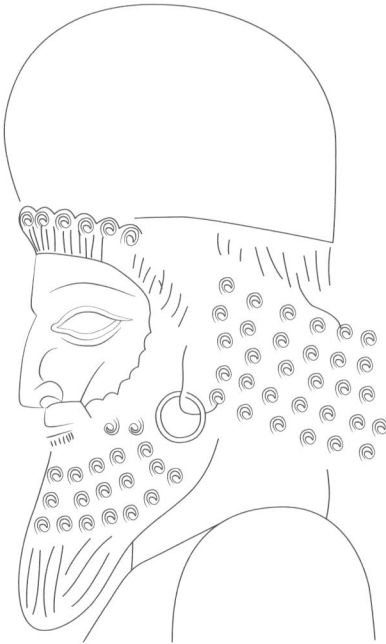

Fig. 9.1—Portrait of Mede.
Chrysantas may have resembled this
Mede from a relief at Persepolis.

As Cyrus II led the battle-hardened Medo-Persian army toward Babylon to add it to the expanding Medo-Persian Empire, Chrysantas felt confident that his forces would be able to defeat any army the Babylonians could muster. However, from what he had heard about the defenses of their great city, Chrysantas suspected that its strong walls and large moat would offer a greater challenge. Events proved his instincts correct. The Babylonians did muster their troops, and the Babylonian king led them out to face the attackers. Afterward, Chrysantas thought the Babylonian military had acted like a tired old man—outdated, sluggish, and poorly maintained. The Babylonians proved no match for the strong, energetic, and confident Medes and Persians. The Medo-Persian troops engaged and quickly put to flight the Babylonians, who broke and scrambled toward the safety of the city's defenses.[2] The mounted troops such as those under Chrysantas cut down hundreds of Babylonians before they reached their destination.

The Medes and Persians had clearly won the first encounter at Babylon, but now they advanced towards Babylon's justifiably famous defenses. Babylon's earlier, more capable kings had built a magnificent city. It was enormous for its time, measuring some 4.5 miles around the primary city, which was protected by the inner wall and moat, and 7.5 miles around the greater but less substantial outer wall (Fig. 9.3). The outer wall presented little difficulty to the attackers. Cyrus picked a vulnerable point, and his troops easily overwhelmed the half hearted Babylonian defenders. The Medo-Persian army then advanced to the much more substantial inner wall and its moat filled with water from the Euphrates.

As they so often did, the troops in the highly mobile cavalry served as scouts, and found the best views of the city's primary defenses to gather the needed information. From the right vantage points, Chrysantas could see that the inner wall was actually a double wall. He estimated one to be twenty-one feet thick and the other twelve feet thick, spaced about twenty-four feet apart; this would enable the Babylonian military to move quickly to wherever the city needed defending. Chrysantas noted how much room the defenses took up, an especially significant matter inside a walled city where space was scarce. He thought the cost to the city was high but undoubtedly worth it; the weak Babylonian army needed all the help it could get. In addition, both walls were fortified with

Fig. 9.2—Cyrus II. Also called Cyrus the Great, founder of the Persian Empire.

towers about sixty feet apart to allow defending archers a good field of fire along the entire face of the walls. These were strong defenses indeed.

Such walls by themselves would have been difficult enough to penetrate, but the builders had naturally taken advantage of the Euphrates River as well. They had dug an enormous moat forty feet wide along the entire length of the wall, connected to the Euphrates where it entered and exited the city (Fig. 9.3). The walls had to stop at the river, of

Babylon

N

Euphrates River

Outer Wall

Canal

0   500   1000
Yards

Moat

Ishtar
Gate

Tower

New
City

Marduk
Temple

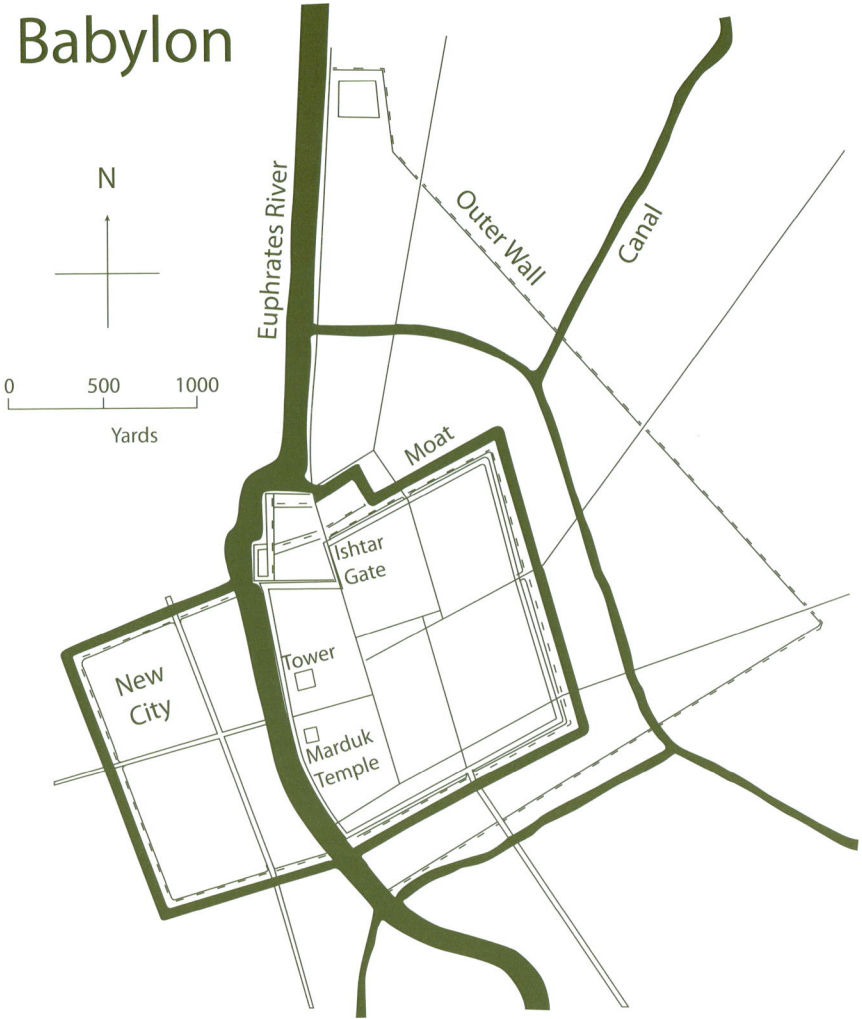

Fig. 9.3—Plan of Babylon. Note original city east of the Euphrates River and New City on the west, both protected by inner wall and moat, plus outer wall offering further defense on east and north.

course, offering the tempting possibility of easier entry at those points. But when the troops tested the depth of the river with long poles, they estimated it at forty feet.[3] Chrysantas whistled. The army had never had to overcome defenses of this magnitude. Getting past them would require great effort, if it were possible at all.

Chrysantas imagined the Babylonians felt secure inside such a defensive system—he knew he would. He didn't have much respect for the Babylonians, but he felt sure even they would have stored up adequate provisions to withstand a long siege. Plus, with a great river literally flowing through the city, the inhabitants needn't fear running out of water. They probably felt confident they could withstand any attacking army for many years.[4]

This challenge set the stage for a somber war council when Cyrus, Chrysantas, allied commanders Gadatas and Gobryas,[5] and other senior officers met to determine their strategy for attacking the city. Cyrus began, "Friends and allies, we have viewed the city on every side. But I am sure I cannot see how anyone could take by storm walls so massive and so high." Chrysantas pointed out the extra defense and provision of water given by the Euphrates, to which Cyrus replied, "Chrysantas, let us not trouble ourselves with that which is beyond our powers; but we must apportion the work among ourselves as quickly as possible, to each contingent its proper share, and dig a ditch as wide and deep as possible."[6]

Cyrus settled on the strategy of entering Babylon by diverting water from the Euphrates using a ditch. If they could divert the river long enough to make the water level drop low enough, a force of attackers should be able to wade into the city at the two points where the river dissected the wall. Theoretically possible, such an unusual strategy relied on many things going right, including a major failure by the Babylonian watchmen to notice the troops as they entered and then summon reinforcements to repel the attack.

Chrysantas didn't like the plan, not because he didn't think it had a good chance of working, but because it gave little opportunity for the Median cavalry to play a meaningful role. He understood, of course, that different types of troops played different roles and, in some battles, almost no role at all. But leaving the cavalry out of such a strategic conquest would hamper the opportunities for Median cavalrymen to play vital roles in the political realities after the battle ended—assuming it would end in victory.

Chrysantas assumed they would conquer the city eventually. If this particular plan didn't work, they would devise some other method to take Babylon despite the challenges. Babylon was a piece of fruit that had passed its peak of ripeness; the Medes and Persians were taking control of the orchard, and their god Ahura-Mazda would surely give them this treat. Along with the victory, Chrysantas also had to maneuver so that his people could get their rightful share of the spoils afterward.

Despite the objections of Chrysantas and a few others in the council, Cyrus moved ahead with the plan. He ordered contingents of his best infantry, the Immortals (discussed below), along with Gadatas and Gobryas to be stationed where the river entered and exited the city. As soon as they saw that water level dropped to mid-thigh, they were to wade into the city and kill the guards. Next, they had to rush to the palace and kill the leadership as quickly as possible, then secure as many fortresses and other key points of control as they could. One unit was charged with opening the Ishtar Gate on the northern side of the city (Fig. 9.3) so the rest of the army could enter and help with the subjection of the city. Chrysantas chafed at the idea of having to wait so long to join the battle. The infantry and allied commanders would surely capture and keep control of the major locations, then the corresponding positions of power afterward. They were no fools; they knew how to play the power game well.

But Chrysantas was a good soldier even more than a good politician, so he and his troops did their part and did it well. They and the rest of the army withdrew, leaving only contingents of Immortals and allies by the river at opposite ends of the city. Cyrus and the bulk of the army moved north to a place near the Euphrates where an earlier Babylonian queen had constructed a lake from what had formerly been a swamp.[7] There the army dug a large canal from the river to the lake, but held off opening the connection from the river to the canal. Cavalrymen despised digging ditches, but Chrysantas' division moved more earth and completed its part faster than any other. Soon the preparations were complete, and the army waited. Cyrus had learned of a coming festival when the Babylonians would likely be drinking and partying through the night,[8] so he held off, hoping that the celebrations would lower the Babylonian watchfulness.

On the appointed night, the Medes and Persians launched their attack. Those upstream opened the head of the canal at the river, diverting much of the water into the lake, thus gradually lowering the water level at the city. When it dropped to the height of mid-thigh, Gadatas, Gobryas, and the

Immortals began infiltrating. At this point the attack was most vulnerable. Had the Babylonians been more alert, they could have trapped and slaughtered the invaders.[9] Since they did not, the attackers got through the river and into the city, and they began making their way toward the palace.

The advance to the palace went exactly according to plan. The attackers met relatively few Babylonians out in the streets. A few resisted and perished quickly. Most fled into their homes. Others called out to the armed men, thinking they were fellow partiers, to which the attackers responded in kind and let them go their drunken way. When they arrived at the palace, the attackers found the gates locked and the guards drinking and warming themselves at a fire. They were quickly overwhelmed and killed. The noise carried inside, and amazingly, the king ordered the gates opened to see what the commotion was. Thus the attackers had easy access to the palace and the chamber where the king and his retinue partied. The king's entire entourage died within minutes. Only the king and a few others even had the chance to draw their daggers in a weak show of resistance.[10]

While this was taking place, the designated group opened the Ishtar Gate as planned, and the rest of the army rushed in. Chrysantas' men and the other cavalry led this second wave. Those who spoke Akkadian rode about as heralds, warning everyone to stay indoors or pay with their lives. Others rode past the closer objectives first to the heart of the city, where they found other partiers still reveling, completely unaware of any trouble. The troops dispersed or killed them, and continued to the citadels at the perimeter of the city to capture as many as possible. They managed to take some, but a few Babylonian commanders caught wind of the attack and secured their commands. By morning, most of these realized the futility of resistance and surrendered.[11] Thus, Cyrus and his army conquered Babylon with almost no destruction and relatively little bloodshed.

Cyrus completed the takeover in his typical firm but generous fashion. He gave permission for relatives to bury their dead, and ordered all inhabitants to surrender their weapons at the citadels. His troops then scoured the city, and in any homes where they discovered weapons, killed all who lived there. Cyrus distributed a good portion of the plunder to the local temples. He transferred the homes and property of those who had been killed in the takeover to those who had carried out and aided the conquest. He then ordered the populace to return to normal life, carrying on their businesses or tilling their farmlands near the city. He also assigned new officials, including those who collected taxes and tribute monies that now, of course, would go to Persia.[12] Chrysantas and Cyrus' other troops had done their work, and their capable and gracious king had done his; Persia would be larger, richer, and more glorious as a result.

HISTORICAL BACKGROUND AND BIBLICAL CONNECTIONS

The Persians followed the Assyrians and Babylonians to become the final great power to rule the ancient Near East from the area in or near Mesopotamia, and they dominated at the conclusion of the Old Testament.[13] The first great Persian king, Cyrus II, combined effective administrative and military leadership to raise Persia to greatness, much like Nebuchadnezzar had done for Babylon centuries earlier. The Persians first dominated the related Medes, who apparently immigrated to the Iranian plateau about the same time as the Persians, sometime after 1500 BC. The Medes rose to power first under the leadership of Cyaxares (625–585 BC). As noted earlier, Cyaxares led the Medes to conquer Ashur in

Fig. 9.4—Alternating Persians (flat-topped headdresses) and Medes, illustrating the two main peoples in the Medo-Persian Empire. Image from frieze at Persepolis (see Map 9.1), the ceremonial capital of Persia.

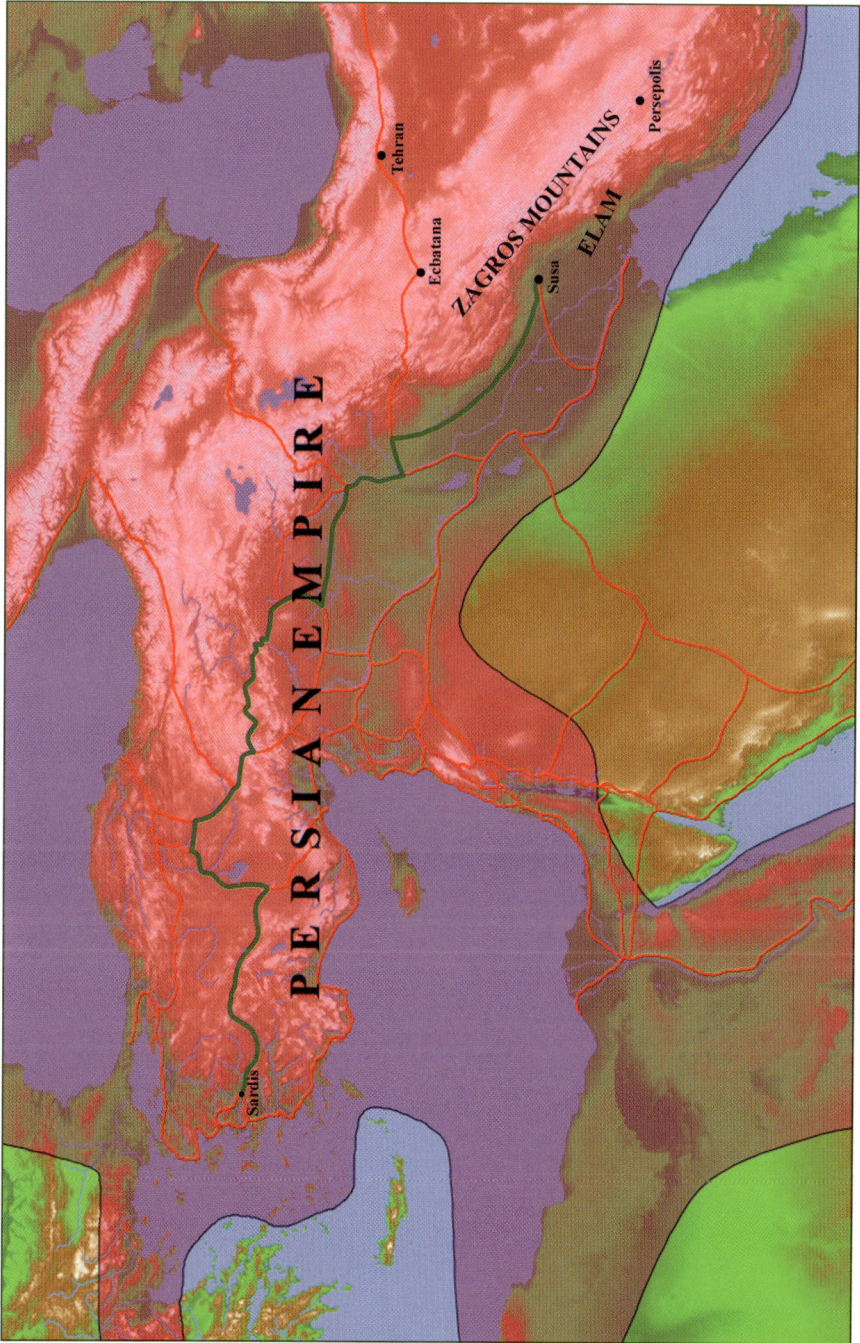

Map 9.1—Persian Empire at its peak, including approximate route of the Royal Road

Tehran

Ecbatana

Susa

Persepolis

ZAGROS MOUNTAINS

ELAM

PERSIAN EMPIRE

Sardis

614 BC and allied with the Babylonians to take Nineveh in 612 BC. By the early 6th century, the last ruler of an independent Media married his daughter to a Persian, and their union produced Cyrus II, also known to history as Cyrus the Great. Cyrus led the Persians in their revolt against Median rule (and Cyrus' grandfather) in 550 BC, after which time the Persians eclipsed the allied Medes in importance.

Eventually, the Persians would control more of the ancient Near East than any of their predecessors. Their territory would stretch from Greece and Asia Minor in the northwest, to Egypt in the southwest, to the Indus River near the border of modern India in the east (Map 9.1), far surpassing the holdings of either Assyria or Babylon.

These conquests started with Cyrus II (559–530 BC; see Fig. 9.2). Following his victory over the Medes in 550 BC, Cyrus conquered Lydia in Asia Minor in 546 BC, and then Babylon in 539 BC (Dan. 5). Cyrus served as God's servant to help restore the Jewish people (Isa. 44:28–45:13) when he encouraged them to return home from Babylon and rebuild their temple (Ezra 1, 5:13–6:3), a practice he followed with other peoples also exiled by Babylon. Cyrus' son Cambyses II (529–522 BC) succeeded his father and conquered Egypt in 525 BC, though he died on the trip home.

The unrelated Darius I (522–486 BC) next took power and further expanded the Persian Empire. The Old Testament records that Darius also supported the struggling Jewish efforts to finish rebuilding their temple in Jerusalem (Ezra 5:6–6:15), which the Jews ultimately completed during his reign (Hag. 1:2; 2:10; Zech. 1:1, 7; 7:1). Among his other projects, Darius established a mounted courier system[14] that dramatically shortened the time needed to send a message the 1,700 miles along the Royal Road from the capital of Susa to the city of Sardis in western Asia Minor (Map 9.1). Rather than the typical ninety days, this "pony express" needed just one week to cover the vast distance. Darius also expanded the Persian Empire westward by conquering much of Greece, but his numerically superior force suffered a decisive defeat on the plains of Marathon in 490 BC in the battle that ultimately gave rise to the modern long-distance race of the same name.

A second attempt to conquer Greece fell to Darius' son, known both as Xerxes I and Ahasuerus (485–465 BC), and presented as the husband of Vashti and Esther in the book of Esther. Xerxes first had to suppress revolts in Egypt and Babylon after taking power, and then organized the largest military force known in antiquity for the second invasion of Greece. During the Persian advance, 300 brave Spartan warriors sacrificed their lives to slow the attacking force at the Thermopylae Pass in east-central Greece in 480 BC. Although the invading Persians eventually managed to reach and sack Athens, their clear numerical and material advantages ultimately failed to overcome the Greeks' tactical superiority and their will to resist. The Greeks won the decisive victory in the naval battle in the Bay of Salamis near Athens. With his naval power broken, Xerxes could not hope to conquer the rest of Greece. By that point, winter was just weeks away, and other priorities in the empire demanded his attention as well. Xerxes fled Greece and ultimately was assassinated. Persian expansion, military supremacy, and its aura of invincibility had all crested and fallen with this historic but unsuccessful invasion.

Artaxerxes I (464–424) succeeded his father and became the last Persian king to overlap with Old Testament history. Artaxerxes commissioned Ezra, the Jewish scribe, to lead a return of Jews to Jerusalem in 458 BC, and the king offered financial support for Ezra's efforts to restore the nation religiously and socially (Ezra 7). In 445 BC, the same king commissioned his official Nehemiah to return to Jerusalem (Neh. 2:1–10) in order to rebuild the city's walls and govern the greatly reduced and impoverished province of Judah. The poor inhabitants of Judah faced severe economic and social challenges (see esp. Neh. 5), caused in part by the Persian tax load. The Jews would continue to struggle with such cultural challenges for the rest of Persian rule, which would last for another century. In the late 4th century BC, Alexander the Great conquered the entire region, bringing the blessings and challenges of Hellenistic culture to the land and people of the Bible. Cultural and military dominance thus shifted west to Greece, ending roughly four centuries of Mesopotamian control that had begun with Assyria and continued through Babylon and finally Persia.

MILITARY ORGANIZATION

Like with the Babylonians, we know less about the Persian military than the earlier Assyrians because the Persians left relatively little visual evidence, leaving us to rely mostly on the limited textual information. The Persian military is better known than the Babylonians', thanks to later Greek historians such as Herodotus (5th century BC) and Xenophon (4th century BC), who describe the Persian military in some detail because of the repeated Persian invasions of their Greek homeland. Describing the Persian military proves challenging, in part because of its long history. The Persians were a major power for roughly two centuries, and their practices clearly changed over time. The following description will focus primarily on the Persian military during the first century of its empire, which corresponds to the period at the end of the Old Testament.

Recruitment and Training

The Persians drew their forces from a wide range of peoples, reflecting the vast area controlled by their empire. The Persians tried to draw the core of their military from Persians, Medes, and Elamites—the peoples native to the Iranian plateau. Some select units were open only to troops from these regions, as discussed below. Ultimately, the Persian military included troops from dozens of other people groups as well, from India to Nubia in Africa to Greece. This wide range appears to have been a source of interest and pride at the time. Darius had a bilingual text inscribed on white marble pillars near a bridge over the Bosporus, which listed "the names of all the nations that were in his army; in which were all the nations subject to him."[15] In Herodotus' later catalogue of troops that comprised Xerxes' force that invaded Greece, Herodotus describes the various units that were drawn from forty-six different peoples.[16]

Some of the different peoples provided different types of troops. Most regions supplied infantry. Maritime nations contributed ships and sailors to the Persian fleet. Cavalry, which played a major role in the Persian military, typically came from Persian nobility or other peoples inhabiting the horse-breeding regions of the Iranian plateau. Elite cavalry units were made up of men from the highest social circles, marked by special dress and privilege.[17]

The Persians drew soldiers from two of the three strata of their society—nobles and bondsmen, with only slaves exempt. The Persians expected adult, free males to give military service, and they trained their youth accordingly. From ages five to twenty, Persian boys learned "to use the bow, to throw the javelin, to ride horseback, and to speak the truth."[18] They then served in the military for four years, and were subject to temporary service until age fifty.[19]

The Persian military usually allowed families to make financial payments in lieu of service, but when the king went on campaign, all had to go. During Xerxes' invasion of Greece, a Lydian named Pythius asked the king to release the eldest of his five sons, since all five were serving in the Persian army. Xerxes "released" the son by having him cut in two, and then had the halves placed on either side of the road so the army would pass through them.[20] Years later, during one of Darius' campaigns, a certain

Persian named Oeobazus, who had three sons in the army, asked Darius if one could be left behind. "'Nay,' said the king, 'you are my friend and your desire is but reasonable; I will leave all your sons.'" Oeobazus rejoiced, but then Darius ordered the throats of all three cut, leaving the father three corpses.[21]

Military Branches

Darius and his fellow Persian kings relied on their military to conquer and maintain the greatest kingdom that part of the world had ever seen. They made extensive use of infantry and cavalry, only some use of chariotry, and had to rely heavily on an effective navy for their invasions of Greece.

Infantry

Curiously, the Persians did not rely as much on heavily armed infantry, as did many other contemporary armies—including the Greeks with their hoplites fighting with spears in phalanx. Most of the Persian infantry were rather lightly armed, with spears as their main weapon. Instead, the Persians relied more on their numerous archers and cavalry, plus a few heavily armed infantry serving as marines aboard ships. One sees the importance of the Persian archers in the predominance of the bow in their relatively few images, and by the warning to the Greeks that Persian arrows would be so numerous that they would blot out the sun in the battle at Thermopylae.[22]

One particular unit of Medo-Persian infantry stood out. Herodotus calls the elite unit of Persian infantry the "Ten Thousand" or "The Immortals" because any member who was killed or fell ill would be immediately replaced to keep their number at exactly ten thousand. This unit served as the royal bodyguard, including while on campaign. Each of these Immortals wore a felt cap and an elaborately decorated, long-sleeved tunic over a coat of scale armor, apparently inferior to Greek armor of the time. In battle, the Immortals carried a bow and quiver, a sword or large dagger, a wicker shield, and a short spear with a counterbalance made of silver or gold (Fig. 9.5). Only Persians, Medes, or Elamites could serve in the Immortals. When on the march, the members of this unit enjoyed superior food, as well as perks such as concubines and attendants. [23]

The Persians used a well-developed organizational system for the Immortals and the rest of their army, with a corresponding corps of officers. The infantry was apparently organized in units of 10,000, 1,000, 100, and 10, with officers over each, often drawn from the nobility. Members of the royal family typically served as high-ranking officers in the various branches of the military. For example, Xerxes appointed eight brothers and half brothers as high-ranking officers, including one who was named admiral of the Persian fleet in exchange for his support when Xerxes assumed the throne.

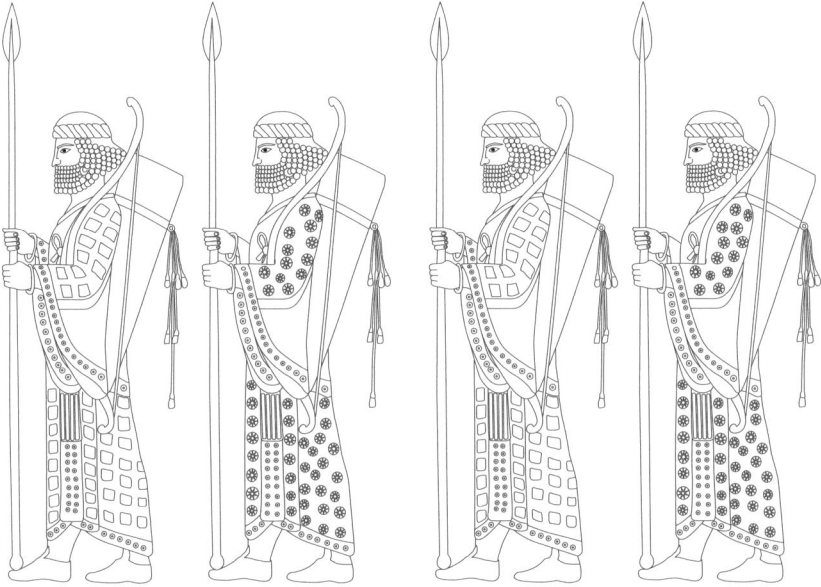

Fig. 9.5—Persian troops, apparently Immortals. Glazed brick from Darius' palace in Susa ca. 510 BC.

Careful organization extended beyond the royal army out into the provinces. Governors called satraps ruled the Persian provinces, but the garrison commanders and treasurers in each province reported directly to the king, who also maintained control through annual visits by a royal inspector called the "King's Eye."[24] Satraps saw to the defense of their regions with units from the royal military, supplemented by regiments of local nobility and mercenaries. The satraps commanded some of these units including mercenaries, but citadels and forts of strategic importance were often commanded by troops paid directly by the king and led by officers who reported directly to the king. Such organization made it more difficult for satraps to rebel.[25]

Chariotry   By the time of the Persian Empire, chariots had largely given way to cavalry as a way of providing mounted troops. Only rarely did the wheeled vehicles play a meaningful role in battle. When they did, it was usually on the fringes of the empire, such as in India, Libya, or Cyprus, using chariots equipped with scythes. These charged the enemy lines in an attempt to disrupt them before the main forces engaged.[26] The king did still use a chariot for hunting (Fig. 9.6), and he, like the Persian god, rode to war in a chariot pulled by special horses.

Fig. 9.6—Darius hunting from chariot. From seal impression.

Cavalry

As noted earlier, the Persians relied heavily on their cavalry, perhaps because their empire originated in the horse-growing Iranian plateau. Cavalrymen usually used harness and saddle cloth for their otherwise unprotected horses, and clothed themselves with iron breastplate and helmet. They carried a bow and arrows, two javelins, an iron club, and a wicker shield[27] (Fig. 9.7). When in battle, the cavalry apparently advanced toward the enemy to fire their bows and javelins. Sometimes they charged in a column rather than a line to smash the center of the enemy line. In such a charge, the troops could then throw their javelins or use them as spears in hand-to-hand fighting, and they developed an armored saddle to help protect themselves during these engagements.[28] Cavalry also operated effectively in the enemy's rear, disrupting lines of supply and communication, or attacking scattered enemy troops, such as those fleeing a battlefield.

Fig. 9.7—Persian horseman throwing javelin. From seal impression.

One finds other details about the cavalry in the Persian records as well. Officers called hipparchs commanded the cavalry. In Xerxes' army, Arab troops rode camels, and in the battle against Croesus of Sardis in 547 BC, the camels' odor spooked the enemy's horses. In the late 4th century, Persian forces occasionally used elephants. By the end of the Persian period, some charioteers had discarded the javelin and used a long, two-handed lance, and thus had become the forerunner of the medieval knight.[29]

Navy

Although land-based troops such as infantry, chariotry, and cavalry would have sufficed to control much of the empire, conquests along the Mediterranean or into Greece required the Persians to use a navy for transport or outright naval battles. The Persians obtained their ships from places like Phoenicia, Egypt, and Greece. Admirals commanded the navy.

The Persian navy consisted of two types of ships. Penteconters, the smaller ships, had perhaps fifty oars. The larger triremes served as the main fighting ships. They had a total of 170 oars arranged in three banks on each side, pulled by oarsmen and kept in cadence by an officer calling a beat, accompanied by a flutist. A captain commanded the vessel, and a pilot in the stern steered. Triremes measured approximately 140 feet long and 20 feet wide, plus another 14 feet for oars on each side. The crews were made up of 200 rowers and deckhands, plus 10 to 30 marines and a few archers. They could travel up to 145 nautical miles per day and reach speeds up to 12 knots (14 miles per hour).[30] They attacked primarily by ramming enemy vessels with the bronze ram on their prow. They sought to destroy or cripple enemy ships, or to have their marines take control of them.

General Information

Size of Army

We know little about the size of the Persian military for most of its history, but we do know a great deal from Xerxes' invasion of Greece in

480 BC. Unfortunately, the numbers recorded for Xerxes' force are so large as to be problematic. Clearly, Xerxes amassed the greatest military force in antiquity; its actual size is less clear. Shortly after repulsing the invaders, the victorious Greeks spoke of 3,000,000 Persians. A generation later, the normally reliable Herodotus listed 1,700,000 infantry, 80,000 cavalry, 20,000 camels and chariots, plus 300,000 Greeks and others added en route. With naval troops, this meant the Persian forces would have numbered over 2,300,000 combatants, plus nearly as many non-combatants.[31]

Such a number appears impossibly large. One author notes that a force that size, with infantry marching ten abreast and cavalry riding five abreast, would have formed a line of march extending over 1,300 miles, more than twice the distance from Athens to the Hellespont, where the Persians crossed from Asia into Greece.[32] Other ancient authors reduced the number of Persian invaders to less than 1,000,000; modern estimates range from 50,000 to 500,000.[33] Whatever the actual number, Xerxes successfully accomplished an amazing feat of logistics and organization to muster that army, although he failed to win his ultimate objective and conquer Greece.

Role of the King

Xerxes personally led the aforementioned campaign, not an unusual event for a Persian king. Like the kings of most other ancient powers, Persian kings varied in their military participation. Some personally fought with their armies, like Cyrus the Great, who ultimately died in battle. Others, such as Xerxes, accompanied the army and made command decisions, but did not personally participate. Xerxes travelled with his force, though not without considerable opulence and luxury, as described below. He made the key decisions for the campaign, and then positioned himself to watch the major engagements. This was intended to motivate the troops, as at Thermopylae, where the Persians won but suffered great casualties. But the king's watchful eye could not guarantee victory. Xerxes positioned himself under a golden canopy to observe the decisive naval battle at Salamis, but he had to witness a crippling defeat rather than a smashing victory.

Role of the Gods

As the Persian kings' involvement in their military reflected the general pattern of the time, so did the Persians' reliance on their gods in all their military activities. When on the march, holy men accompanied the king, along with altars and sacred fire. Xerxes used these to offer libations at sunrise before the battle at Thermopylae.[34]

The Persians differed from their predecessors in that they often treated conquered peoples more kindly, including aiding their worship, as discussed earlier in the chapter. Cyrus made sure to contrast his own religious zeal with that of his Babylonian predecessor in the text of the Cyrus Cylinder, justifying Cyrus' conquest of Babylon in 539 BC. Cyrus described his devotion to the gods by saying, "I sought daily to worship (Marduk). . . . I kept in view the needs of Babylon and all its sanctuaries to promote their well-being."

WEAPONS

Information about Persian weaponry is scarce. Texts and pictures suggest that the spear served as their most common short-range weapon, and the bow their most common long-range weapon. For example, Darius described himself as a good bowman and spearman, and the daric, his gold coin that circulated widely up until the time of Alexander, shows a figure, apparently the king, using one or both of these weapons (Fig. 9.8). Additionally, the Persian guardsmen (apparently Immortals) shown in reliefs at Susa and Persepolis also appear with spear and bow (Fig. 9.5). Other weapons named in texts include swords, daggers, iron clubs, javelins, and slings. Some nomads fought with lasso and dagger.

TACTICS

Motivation

The Persians appear to have fought their wars for the same reasons other nations did—usually for power and wealth. A new king often had to reassert his nation's power by subduing rebellions that broke out after the preceding king had died. Subjected nations often used the change in power to try to free themselves from the required annual tribute. Darius in particular faced such rebellions after a pretender named Gaumata assumed power following the death of Cambyses in 522 BC. Darius led an alliance of noble families that took power from Gaumata, and had to put down the many rebellions that broke out during the ensuing turmoil.

Persian kings also fought to gain wealth. For example, in 516 or 515 BC, Darius conquered a territory called Hindush along the Indus River in what is today Pakistan. From this one region, the Persians received annual tribute of 360 talents of gold dust.[35] Darius' predecessor Cambyses conquered Egypt in 525 BC. He must have been motivated at least somewhat by the wealth of Egypt, but he justified his actions by making differing claims about some offense that had led to the war.

Fig. 9.8—Persian daric showing Darius(?) with spear and bow.

Strategy

As was typical for armies of the time, the Persians campaigned from spring until fall and then stopped for the winter. Xerxes' apparent schedule for invading Greece illustrates the pattern well. He left Susa with his army around April 481 BC and followed the Royal Road westward across the heart of the empire (Map 6.1). He reached Sardis around October and wintered there. Then, in March of 480 BC, the army resumed its journey to Greece and traveled all the way to Athens before setbacks including the approaching winter caused him to pull out in the fall of 480 BC.

Season for War

Earlier, Cyrus had used this typical annual calendar to his benefit. He and Croesus of Sardis fought at Sardis until the onset of winter in 547–546 BC, when Cyrus appeared to withdraw. Croesus dismissed his foreign mercenaries and made plans to resume in the spring, only to have Cyrus return in November and capture the Lydian capital.[36]

Xerxes' approach to Greece, described above, involved many hundreds of miles of marching. He and his army marched some 1,600 miles from Susa to Sardis before stopping for the season, and then set out again in the spring to the Hellespont to cross from Asia into Europe. To get his enormous force across the nearly mile-wide Hellespont, Xerxes' engineers built two pontoon bridges. One used 360 ships to span the 4,220 yards of water; the other needed 314 ships to cross 3,700 yards. Each bridge used two flax and four papyrus cables, plus planks laid crossways on the cables heaped with earth to form the roadway, and hedges on the sides to keep the animals

The March

from spooking. Herodotus records that when a storm destroyed the bridges, Xerxes had the engineers responsible for the project beheaded. Xerxes also commanded his men to punish the Hellespont by scourging it with whips and branding it with hot irons before rebuilding the bridges. When the new bridges were ready, it took seven full days and nights for the force to cross.[37]

The order of troops during this crossing may suggest the general order of march for the Persian army. One thousand select cavalry led, followed by 1,000 infantry with spears reversed. Next came the sacred chariot of the Persian god Ahura-Mazda drawn by eight white horses and guided by a charioteer walking behind the chariot, "for no mortal man may mount into that seat."[38] Next came the king in his chariot (or in his carriage if he wished to ride rather than stand). Another 1,000 infantry followed with spears pointed normally, then another 1,000 picked cavalry. Next came 10,000 select infantry (apparently the Immortals), 1,000 with golden pomegranates for counterbalances, the other 9,000 with silver. Another 10,000 cavalry followed, and then the rest of the army.

Food and Logistics

The bridges over the Hellespont represented only one of many logistical challenges that Xerxes had to face in getting his large force to Greece. Roads and other pontoon bridges also had to be built. Some rivers required ferries. The Royal Road needed adequate staging posts stationed a day's journey apart.[39] One canal took three years to cut.

Another great logistical challenge came from supplying such a force with adequate food and water, sometimes over long periods on foreign soil. Xerxes arranged for large stores of grain and piles of salted meat, as well as medical supplies like myrrh and cotton bandages, to be stockpiled along the way. Drivers, supply teams, and pack animals carried goods, and personnel such as tailors, smiths, and saddlers carried supplies and provided support for the army.[40]

A large royal party accompanied the army—but its members didn't have to live like most of the army. The king's family, including his mother, wife, children, and servants, often accompanied him. While the rest of the army drank local water, the king and his party drew from silver urns filled with boiled "golden water." The royal party also ate the best foods served in great luxury— in gold and silver vessels inlaid with gems, served on tables and chairs overlaid with gold or silver. Years later, the royal party of Darius III enjoyed the attentions of 365 pages, 40 perfume makers, and 70 wine strainers while on campaign. The king also brought along his war chest. Darius III needed 600 mules and 300 camels to carry his money.[41]

The Persians further advanced their military efforts with information tion gained through paid spies and by influencing the actions of others with ample bribes. Xerxes used money to motivate many Greek cities outside of Sparta and Athens to desert the Greek cause and join with his invading force. One author described these efforts as follows: "Any successes that were achieved in the last hundred years of Achaemenid (Persian) rule came largely through intrigue and bribery, and by tampering with the loyalty of mercenary leaders on the opposite side."[42] *Intelligence*

Battle Tactics

Since much of our knowledge about the Persian military comes from Greek historians writing about two failed Persian invasions of their homeland, information about successful Persian battle tactics is hard to come by. Usually, the texts describe Persian defeats. For example, in the battle of Marathon in 490 BC, the Greeks numbered about 9,000, with the Persians perhaps two or three times that. The Persians relied heavily on their archers to neutralize the opposing Greek infantry. The Greeks had no cavalry, and since the accounts tell of no Persian cavalry engaging, it may not have been present. The Greek infantry compensated for the fierce Persian archery by closing at a run to reduce the time they would have to face the Persian arrows. The Greeks purposely left their center weak so the Persian infantry would penetrate it. When they did, the Greek wings enveloped the Persians and decimated them. The Persians lost 6,400 men in the battle, the Greeks only 192.[43] *Pitched Battle in Open*

A generation later at Thermopylae, the Persians eventually defeated the Greeks holding the narrow pass, but again at a very high cost. The Persians could not defeat the 6,000–7,000 Greeks that initially defended the site until they exploited a path that led up and around the pass. The Immortals fought their way along the path and made their way to the rear of the Greek position. The Greek commander Leonidas chose to save most of his force by sending them away and staying with just 300 Spartans to delay and kill as many Persians as possible. All 300 Spartans died, but so did as many as 20,000 Persians.[44]

The existing sources record many more Persian victories when attacking various cities throughout their empire. Cyrus the Great helped launch the Persian Empire by capturing the city of Babylon in 539 BC. As described in this chapter's opening story, Cyrus had initially approached the city and defeated the Babylonian army, which then retreated into the city. When subsequent direct attacks against the *Attacks on Cities* fortifications failed, Cyrus left contingents near where the Euphrates entered and exited the moat that protected the city. He pulled back the rest of his force upstream and had the troops dig a channel to divert the Euphrates into a lake temporarily. The Persians diverted the river during a festival when Babylonians were likely to lower their guard, and their plan worked. Their men were able to wade through the lowered water and enter and conquer Babylon.[45]

Cyrus did not destroy the conquered city, and by 522 BC Darius had to re-conquer it. Darius also won with the help of an unusual strategy, this time involving a memorable act of selflessness by one of his men. The Persian army had laid siege to the city for twenty months, but failed to penetrate it. Then a Persian named Zopyrus sought to pose as a defector in order to gain entrance into the city. He cut off his own nose and ears, shaved his head, and scourged himself so he could present himself to the Babylonians as a victim of Darius' punishment. He was granted entrance into the city, and won command over a Babylonian military force. He led that force to victories over groups of Persian troops in three increasingly large, pre-arranged battles, after which he got himself made chief of the city's defenses. He then opened two of the city gates to the Persians, who captured the city.[46]

Persian attacks on many other cities followed more conventional strategies. Cyrus used an engineering corps to construct and use "machines" (apparently siege engines) and scaling ladders to attack one city and siege engines and battering rams for others.[47] They also used siege ramps and blockades and dug tunnels under fortifications to penetrate cities, though in one case, a clever defender used a bronze sheet from a shield to thwart Persian sappers in the process of digging tunnels. This metal smith laid the bronze sheet on the ground and struck it to check the sound it yielded. Dull sounds meant solid ground, but sharp reports indicated tunnels, enabling the defenders to repulse the attacks.[48]

Like other armies, the Persians preferred to avoid costly sieges of heavily fortified cities whenever possible. They often sought to induce a city to surrender with the promise that surrender would avoid destruction of the city. By contrast, resistance would lead not only to destruction of their homes and temples, but also to the giving of their land to others, enslavement of the population, and, in at least one case, castration of the males.[49]

After the Battle
Although the Persians earned the reputation for demonstrating relative kindness in their treatment of conquered foes, such was not always the case. Sometimes they resettled conquered populations like the

Assyrians had, though not on the same scale. The Persians occasionally massacred the population of a city when angered by some dishonorable act such as treachery. After Darius re-conquered Babylon through the long and difficult siege described earlier, he destroyed the city's walls and gates, then impaled 3,000 of its leading citizens. He then shifted and demonstrated kindness by reportedly supplying 50,000 women for the men of the city who had lost their wives during the long siege.[50] The Persians also demonstrated their wrath following their costly victory at Thermopylae. On their subsequent campaign through central Greece, they burned all the towns they came across and raped the women. When they captured the Acropolis at Athens, they burned and looted the temple, and slaughtered those who had taken refuge there.[51]

More commonly, though, the Persians demonstrated restraint. For example, when Cyrus the Great conquered Babylon as described earlier, the historians make no mention of slaughter or looting. But when his forces conquered Sardis, he apparently had trouble keeping his troops from these common activities.

CONCLUSION

Thus we see that the Persian military was organized and used weaponry and tactics similar to those of the other ancient Near Eastern armies treated earlier. With the notable exception of cavalry largely supplanting chariotry, these nations generally relied on infantry and equestrian troops, fighting at the direction of their kings and for their gods. They used spears, swords, and bows to attack, and defended themselves with shields and armor. When their armies were strong, they met opposing armies in the field, or attacked fortified enemy cities. They fought for their gods, glory, and riches, but none could establish a perpetual kingdom. All ultimately fell to the next great power.

NOTES

1   According to the Greek historian Xenophon, Chrysantas was a member of Cyrus' war council when the allied Medo-Persian army met to discuss strategy before conquering Babylon in 539 BC (*Cyr.* 7.5.8–9). Xenophon does not record Chrysantas' ethnicity or position, but this chapter presents him as a major Median cavalry officer.

2   *Her.* 1.190.

3 Xenophon includes one advisor's response to Chrysantas during the war council regarding the depth of the river: "Its depth is such that two men, one standing on the other's shoulders, would not reach the surface of the water, so that the city is better defended by the river than by its walls" (*Cyr.* 7.5.8).

4 Herodotus writes that the Babylonians indeed felt exactly that (1.190), and Xenophon records that the defenders on the wall "laughed (Cyrus') siege-works to scorn, in the belief that they had provisions enough for more than twenty years" (*Cyr.* 7.5.13).

5 According to *Cyr.* 7.5.24, two officers with these names were to lead those who first penetrated the city to the palace since they were familiar with the city. This suggests that they may have been allied with the Babylonians earlier but now had joined the Persians.

6 Dialogue from *Cyr.* 7.5.7–9. At this point, the accounts of Xenophon and Herodotus diverge. Xenophon has the attackers digging a ditch around the city and erecting siege works, whereas Herodotus says that they dug a canal from the Euphrates into a lake, apparently upstream from the city (*Her.* 1.191).

7 *Her.* 1.191.

8 *Cyr.* 7.5.15.

9 *Her.* 1.191.

10 *Cyr.* 7.5.26–30.

11 *Cyr.* 7.5.31–33.

12 *Cyr.* 7.5.34–36.

13 For a helpful review of Persian history, see Edwin M. Yamauchi's "Persians" in Hoerth, et al, eds., *Peoples of the Old Testament World*, 110–20.

14 According to Herodotus, "these (messengers) are stayed neither by snow nor rain nor heat nor darkness from accomplishing their appointed course with all speed" (8.98). A version of this statement is now inscribed on the James Farley Post Office in New York City, and is sometimes used as an unofficial motto of the U.S. Postal Service.

15 *Her.* 4.87.

16 *Her.* 7.61–88.

17 Sekunda, *Persian Army*, 56–57.

18 *Her.* 1.136.

19 Strabo 15.3.19.

20 *Her.* 7.38–39.

21 *Her.* 4.84–85.

22 *Her.* 7.226.

23 *Her.* 7.83.

24 Oates, *Babylon,* 136–38.

25 Sekunda, *Persian Army,* 19–20.

26 Dalley, "Ancient Mesopotamian Military Organization," 422; Sekunda, *Persian Army,* 25, 29.

27 Cook, *Persian Empire,* 102.

28 Sekunda, *Persian Army,* 22, 25, 54–56.

29 Sekunda, *Persian Army,* 29.

30 Yamauchi, *Persia and the Bible,* 199.

31 Cook, *Persian Empire,* 113–14.

32 Yamauchi, *Persia and the Bible,* 195.

33 Cook, *Persian Empire,* 114–16.

34 Cook, *Persian Empire,* 104; *Her.* 7:223.

35 *Her.* 3.94.

36 Yamauchi, *Persia and the Bible,* 82.

37 *Her.* 7.33–36, 56.

38 *Her.* 7.40–41.

39 *Her.* 5.52–53.

40 Cook, *Persian Empire,* 116.

41 Cook, *Persian Empire,* 105.

42 Cook, *Persian Empire,* 107.

43 Yamauchi, *Persia and the Bible,* 164–70. Sekunda, *Persian Army,* 14.

44 Yamauchi, *Persia and the Bible,* 203–06.

45 See Dan. 5, *Her.* 1:190–91, and *Cyr.*7:5.1–34.

46 *Her.* 3.151–59. Herodotus also records the earlier Babylonian taunt that the Persians would "take our city when mules bear offspring." Since mules are sterile, the taunt assumed it could never happen. But then, in the twentieth month of the siege, one of Zopyrus' mules actually gave birth, and he hatched the plan already described.

47 *Cyr.* 6.3.8; 7.2.2; 7.4.1.

48 *Her.* 4.200.

49 *Her.* 6.9.

50 *Her.* 3.159. Herodotus wrote that the Babylonian men, "fearing for their food, had strangled their own women."

51 *Her.* 8.51–53.

For Further Reading

GENERAL

Bonnet, Hans. *Die Waffen der Völker des alten Orients* (*The Weapons of the Peoples of the Ancient Orient*). Leipzig: J. C. Hinrichs'sche, 1926 (in German).

Eph'al, Israel. *The City Besieged: Siege and Its Manifestations in the Ancient Near East.* Vol. 36 of *Culture and History of the Ancient Near East.* Thomas Schneider et al, eds. Leiden: Brill, 2009.

Gabriel, Richard A., and Karen S. Metz. *From Sumer to Rome: The Military Capabilities of Ancient Armies.* Contributions in Military Studies 108. New York: Greenwood, 1991.

Gonen, Rivka. *Weapons of the Ancient World.* Cassell's Introducing Archaeology Series 8. London: Cassell, 1975.

Hallo, William W., and K. Lawson Younger, Jr., eds. *The Context of Scripture.* 3 vols. Leiden: Brill, 1997–2002.

Hoerth, Alfred J., Gerald L. Mattingly, and Edwin M. Yamauchi, eds. *Peoples of the Old Testament World.* Grand Rapids: Baker, 1994.

Pritchard, James B., ed. *Ancient Near Eastern Texts Relating to the Old Testament.* 3d ed. Princeton, NJ: Princeton University Press, 1969.

_____. *The Ancient Near East in Pictures Relating to the Old Testament.* Princeton, NJ: Princeton University Press, 1954.

Seevers, Boyd. "The Practice of Ancient Near Eastern Warfare with Comparison to the Biblical Accounts of Warfare from the Conquest to the End of the United Monarchy." Ph.D. diss., Trinity Evangelical Divinity School, 1998.

Stillman, Nigel, and Nigel Tallis. *Armies of the Ancient Near East 3,000 BC to 539 BC.* Worthing, Sussex: Flexiprint, 1984.

Yadin, Yigael. *The Art of Warfare in Biblical Lands in the Light of Archaeological Study.* 2 vols. New York: McGraw-Hill, 1963.

CHAPTERS 1–2: ISRAEL

Hobbs, T. R. *A Time for War: A Study of Warfare in the Old Testament.* Old Testament Studies 3. Wilmington, DE: Michael Glazier, 1989.

_____. "Aspects of Warfare in the First Testament World." *Biblical Theology Bulletin.* 25 (1995): 79–90.

Liver, Jacob, ed. *The Military History of the Land of Israel in the Days of the Bible.* Jerusalem: Ma'acarot, 1964 (in Hebrew).

Rodriquez, Seth M. "The Arsenal of the Hebrew Kings and Their Neighbors: A Description of Biblical Weapons in the Iron Age." Ph.D. diss., The Southern Baptist Theological Seminary, 2009.

Seevers, Boyd. "The Practice of Ancient Near Eastern Warfare with Comparison to the Biblical Accounts of Warfare from the Conquest to the End of the United Monarchy." Ph.D. diss., Trinity Evangelical Divinity School, 1998.

Ussishkin, David. *The Conquest of Lachish by Sennacherib.* Tel Aviv: Tel Aviv University Institute of Archaeology, 1982.

Yadin, Yigael. *The Art of Warfare in Biblical Lands in the Light of Archaeological Study.* 2 vols. New York: McGraw-Hill, 1963.

CHAPTERS 3–4: EGYPT

Breasted, James H., ed. *Ancient Records of Egypt.* 5 vols. Repr., London: Histories & Mysteries of Man, 1988.

Faulkner, R. O. "The Battle of Megiddo." *JEA* 28 (Dec. 1942): 2–15.

_____. "Egyptian Military Organization," *JEA* 39 (Dec. 1953): 32–47.

Hayes, William C. "Egypt: Internal Affairs from Tuthmosis I to the Death of Amenophis III. - IX. The Army, Navy, and Police Force." Pages 363–72 in *The Cambridge Ancient History.* 3d ed. Cambridge: Cambridge University Press, 1973.

Hoffmeier, James K. "The Annals of Thutmose III." Pages 7–13 in *COS, Vol. II: Monumental Inscriptions from the Biblical World.*

Kitchen, K. A. "The Battle of Qadesh—The Poem, or Literary Record." Pages 32–38 in *COS, Vol. II: Monumental Inscriptions from the Biblical World.*

Lichtheim, Miriam. "The First Campaign: The Battle of Megiddo." Pages 29–35 in *AEL, Vol. II: The New Kingdom.*

Littauer, M. A., and J. H. Crouwel. *Chariots and Related Equipment from the Tomb of Tutʻankhamūn.* Vol. VIII of *Tutʻankhamūn's Tomb Series.* Edited by J. R. Harris. Oxford: Griffith Institute, 1985.

McDermott, Bridget. *Warfare in Ancient Egypt.* Stroud, UK: Sutton Publishing, 2004.

Nelson, Harold Hayden. *The Battle of Megiddo.* Chicago: University of Chicago Press, 1913.

Schulman, Alan R. *Military Rank, Title, and Organization in the Egyptian New Kingdom.* Berlin: Bruno Hessling, 1964.

_____. "Military Organization in Pharaonic Egypt." Pages 289–301 in Vol. 1 of *Civilizations of the Ancient Near East.* Edited by Jack M. Sasson. New York: Charles Scribner's Sons, 1995.

Wilson, John A. "The Asiatic Campaigns of Thut-mose III. The First Campaign: The Battle of Megiddo." Pages 234–238 in *ANET.*

Wolf, Walther. *Die Bewaffnung des altägyptischen Heeres.* Leipzig: J. C. Hinrichs'sche, 1926 (in German).

CHAPTER 5: PHILISTIA

Bierling, Neal. *Philistines: Giving Goliath His Due.* Marco Polo Monographs 7. Warren Center, PA: Shangri-La, 2002.

Dothan, Trude. *The Philistines and Their Material Culture.* New Haven: Yale University Press, 1982.

_____, and Moshe Dothan. *People of the Sea: The Search for the Philistines.* New York: Macmillan Publishing, 1992.

Howard, David M. Jr. "Philistines." Pages 231–50 in *Peoples of the Old Testament World.* Edited by Alfred J. Hoerth, Gerald L. Mattingly and Edwin M. Yamauchi. Grand Rapids: Baker, 1994.

Sandars, N. K. *The Sea Peoples: Warriors of the Ancient Mediterranean 1250–1150 B.C.* Rev. ed. London: Thames and Hudson, 1985.

CHAPTERS 6–7: ASSYRIA

Dalley, Stephanie. "Foreign Chariotry and Cavalry in the Armies of Tiglath-pileser III and Sargon II," *Iraq* 47 (1985): 31–48.

_____. "Ancient Mesopotamian Military Organization." 1:413–22 in *Civilizations of the Ancient Near East.* Edited by J. Sasson. New York, 1995.

Eph'al, Israel. "On Warfare and Military Control in the Ancient Near Eastern Empires: A Research Outline." Pages 88–106 in *History, Historiography and Interpretation: Studies in Biblical and Cuneiform Literatures.* H. Tadmor and M. Weinfeld, eds. Jerusalem: Magnes, 1983.

Grayson, A. Kirk. "Assyrian Civilization." Pages 194–228 in *The Assyrian and Babylonian Empires and Other States of the Near East, from the Eight to the Sixth Centuries B.C.* Vol. 3, part 2 of *Cambridge Ancient History.* 2d ed. Edited by John Boardman et al. Cambridge: Cambridge University, 1991.

_____. "Assyrian Rule of Conquered Territory in Ancient Western Asia." 2:959–68 in *Civilizations of the Ancient Near East*. Edited by J. Sasson. New York, 1995.

_____. *Assyrian Royal Inscriptions*. 2 vols. Records of the Ancient Near East. Edited by Hans Goedicke. Wiesbaden: Otto Harrassowitz, 1972–1976.

_____. *The Royal Inscriptions of Mesopotamia. Assyrian Periods*. Vol. 2. *Assyrian Rulers of the Early First Millennium BC I (1114–859 BC)*. Toronto: University of Toronto, 1991.

_____. *The Royal Inscriptions of Mesopotamia. Assyrian Periods*. Vol. 3. *Assyrian Rulers of the Early First Millennium BC II (858–745 BC)*. Toronto: University of Toronto, 1996.

Madhloom, T. A. *Chronology of Neo-Assyrian Art*. London: Athlone, 1970.

Saggs, H. W. F. "Assyrian Warfare in the Sargonid Period." *Iraq* 25 (1963): 145–54.

_____. *The Might that was Assyria*. London: Sidgwick & Jackson, 1984.

Shanks, Hershel. "Destruction of Judean Fortress Portrayed in Dramatic Eighth-Century B.C. Pictures." *BAR* 10:2 (Mar/Apr 1984): 48–65.

Ussishkin, David. *The Conquest of Lachish by Sennacherib*. Tel Aviv: Tel Aviv University, 1982.

_____. "Defensive Judean Counter-Ramp Found at Lachish in 1983 Season." *BAR* 10:2 (Mar/Apr 1984): 66–73.

CHAPTER 8: BABYLON

Arnold, Bill T. "Babylonians." Pages 43–75 in *Peoples of the Old Testament World*. Edited by Alfred J., Hoerth, et al. Grand Rapids: Baker, 1994.

Grayson, A. K. *Assyrian and Babylonian Chronicles*. Vol. 5 of *Texts from Cuneiform Sources*. Edited by A. Leo Oppenheim. Locust Valley, NY: J. J. Augustin, 1975.

Oates, Joan. *Babylon,* rev. ed. London: Thames & Hudson, 1986.

Saggs, H. W. F. *The Greatness that was Babylon: A Sketch of the Ancient Civilization of the Tigris-Euphrates Valley.* New York: Hawthorn, 1962.

_____. *Babylonians.* Peoples of the Past. Norman: University of Oklahoma, 1995.

CHAPTER 9: PERSIA

Allen, Lindsay. *The Persian Empire.* Chicago: University of Chicago, 2005.

Campbell, Duncan B. *Ancient Siege Warfare: Persians, Greeks, Carthaginians and Romans 546–146 BC.* Elite 121. Oxford: Osprey, 2005.

Cook, J. M. *The Persian Empire.* New York: Schocken, 1983.

Herodotus: With an English Translation by A. D. Godley. The Loeb Classical Library. T. E. Page, et al, eds. Cambridge, MA: Harvard, 1960.

Sekunda, Nick. *The Persian Army 560–330 BC.* Elite 42. London: Osprey, 1992.

Yamauchi, Edwin M. "Persians." Pages 107–24 in *Peoples of the Old Testament World.* Edited by Alfred J., Hoerth, et al. Grand Rapids: Baker, 1994.

_____. *Persia and the Bible.* Grand Rapids: Baker, 1996.

Xenophon's Cyropaedia: With an English Translation by Walter Miller. The Loeb Classical Library. T. E. Page, et al, eds. Cambridge, MA: Harvard, 1960.

Figures and Maps Index

Chapter 5: Philistia

Figures

Chapters 6–7: Assyria

Figures

Subject Index

Scripture Index